move
Architecture in Motion

Birkhäuser
Basel · Boston · Berlin

move

Architecture in Motion – Dynamic Components and Elements

Michael Schumacher Oliver Schaeffer Michael-Marcus Vogt

■ Contents

Contents

■ Preface

Eppur si muove – And yet it does move! Galileo Galilei uttered these words referring to the orbit of the Earth around the sun. In the early 17th century, what is now common knowledge was so revolutionary for our conception of the world that it was regarded as heresy and grounds for religious prosecution. Today the notion that we as humans live on a body that moves at high speed through an unimaginably large, seemingly limitless space seems self-evident.

Perhaps this is the origin of our fascination with movement in general. Our actual experience of standing on this body that is planet Earth is quite different, namely that it is stable and does not move. Given this perceived reality – and herein lies the essence of architecture – we erect our houses to be similarly immobile and hopefully stable. The architect's task is to erect a building on this apparently stable ground that is durable and lasting, both in terms of materials and construction as well as aesthetic quality, a building that in a broader sense is materially and culturally sustainable. But however stable and durable buildings may be as a whole, they also contain movable elements, not least so that we can use them. In fact in many cases these moving parts are a prerequisite for the building's durability. This book is concerned with such moving parts. It examines architectural elements that are movable in terms of their purpose, their composition, their form and their meaning.

As we know from windows and doors, escalators and elevators, shutters and sliding walls as well as from all manner of windbreaks or sun louvres, each of these elements has its own function and structural as well as aesthetic logic. As the title suggests, this book is not solely concerned with movement in itself but about movement in the context of architectural and aesthetic aspects: it examines movements and constructions that on the one hand help make our buildings more useful and more energy-efficient and on the other contribute towards richer, more aesthetic and more haptic experiences.

In film, the aesthetics of movement have always played an important role. In James Bond films, vast craters are made to open, not with the economy and efficiency an engineer might choose but in such a way that their drama and spectacle are heightened.

This book showcases successful examples of how movement can be practical, sensible and not least also "poetic". In addition, it aims to serve as a practical reference by illustrating basic geometric principles and detailing key aspects for consideration when designing with materials, forces and dimensions. Its underlying intention is to communicate the guiding principles behind the conceptual approaches to this topic.

The creation of this book aroused a great deal of interest, moving many people to invest their valuable time and commitment. First and foremost we would like to thank the authors who have contributed essential chapters to this book. Likewise, our thanks go to the many members of the Institute of Design and Building Construction for their round-the-clock application in the meticulous production of drawings and crafting of precise formulations. The team at the publisher are to thank not only for their competent assistance but also for their supportive involvement, and naturally the realisation of this project would not have been possible without the vision and financial support of the sponsoring companies. Last but by no means least, thanks are due also to the architectural offices and engineering firms whose exemplary projects are shown in the pages of this book.

We hope that this book contributes to resolving some of the pressing problems facing "Spaceship Earth" and, alongside the seriousness of these issues, to promoting beauty and the concomitant sense of pleasure that good architecture can provide.

Michael Schumacher, Oliver Schaeffer, Michael-Marcus Vogt
Leibniz University Hanover, November 2009

■ The poetics of movement in architecture

Michael Schumacher

One's finger slides over the smooth, cool surface of the iPhone and finds the slight depression of the home button. A measured amount of pressure, a tactile response and the screen lights up. "Slide to unlock" appears within a graphic bar unmistakably designed to look like a slider. One's finger gently touches the glass surface and without any resistance or friction the virtual switch follows one's finger and slides to one side: the device is ready for use. The calendar appears and one can scroll through the day with one's thumb. If one scrolls too energetically, the list of 24 hours of the day hits the top or bottom and rebounds lightly. There is no actual need for this effect as there is no mechanical movement involved. A narrow black bar on the left-hand side moves gradually with the hours in the opposite direction to the scrolling movement, and appears to act like a counterweight.

When surfing the internet, this most wonderful 21st-century machine, everything appears tiny on the small screen. To get a closer view one "pulls open" a section of the so-called "window" between finger and thumb. The image or text expands until here too a rebound-effect marks the limits of the zoom, dispelling the momentary impression that one can zoom in ever closer into the molecular structure of the universe, as shown so evocatively by Ray and Charles Eames in their film *Powers of Ten*. While not everything is possible, this perfected product of the electronic age epitomises the poetics of movement – paradoxically a kind of movement whose "natural" environment is that of the physical world where things actually move and have mass and volume. So

why do we find this so fascinating? What makes movement beautiful and interesting and when is it clumsy and boring?

Movement and speed

An immanent part of movement is the speed at which movement takes place. Without speed, or a change between two different states, there is no movement. Movement results from a change in position from a stationary condition via acceleration and deceleration to a new stationary condition. The change in speed generally follows the laws of physics, increasing evenly in a linear pattern, then decreasing evenly again until it stops. This characterises how we open a door, pull out a drawer or close the window shutters of a house. This progression from the stationary via a more or less continuous increase in speed until a turning point is reached and speed decreases again can be designed. Perfectly even movement that starts and stops suddenly is for us unnatural. Such extremely controlled movement can be seen, for example, when a CD or DVD tray opens and closes. This aspect of movement is dramatised in Stanley Kubrick's world-famous science fiction film *2001 – A Space Odyssey*. The last surviving astronaut of the mission shuts down HAL, the all-powerful board computer, by removing its cognitive circuit modules. These entirely clear modules (with no circuit boards, just fascinating emptiness) slide silently and with the same slow evenness out of their sockets. HAL gradually starts to lose its memory, its voice becoming ever deeper until all it can remember is a children's song. The slow, even

regularity of the sliding movement lends it a magical quality and communicates powerfully the dramatic act taking place in the film.

Movement and form

Moving things like all things are characterised by specific forms. But the definition of form is more complex than with static objects as its form changes with movement. In architecture this has to do principally with the functional control and design of three states: closed, open and the state in-between. A door when closed fits perfectly in its frame. When it is opened, it often comes to rest at some arbitrary position that is rarely a "good" position. In a sense, the door is waiting to be closed, to be returned to its "good" position. Doors in the thick walls of old castles or manor houses often have an open position that is more aesthetically pleasing. The wonderful toy spheres devised by Chuck Hoberman enter into a different relationship between form and movement. In the initial state, one sees a complex articulated ball made of two colours, one of which dominates. If one moves the ball, for example by throwing it into the air, it changes colour. Through a complex inversion movement, the inward-facing colours swap position with the outward-facing elements. The phase in-between is not a sphere but a kind of star. Now the construction is revealed and we can see that the form is conditioned by its movement and could not be any other way. Although the form and the movement is in itself simple, it appears complex and unfathomable. Therein lies its poetry.

2001 – A Space Odyssey, MGM, 1968

Mercedes SLK-Class, 2004: the folding vario-roof opens and closes within 22 seconds

The upswing of the doors of a Lamborghini have the same intention. It surprises and fascinates us to see how the complex form of a car door can fit so seamlessly into the bodywork, so that when closed it becomes the very expression of elegance. Again, science-fiction films provide many examples for the relationship between form and movement over and above its practical function. Giant doors with matching wedged-shaped profiles clamp together, their interlocking form signifying clearly and unmistakably that passage is barred.

The wonderful elevator doors in the 1970s German TV production *Raumpatrouille* that did not meet in the middle like normal lift doors but closed diago-

nally may have been impractical but certainly exerted a greater fascination. The advent of computer-aided design and production in the automobile industry has allowed manufacturers to develop cabriolets with a hard roof. Here one can clearly see the relationship between form and movement, the fascinating possibilities as well as the degree of complexity. The car needs to look good when the roof is open and when it is closed. The change between the two should take place quickly but nevertheless remain as simple as possible so that it is still realisable with mechanical means. Ideally, too, there should be room left over in the boot. Here, the technical possibilities and the serial production of

cars have led to concepts that are technically and formally more advanced than similar tasks in the architectural realm, for example skylights or stadium roofs.

Movement and mass

As a child I went to school by bus. The buses were articulated and the best place to stand as a child was at the bend. The round platform swivelled as the bus turned a corner (surprisingly, much less than expected). Much more exciting, however, was the ponderous but nevertheless pronounced bounce that resulted when the mass of the two halves of the bus rode over a bump in the road. The kind and

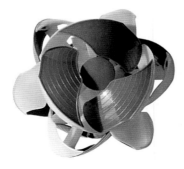
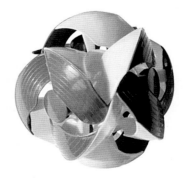

Switch Pitch, Hoberman Designs, 2004

beosound 3200, Bang & Olufsen, 2003

character of a movement is directly related to the mass that is moved. This is a product of basic physics: an elephant moves differently to a fly. Alongside being subject to the laws of nature, many other aspects play a role in the context of architecture. Large masses are more difficult to set in motion as well as to halt once moving. As ever in architecture, the mass of an element needs to be taken into account both in terms of construction as well as design. Excessively heavy doors in schools and children's nurseries are at best annoying and at worst render the building unusable. While motorised openers are, of course, available, they do not help in all situations and doors that suddenly open towards us we often find disconcerting. For architects, the need to consider the implications of mass in the design of moving architectural elements is comparatively new.

Movement and sound

Movements produce sounds. They result from vibrations caused by a movement which are transmitted through the air. These are so to speak the natural sounds of a movement. In comics such sounds are portrayed by words such as "groan", "creak", "screech" or "skid". In the case of cars, sound has always been an important aspect – even, or perhaps particularly, when not moving. The "docile thrum" of an eight-cylinder engine awakens very different associations to the aggressive purr of a six-cylinder. The solidity of the sound a car door makes as it closes conveys a sense of quality. The days in which the sound of a car was dependent on the geometry

of the exhaust manifold are long gone. Today almost as much time is spent on perfecting the sound as the form. Sound designers examine the sound when idle, when accelerating and at top speed. While without doubt much of this can be attributed to decadence, it shows how important the combination of movement and sound is and that one needs to be aware of the relationship between them. In the building sector, less attention has been paid to the sound of movement than in the automobile industry. The sound servomotors make as they open a window is usually left to chance, and the sound is more often than not correspondingly unpleasant. The thin profiles of the facade vibrate and transmit vibrations well, amplifying the sound of the small motors considerably. Other sounds in architecture include warning signals: to prevent people from getting trapped, the process of closure is often accompanied by a piercing sound that rapidly dispels all enjoyment of the movement itself. Sound always accompanies movement and one can exploit its dramatic potential to underline rather than disrupt the beauty of a movement.

This book is about the beauty of movement. Most movements have a practical purpose: either to effect a desired change of use or to adapt to external conditions such as weather, light and so on. Movements become poetic when they go beyond the purely practical, when they make more of the possibilities they hold and in turn heighten their potential. Investing movements with an element of beauty is a matter of conscious emphasis, a slight embellishment rather than the mechanical optimum.

This does not have to imply higher costs; on the contrary, the use of moving elements aims to increase the usefulness and therefore the long-term sustainability of buildings or to improve their energy efficiency. The systematic development of new materials in the industry will increase the potential for moving components in architecture.

The poetry of a movement is not automatically a by-product of its functional or economic optimisation. Making movements attractive increases the useful value of objects significantly so that they form part of our cultural identity. If we do things an interesting way, in a way that gives us lasting enjoyment, we appeal to our sense of being as a whole – and that includes our sense of poetry.

A Theory and planning

■ 1.1 Exploring space – Creating space – Dancing space

A choreographic conception of movement in architecture
Isa Wortelkamp

The terms exploring, creating and dancing describe practices that are essential for the choreographic conception of movement in space. All are integral to the work of the Swiss dancer and choreographer Anna Huber whose performances relate to specific spaces. Perhaps more than any of her contemporaries, Huber seeks a dialogue between the built elements and enclosure of architectural space and the immediate space of her body, changing the way they connect and interact through her movements. In direct contact with the architectural elements, their materials, structures and compositions, a vocabulary of movements emerges that she choreographs on site and for the specific architectural environment. The dialogue between dance and architecture, as characterised by Huber's choreographic works, began in the 1960s during the postmodern dance movement. As dance began to leave the realm of the theatre stage and started to take place in churches, sports halls, industrial buildings or galleries, an examination of the built context became a fundamental part of choreographic work. Characteristic for this development is the work of the American dancer and choreographer Trisha Brown. In her performance *Equipment Pieces* (1968 – 72), the dancers walk upright down the side of a wall towards the spectators or parallel to the floor along the walls of the Whitney Museum in New York. In *Primary Accumulation* (1972) the performers line pathways or swim on the surface of Loring Park Lake in Minneapolis. Brown's choreographic works take place in locations that facilitate a different view of architecture and direct our attention away from the everyday and familiar pattern of

things. Walls, roofs and ceilings, rivers and roads become a space for dance, altering our perception of architecture: "I have in the past felt sorry for ceilings and walls. It's perfectly good space; why doesn't anyone use it?" (Brown, quoted in Stephano 1974)

Exploring space

In Anna Huber's series of works entitled *Umwege* (Detours), she focuses on apparently neglected spaces as the basis for her choreographic creation. Huber explores the corners and niches, walls and angles of spaces that are generally unused or at least are normally used differently to they way in which she explores them with the winding and agile movements of her supple body. A series of choreographies followed in buildings by architects such as Peter Zumthor, Jean Nouvel or Zaha Hadid, architecture that already embodies a sense of dynamism and mobilisation, as well as in various building sites. Together with the composer Fritz Hauser, Anna Huber develops movements that respond to specific architectural situations. The concept for *Umwege* came about in the thermal baths in Vals, Switzerland, and was followed by further performances in places such as Potsdamer Platz Underground Station and the Academy of Arts in Berlin (2002), the Maison des Arts in Créteil near Paris (2003), the Cultural and Congress Centre in Lucerne (2003), the former fire station at Vitra's works in Weil am Rhein (2003), the Art Museum in Stuttgart (2006) and the Parchi di Nervi in Genoa (2007).
Each choreographic creation follows an exploration of the architectural space. The choreographer de-

scribes this process of exploration as one that involves all the senses, a "feeling and sensing of different materials, surfaces and surface qualities" (Huber, 2009). Her inquiries into the nature of the space are manifold: "What does the room offer? How is it structured? Does it have a pre-existing structure or is it just an arbitrary, non-specific space? Does it or did it serve a particular function that may influence my research and perception? What is the history of the space? What is the energy and dynamism of the space?" (Huber, 2009). These lines of enquiry are her first means of approaching the space, her way of understanding and acquiring a feeling for the space. Huber practices being present in the space, occupying, moving around and residing in it, picking up all aspects of the space that the architecture has to offer in one form or another, allowing herself to enter into a relationship with the space, whether through her actions or in her imagination. Anna Huber describes this preoccupation as follows: "I'm interested in man's basic desire to settle somewhere, to find his place, to settle in and make himself comfortable." (Huber, 2009). In the process she traces the positions, actions, paths and patterns of movement that the different means of ordering the space suggest: the movements anticipated in the architect's design, which the choreography then updates and transforms.

Creating space

How can one describe the process of choreographic creation and how does it relate to the architect's creation? The choreographer assimilates and adapts

Umwege (Detours), Anna Huber, thermal baths, Vals, Switzerland, 2002

Eine Frage der Zeit (A Matter of Time), Anna Huber, premiere, Berlin, 2000

Umwege (Detours), Anna Huber, Potsdamer Platz, Berlin, 2002

an existing space, one that is not only based and builds on a pre-existing design but – and this is the point I wish to make – can also be read as a design for movement. It contains and defines different possibilities of moving through the space, of interacting with it, of being in it, of taking up occupancy and of traversing it. If architectural design aims to create a specific form for the buildings we live in (Hahn, 2008), dance transforms this form into movement which it in turn shapes and forms. In this sense, dance interacts with the architect's creation in the same way as it does with a choreographic script or rule, although reading it differently, as it were back to front.

Continuing this train of thought, Huber's dance can be understood as a – physical and moving – manner of reading that picks up and picks out the architectural creation and conveys it anew in and through its movements: not in the sense of translating and implementing a clear set of uniform movements but rather in the sense of accepting its invitation to dance. Dance creates something new in the space in which it takes place. This idea corresponds to Michel de Certeau's theory of walking in which the play of steps can itself be conceived as the "creation of spaces" (De Certeau, 1984).

In the same way that every creation embodies something of the designer, Huber choreographs with her understanding of dance and architecture, her knowledge of the movement, technology, anatomy and motor functions of her body. Her art of dancing interacts with the art of architecture by drawing on

its structures, materials, elements and compositions. Axes, views, directions and paths offer motivations for movements. Huber's particular interest is in the tension between macro- and micro-structures. "In the thermal baths in Vals, for example, strips of stone have been layered both indoors and outdoors. I could insert my body into the lines and spaces between them. While exploring one of these walls, I suddenly became aware of the small, almost playful drawings formed by the veins in the stone. The austere, clear structure of the building gives way to organic, almost archaic forms and figures. I found that inspiring: on the one hand there is the theoretical and abstract and then suddenly entirely different forms and directions are revealed. [...] My experience of these small drawings in the stone stimulated me to research how I could translate these into movement." (Huber, 2009). The performance brings about a change and shift in the relationship between body and space. When one sees Huber dance, the familiar becomes unfamiliar and the unfamiliar familiar. One's perception follows the detours and stray paths and correspondingly discovers that one's own position and point of view has in turn been set in motion.

Dancing space

Anna Huber creates spaces by turning what is down upwards and what is up downwards. She bypasses the order and arrangement of the space, reading it from right to left, turning it on its head: "I play with the balance of forces, for example with a wall.

I might support myself on the wall or press myself at an angle against it. I try and reverse the play of forces in my head by asking myself whether I am leaning against the wall or holding up the wall. I want to communicate this sense of inversion to the spectators so that they suddenly think: she has to hold up the wall otherwise it will fall over!"

Huber subverts perception, dancing architecture, not by following the rules, but by misreading them, her choreography interpreting movements "wrongly" or "incorrectly". This too corresponds to another of de Certeau's thoughts in which reading is seen as an activity that itself changes, forgets and invents (De Certeau, 1984). Here the choreographer breaks with the tradition of reading in the sense of a solely passive practice of consumption. De Certeau posited instead that reading is active and productive. "The reader invents in texts something different from what they 'intended'. He detaches them from the origin, now lost or incidental. He combines their fragments and creates something un-known in the space organized by their capacity for allowing an indefinite plurality of meanings." (De Certeau, 1984). When Huber dances the architectural "text", she reorders what is known and what is familiar and through her dance and her movements brings about another understanding of dance and architecture. Through an inversion and reversal of prevailing paths and patterns, through a new coding and re-functioning of everyday spaces, dance refers to the potential of architectural spaces, which from a dance theory perspective can be seen as choreographic potential. Dance, which is able to turn this potential into a motor for movement is able to contribute towards sensitising the senses: that particular kinetic sense which allows us to perceive a space as a possibility for movement. It is at this intersection where we should seek a dialogue between architecture theory and dance theory, a dialogue oriented around the architect's and the choreographer's practices of exploring, creating and dancing.

Timetraces, Anna Huber, performance for a specific place

Die anderen und die Gleichen (The Others and the Same), Anna Huber, premiere, Berlin, 1999

■ 1.2 The dynamics of nature

Stefan Bernard

It's something we all remember: that rush of light-heartedness that seizes us as we wander through woods in springtime. Winter has passed and light gently spills through the still-sparse canopy, setting in motion an impressive process: the ground, still dark from the leaves covering the woodland floor, absorbs the warmth of the sun, initiating metabolic processes that mark the beginning of an impressive natural spectacle. It is the hour of the spring-flowering plants, that now absorb their ration of the sun's energy for photosynthesis. Carpets of white wood anemones push through the leaves as if remains of snow from winter, the crimson blossoms of the corydalis, the blue of the liverwort or the yellow of the celandine providing patches of colour. The lightness of being and the force and dynamics of nature reveal themselves in their most pleasant form. The blaze of colour is, however, short-lived and springtime quickly passes, not made to last. The leaves on the trees grow rapidly larger, filling out the woodland canopy visibly until it forms a roof. A space is created, dense and defined as if almost architecture. What was a Gothic cathedral is transformed into a medieval crypt. The little sunlight that penetrates the canopy and reaches the woodland floor is barely sufficient for many plants and the surviving herbaceous layer of vegetation is at best unremarkable.

Towards the end of summer, the pattern changes again. As the amount of sunshine gradually decreases, so too does the metabolic activity of the trees. The production of light-absorbing and energy-generating chlorophyll ceases, marking the end of the intense green of the leaves. The abscission begins – the shedding of leaves and fruit – and yellows and reds begin to dominate, lending the autumnal woodland its own melancholic atmosphere. Until the first snow falls. Until the next spring arrives.

Nature as a cyclic system

Changeability is an immanent part of human existence, and of nature too: high and low tide; full and new moon; bud, blossom, fruit; mornings and evenings; day and night; the seasons of the year. The list of examples goes on and on.

What these all appear to share is the fact that the vast majority of natural processes that affect our daily lives reoccur at regular intervals: the larva becomes a chrysalis, then a butterfly, before spawning new larvae. They are regular, cyclic and self-contained processes within the larger order of

Garden in the monastery at Eberbach, Bernard und Sattler Landschaftsarchitekten, Rhinegau, Germany, 2008

things. A coming and going. Grandfather and grandson. What we see as human beings at a particular moment in time is a snapshot, a film-still as it were of a continuous, ongoing process. The time span, the duration, of these individual processes is likewise remarkably consistent. A day, a week, a year, the phases of the moon. The repetitive and regular recurrence of these processes is essential for their continued existence. Their cessation would be their end. This repeating pattern also makes it possible to eradicate "errors" in the system and to adapt to changing conditions. A kind of in-built fine-tuning, as we have learned from Charles Darwin.

This regularity, the certainty of recurrence, the knowledge that spring will follow winter offers mankind, without doubt, a sense of reassurance in its dealings with nature. Nature as the phoenix, an ever regenerating phenomenon. In fact, our very human existence is grounded precisely on this trust in regularity, in the confirmation of our habitual patterns and pre-judgements, in the expectation of fulfilment of our hopes. Anything else leads to "problems" that we have to then laboriously solve, as Karl Popper once put it.

Interestingly, it is precisely this aspect that also feeds our fear of the dynamics of nature. Alongside the regularity, predictability and reliability of natural recurring cycles – the fragrant flowers and pretty birdlife, the pleasant breeze in summer and the warmth of autumn sunshine – nature can also present an ugly face. The good, predictable, reassuring pattern of change is accompanied by a sinister, unpredictable and devastating dynamic that can

potentially have fatal or existential consequences. "Does the flap of a butterfly's wings in Brazil set off a tornado in Texas?" Edward N. Lorenz's phrase, although originally meant in a different context, is a fitting example. One need only recall the sundrenched, romantic beauty of the South Seas shortly before the tsunami struck. Our comprehensible, safe and ordered world is constantly accompanied by a precipitous sense of uncertainty and chaos.

Our relationship to nature is, therefore, characterised on the one hand by an awareness of its recurring, familiar and reliable character, and on the other by a residual risk of incalculability. This explains, perhaps, to a degree our love-hate relationship to nature, as well as our perpetual desire to tame nature, to control it, cultivate it and confer order on it.

The garden – nature tamed
The word paradise originates from the old Iranian word *pairi daêza* – which translates literally as "bounded area". The word "garden" has its linguistic roots in Gothic times and denotes an enclosure bounded by a fence of twigs (*Gerte* in German). The enclosure was designed to protect the cultivated land and its inhabitants from the dangers of the surrounding wilderness. Gardens therefore represent "good" and pleasant natural environments from which dangers are banned: gardens are tamed, ordered and controlled nature. The characteristic dialectic between cyclic regularity (security) and danger (insecurity) is, for the most part, cancelled out. Only the dynamics of changeability cannot be conquered! This awareness is expressed most

vividly in the medieval pomarium or orchard. Located within a monastery, this fulfilled the dual function of an orchard and a cemetery. The monks were buried in the pomarium while the trees – predominantly fruit trees – grew and withered in their rhythmic cycle of bloom, fruit and winter dormancy symbolising the pattern of creation, death and resurrection.

The garden as an expression of culture tries, therefore, to omit the aesthetic category of danger, of unpredictability. It lacks the simultaneity of beauty and ugliness, of creation and destruction, of order and chaos. This is the key difference to "real" nature, and what makes it so pleasant and attractive for us as human beings.

Change as a design principle
The aspect of changeability is ever present in garden and landscape architecture and a conscious and deliberate consideration of "the dynamics of nature" is a necessary and integral part of the design process. The world outdoors is far too complex and the vegetative material used so possessed by its own dynamics and conditioned by unpredictable factors that it is impossible to keep it in check over long periods of time. The same applies to the dynamics of the users of gardens and parks whose actions – even in civilised times – can only be predicted and controlled to a certain degree.

It is, perhaps, specifically this more natural (and somewhat relaxed) attitude to working with the unpredictability of nature that characterises the process of designing landscapes. Outdoor environments

and their perception are subject to constantly changing conditions: a sunny morning or a misty daybreak, the sweltering midday heat or a cool breeze, loutish adolescents or happily playful children. The changing seasons too result in changing structural hierarchies among the plants, for example the cherry blossom in springtime gives way to the resolute majesty of the plane trees in summer and autumn. Changes over long periods of time likewise alter the spatial appearance of a garden: what begins as an open, sunny garden with small, delicate young trees will over time develop into an imposing, shady, spatial agglomeration formed by a cluster of 100-year-old beech trees.

The design of gardens and landscapes always takes place with an awareness that the end result, in addition to the inability to control how others perceive it, can only be more or less governed – it is an approximate art. While much can be directed by design to develop in an orderly manner, other things will simply just happen. The composition and design of landscapes is, therefore, in its core always accompanied by a certain degree of fatalism. To a certain extent, it can be regarded as an aesthetic of incomplete control, though the spatial constellations that result are by no means less stimulating. Can then such a restrained approach to design that is sensitive to change, indeed that embraces (and expresses) change, offer an example for the architectural design of buildings? After all, architectural design typically aims to produce constructions that remain the same over longer periods of time, an approach that in principle would seem to exclude the possibility of change. If one is nevertheless willing to consider the "dynamics of nature" as a conceptual basis for architectural design and construction, one must first ask oneself what kind of dynamics and what degree of change one wishes to strive for? Is it the notion of a tamed, orderly (built) environment accompanied by a controlled, carefully orchestrated dynamism? A notion of changeability that emphasises the pleasant, desirable effects of nature and attempts to minimise the dangerous side effects – a kind of "changeability lite"? Or is the aesthetic intention to express a "truthful" sense of nature, untamed and willing to accommodate consequences that one can only estimate? A form of nature that may at any time get out of hand.

While the question is perhaps rhetorical, it is one that, now as then, has lost nothing of its frightening attraction.

■ 1.3 Motion in photography and film

Frank Möller

To learn more about movement in space it can be instructive to take a look at the extensive fund of knowledge that photography and film have to offer, not least because these media relate closely to our own mode of visual perception.

Simplifying things somewhat, this topic can be approached from two different points of view.

Firstly, the movement of a viewer through (architectural) space and the representation of his or her subjective impressions: a room is crossed and then reassembled out of the viewer's individual impressions to form an experience of the space, or as Siegfried Giedion expressed it in his book *Space, Time and Architecture*:

"The essence of space as it is conceived today is its many-sidedness, the infinite potentiality for relations within it. An exhaustive description of an area from one point of reference is, accordingly, impossible; its character changes with the point from which it is viewed. In order to grasp the true nature of space the observer must project himself through it."

Secondly, the aesthetic representation of moving objects, of dynamically changing processes or structures that take place in full view of the viewer, affecting the space around them.

The flying eye

In the history of art and media, our individual, subjective view of space has become successively more dynamic. The invention of perspective in the Renaissance, the large panoramas and later film all testify to an increasing desire to experience the dynamism of space.

Ever since a day in 1908, when a film camera was first detached from its tripod and hung from a gantry or placed on tracks, it has been made easier for the viewer to identify with the "point of view" of the camera and to enter into a relationship with photographed spaces. This dynamic interaction is also supported by the backdrop and scenery. An examination of sketches drawn by Ken Adam, the production designer for films such as *Dr Strangelove: or How I Learned to Stop Worrying and Love the Bomb*, *Barry Lyndon* or *Goldfinger*, reveals how the subjective view becomes the directive for the design of space. His sketches, made with a fat fibre-tip marker, clearly show where the camera stands and the focal length to be used. As such they already embody the dynamism of the moving picture.

This dynamism is heightened as soon as the camera starts moving, and with it the viewpoint of the viewer. Although camera movements generally take the viewer on a journey lasting only a few seconds, they immediately reveal through their representation of space, architecture and the city, which possibilities exist for perceiving space and the ways in which spaces can be portrayed through movement. The cameraman Michael Ballhaus relates his particular approach in the book *The Flying Eye* as follows:

"I like to move the camera, to narrate with the camera's movement, for example, to relate the emotions of the actors or what is happening in the story."

The 360° circle shot that Michael Ballhaus employed in Rainer Werner Fassbinder's film *Martha* and went on to utilise many times, or the related technique used by the Wachowski Brothers for the "bullet time" scene in the film *The Matrix* show just how influential dynamic perspective can be for the narrative.

The "bullet time effect" differs slightly in that it is not realised using true camera movement. Instead, a succession of individual frames of a scene are taken by several different cameras and subsequently assembled to simulate camera movement. In general, the ongoing development of imaging technologies plays a not insignificant role in pushing forward our conception of time and space.

From the studies of movement undertaken by Eadweard Muybridge, one of the founders of serial photography, to modern-day film effects such as "bullet time" or the "time slice", imaging techniques have expanded our perception and our understanding of space and time. John Gaeta, one of the protagonists of the new film techniques, describes a central aim of this development as follows:

"The tension lies in reinterpreting the moment: we want to depict the moment in a way in which we cannot see it in real life."

The grace of turning

In the history of film there are many examples of the aesthetic representation of moving objects. One particularly monumental sequence is the initial depiction of outer space in Stanley Kubrick's *2001: A Space Odyssey* in which Space Station 5 slowly re-

Bullet time describes a special effect used in films in
which the camera revolves around an object that appears
to be "frozen in time".
The "bullet time effect" is not realised using true camera
movement. Instead, a succession of individual frames of a
scene are taken by a series of different cameras and
subsequently assembled to simulate camera movement.

Shooting of the film *The Matrix*, 1999

For his artworks the Japanese artist Tokihiro Sato uses extremely long exposures of one to two hours. The points of light in his photographs are created by reflecting sunlight into the camera using a mirror.

#87 Shibuya, Tokihiro Sato, 1991

Right: #385 Kokuritsu-Soko 3, Tokihiro Sato, 1999, Haines Gallery, San Francisco

volves like a giant Ferris wheel. Kubrick underscores this scene with a passage from a famous waltz, remarking:
"It's hard to find anything better than the 'Blue Danube' for depicting the grace and beauty in the turning."
The expression of spaces in film can change dramatically when elements that define space are set in motion. Particularly where architectural constructions in film are concerned, filmmakers are comparatively free to turn such spatial experiments into filmic reality. Film sets do not have to be designed to support real loads or be made of real materials. They do not need to withstand years of use or carry a second storey and are not exposed to the elements over a long period of time. In film it is possible to realise spatial concepts that are not static but can appear movable and transient. It is rarely necessary to construct a solid, inhabitable space; in most cases film sets serve only to frame precise theatrical mechanisms.
Accordingly, large-scale transforming spaces have been the subject of countless sci-fi scenes and James Bond films. The sets of the early Bond films all appear to have an underlying agenda, that to this day lends them the aura of a dark, modern-day version of Alice in Wonderland: things are not what they at first seem to be and scenes abound with false floors and secret mechanisms. There are swimming pools that turn into shark tanks and vast, artificial crater lakes that shift to one side to make room for a rocket launching pad. As soon as the main room in Auric Goldfinger's house changes first

from a Frank-Lloyd-Wrightesque living room to a lecture room, then to a deadly prison, there is no mistaking that James Bond is up against an adversary of equal stature.

A sculpture in time

In addition to the examples discussed here, there are an almost inexhaustible number of fascinating works in both film and photography from which one can learn about movement in space.
Among these are some that have managed to distil both of the aforementioned approaches to movement in space into a single film sequence or a single image.
The interiors of Space Station 5 in Stanley Kubrick's *2001 – A Space Odyssey*, which was designed as a giant centrifuge that rotates around its centre to artificially create a sense of gravity, are among the most spectacular and beautiful moving spaces ever made in the history of film. The film sequences illustrate Stanley Kubrick's meticulous capacity for invention, constructing a space that creates a different kind of gravitation and a form of movement that corresponds to these conditions.
With the help of the centrifuge, it was possible to unite both perspectives – movement through space as well as the representation of movement itself – in a single, brilliantly-conceived film set.

There are few more compelling examples of the combination of both phenomena in a single image than the beautiful photographs taken by the Japanese sculptor and photographer Tokihiro Sato. Whether

an urban square, interior or picturesque natural setting, the artist walks through the spaces, gauging their size, all the while photographing the scene with a long time exposure. Although the artist himself is not actually visible in the photo, the image contains an exact record of his changing position and with it his physical range.
"I only photograph landscapes, certain objects, and light. Nevertheless, these photos still have a distinctly human quality. The light becomes corporeal, while the traces of light that I create as I move embody passing time, creating a sculpture in time."
Tokihiro Sato

1 Giedion, Sigfried: *Space, Time, Architecture*, 5th edition, Cambridge, Mass., 2003.
2 *Das fliegende Auge*, Michael Ballhaus in conversation with Tom Tykwer, Berlin 2002, cover text.
3 „Kino wird sich grundlegend verändern", Interview with John Gaeta, *SPIEGEL Online*, 8.5.2008.
4 Castle, Alison (Ed.): *The Stanley Kubrick Archives*, Cologne 2008, p. 33.

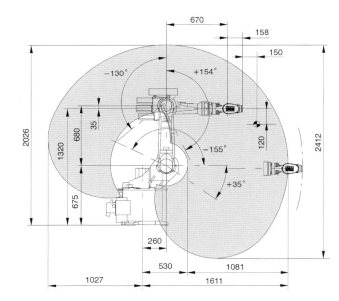

The work envelope of an industrial robot

■ 1.4 On the relationship between robots and space

Jan Zappe

Robots are pieces of mobile architecture. Their relationship to architecture is manifold and varied and can be regarded from many different perspectives. A robot can, for example, be understood as a small architectural model for a gigantic mobile building that is able to change its form. Alternatively, it could be part of an architectural interior that actively shapes space in the function of an integral device or piece of dynamic furniture. More conventionally, robots are understood as items of machinery in industrial production plants. As an integral part of an assembly line inside of the industrial factory building they, along with the other technical equipment, form a functional unit that is optimised for maximum efficiency. Through its location and the cooperation between people and robots on the factory floor, numerous spatial and architectural phenomena already arise. However, if one thinks beyond this scenario and imagines robots in other public or private environments, a much broader range of relationships to space emerges. At present,

SSRMS – Space Station Remote Manipulator System, NASA/CSA, 2005

A

1

AT-AT, All Terrain Armoured Transport, walking fighting machine from the *Star Wars* films; mobile robotic architecture with crew, 1980

juke_bots, Robotic DJ installation by robotlab, 2001

The projects by the artists at robotlab make experimental use of standard industrial robots for art installations and performances. In their exhibitions, the machines which normally carry out repetitive tasks in factories become autonomous protagonists. As painters, writers, dancers or disc jockeys they make inroads into artistic fields that are traditionally the realm of human creativity and expression.

however, such situations are rare in everyday life and the following text refers, therefore, to other public spaces such as museums or theatres – contexts in which robots are occasionally to be found. What happens when an industrial robot becomes an exhibit in an exhibition? Firstly, the machine occupies a lot of space. To ensure precise movement, the robot is fixed to a large and sturdy footing that provides sufficient counterweight for the weight of the robot's moving arms. It is also surrounded by a barrier that stops visitors from being struck by the robot – for example, wires or ropes strung between posts, or possibly acrylic glass partitions. The presence of the robot as a static object along with its surrounding installations is, therefore, in itself a drastic, architectonic intervention in the exhibition space. The robot literally occupies this space; it stands its ground.

A robot also affects its environment in another, more significant way: through movement. Every point in space that the robot is able to reach through the anatomy of its hand is defined as its work envelope. This is the robot's physical range of reach, its sphere of action and its space of possibilities. Although all the robot's actions take place within this sphere of action, it can still influence its wider environment through its impact as an image as well as the sound it produces. A robot's movements attract attention, exert a certain fascination and stimulate the imagination. The movement of the articulated arm of a robot has a dynamism that, unlike other specialised industrial machinery, is almost organic, lending it an intrinsic being

that is further underlined by its distinctively anatomical appearance. This intrinsic being is defined as its unique nature to appear to another living being as related, although it actually contains little of the latter and is inherently so very different that one can scarcely conceive what it constitutes. Here we must differentiate between an "intrinsic" being and a "living" being. Given the differences between robots and living beings, I will refrain from even attempting a definition that robots constitute a new form of living being but rather focus on the dynamic means with which a robot can transform space and through which it communicates its intrinsic being. With the invention of the robot, a parallel definition of an intrinsic being has emerged that is distinct from that of a human or animal. This term designates the robot as a being that is simultaneously lifeless yet lively.

The space a robot can influence becomes the place of its actions. It is not just the architectural constellation of the geometry of the building and the geometry of the robot itself but also a scenery in which events take place that the robot influences through its actions, a place in which the geometry of the space interacts with the changing geometry of the robot. It is through these interactions that a machine in an exhibition becomes a point of communication in a museum.

How do the actions of a robot in an exhibition differ from those in an industrial context where robots are more commonly deployed? On the factory floor, robots are always considered in the context of a predefined perspective, whether by a programmer, a

shift worker or a visitor to the works: all activities are oriented around the manufacture of a particular product. In the production process, the robot must fulfil a set of predefined actions as quickly and precisely as possible. The determining factor for the production hall is the production process, not the robot or those observing it. In this case the role of the robot is determined by its functionality.

In an exhibition space, by contrast, there is no set functionality. Here, the robot in the exhibition becomes a medium that facilitates communication with visitors through its movements. This communication is part of its intrinsic being. As a medium this goes further than simply being a machine with media-related functions. This additional quality, which sets it apart from other technical apparatuses for communication, is a product of the robot's universal, signifying "physicality". This physicality, expressed through its movements and configurations, is a sign that goes beyond the primary meaning and simultaneously communicates itself and its intrinsic being. It is not just what it stands for and does but also what it means and what it implies through itself as well as what it produces. In robots, the physical and the symbolic fuse together: it is a sign and an object in one. The robot enters into a symbiosis with the exhibition space, and respectively with its architectural container, into which the machine introduces its own specific communicative quality.

As a result, a robotic installation has the character of an event and is more closely related to interactive art forms and performance than to pictures or

bios [bible], Bible Scribe by robotlab, 2007

bios [bible], calligraphy written by the hand of a robot

sculptures which are physically static. Their actions are ephemeral moments that tell a story or describe actions; the configurations that result are as it were *tableaux vivants* of contemporary media art. For this reason robots are frequently utilised on stage in the context of theatre or dance performances where spatial presence is similarly created through movement. While a robot in an exhibition or on stage fulfils a functional purpose just as it does on the factory floor, the symbolic value of its actions are not reduced to capacity and throughput as they are in an industrial context. Its relationship to space is profound but, particularly with regard to its architectural surroundings, does not necessarily have to be functional or productive. Conversely, robots can also directly intervene in architecture, for example in the demolishing or the assembly of a building. Robots can also be integrated into architecture, for example to move walls or open doors, directly manipulating the geometry of a space. In the latter case, the robot becomes part of the architecture – rather than being a function contained within the building, it becomes an integral part of the building's functionality.

Despite the fact that there are now millions of robots, they have had little appreciable impact – in any of the aforementioned senses – on everyday public and private spaces, hence the focus here on industrial, exhibition and performance spaces. In domestic or service sectors, the use of robots is likewise an exception. As a consequence, the relationship we have to robots is largely one of unfamiliarity – we are fascinated, awed and wary of ro-

bots all at the same time. Although robots exist and, through their productivity, have had a major impact on society, they are largely invisible so that we are mostly unaware of them. Here too lies a similarity with architecture: although it is most definitely visible and plays a major role in determining our living environment, its silent presence and familiarity means that we seldom give it much attention. The inconspicuousness and static nature of architecture is a discreet quality that could potentially be transformed by the development of mobile robotic architecture which would help architecture emerge out of the shadow of immobility. In today's society, the impact of both robots and architecture is abstract, although both exert a strong presence in space. Robots continue to operate in the backyards of society, in factories and research laboratories, as if in the subconsciousness of our culture.

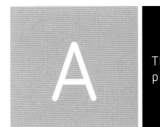

A Theory and planning

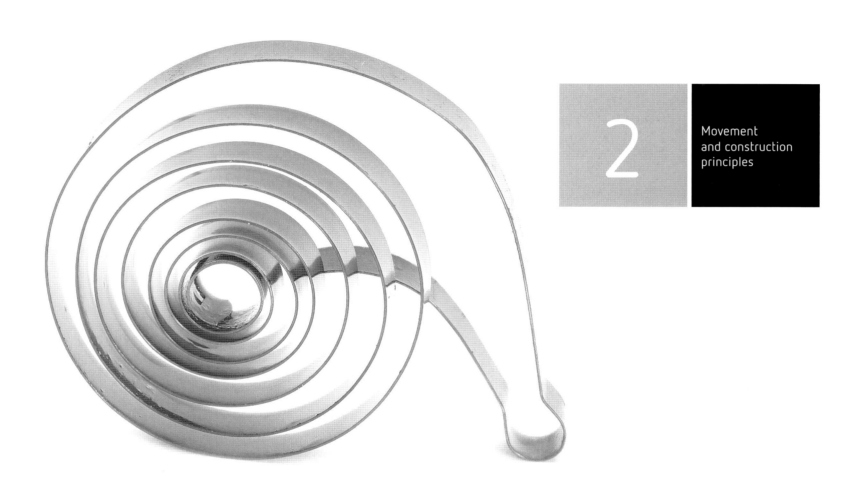

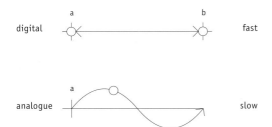

■ 2.1 The principles of designing movement

Over the ages, architecture has brought forth a wide-ranging canon of design principles that address how to design good, man-made built environments at all scales. These principles describe the respective, culturally-specific understanding of well-designed architecture. Almost exclusively, however, they concern building structures or building elements that are permanent, fixed or immobile. Little thought is given to the design possibilities afforded by changing individual parts of a building over the course of time. The following examination offers a systematic breakdown of aspects and parameters that inform the good design of mobile and movable architecture. As a starting point, it is instructive to undertake a morphological analysis of other design disciplines that also deal with movement and space in a wider sense, for example choreography or film montage.

Digital and analogue movement

The way in which movements take place can be divided into two fundamentally different types, depending on whether the movement effects a change of state from A to B or whether the movement is itself the intention. The first of these can be described as digital movement. In such cases, the start and end states are the key formal characteristics of movement. The transition between the two serves purely the change of state and is for the most part unimportant. In architecture, this is the most common type of movement: a door is either open or closed. The process of opening the door is irrelevant in design terms, even when the process itself necessitates high-precision technical fittings. However, as soon as the specifics of the mechanism of opening or closure become more apparent, the construction-

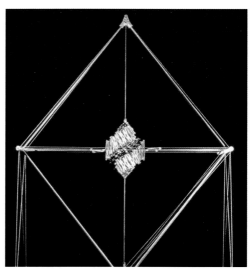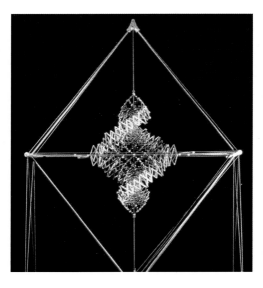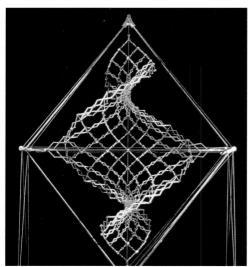

Expanding Helicoid, Hoberman Associates, 1998

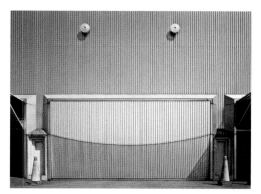
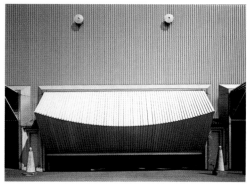

Ernsting's Family Distribution Depot doors, Santiago Calatrava, Coesfeld, Germany, 1985

al dimension can acquire design potential. This might be the case when an open door comes to rest in an unusual position, or when the door's particular construction produces a specific opening sequence. By way of example, the slow movement of a heavy, armoured door to a strongroom communicates an immanent sense of gravity and security. If the sequence of the change of state acquires a quality in its own right, then this movement can be described as being analogue. In this second type of movement there is typically no clear start or end state. Movements of this kind often follow a repeating pattern which can be described as a rhythm. In architecture, a suitable example would be shading louvres that react to the position of the sun. The slow but continuous change in the angle of the louvres is characteristic for this type of movement. With the excep-

tion of wind rotors there are very few examples of architectural elements that move continuously at a perceptible speed in an analogue fashion.

Speed

The speed of movement is critical for our perception of movement altogether. The human eye can sense around 30 impulses of light per second. This effect is used in film technology to simulate the effect of movement by presenting a series of separate frames in rapid succession at a rate of at least 24 frames per second. Similarly, we are also unable to make out fast-moving real objects precisely. Either the moving object appears blurred or else we perceive it only in terms of before and after, much like the digital sense described above. For example, a grasshopper sitting in the grass that

we can see clearly disappears from one moment to the next.

If the speed of movement lies within a range we can perceive visually, numerous factors influence our subjective estimation of its speed. This depends, among other things, on the size of the stimulus, how far away it is, its brightness, its own speed, the moving object's surroundings and the type of movement. Furthermore, optical effects can also create the illusion of movement. These include the aforementioned stroboscopic effect, that is the rapid succession of distinct individual stimuli, or an induced sense of movement through a change in the frame of reference. Train passengers see this phenomenon when looking out of a carriage window in a railway station: it is not always clear which train is moving, one's own or the neighbouring train outside.

Abismo steel rollercoaster, Madrid, 2006

The estimation of whether speed of movement is fast or slow is therefore highly subjective and we are generally unable to say at what speed an object is travelling. If an object moves with respect to the viewer at a rate of less than 1/3° of an optical angle per second, the eye is unable to perceive that it is actually moving. The change in position can only be identified by mentally comparing two or more memorised states. A snail travels a distance of around 3 m in an hour, but we are rarely aware of it actually moving.

Acceleration
Where the speed of movement is perceptible to the human eye, changing the speed through positive or negative acceleration can be an elementary means of design. Although we are only able to determine the speed of other objects indirectly through perception, our sense of balance allows us to directly sense the acceleration of our own body. Acceleration is given in m/sec², that is the change of velocity in metres per second every second. 59 m/sec² corresponds to six times the acceleration of a free-falling

body, or 6 g for short. This represents the maximum speed of vertical acceleration that most people can tolerate (trained pilots can raise their tolerance to up to 10 g). Beneath this tolerance level, our perception of movement is determined primarily by acceleration. For example, the linear acceleration curve of an electric vehicle differs significantly from the flattened parabolic curve typical of petrol-driven vehicles, lending the electric vehicle a quite different and more direct driving experience. Acceleration is also relevant for indirect sensory perception. In general, gentle acceleration and deceleration is perceived as being harmonious, or even elegant. The damping mechanism of a car tailgate serves more than just safety and noise-reduction; it also appeals to our appreciation of well-designed movement.

Serial repetition
The serial coupling, or at the very least the repetition, of movable building elements is very common in architecture. In addition to the economic benefit of serially producing complex building elements, this approach also presents numerous design op-

tions. The way in which elements are coupled in series can have a great effect on the overall appearance. The movement of an individual window shutter is nothing extraordinary. Taken together, however, the opening and closing of many individual shutters, at once or individually, creates a varied and modulated appearance that can change throughout the day. In simple cases, the serial arrangement is such that all the individual elements are interlinked so that they move according to a predetermined pattern. The connection may simply be a product of its mechanical configuration or controlled by a central control system that directs all the elements synchronously. Greater variety is possible if all the individual parts can be moved and controlled independently. The coordination of movement may be controlled centrally and apply to all the elements according to a specific pattern, or controlled locally at each element in response to local conditions. With regard to the external appearance, one can differentiate between two different design strategies: choreographed movement follows a predetermined plan while individual movement means

Jocelyn Vollmar as Myrthe in *Giselle*, San Francisco Ballet, 1947

Sculpture 55A, Santiago Calatrava

that each element can be moved entirely independently. And when the activity of a single element responds to the movements of neighbouring elements, the overall combinatory effect can acquire a swarm-like quality.

Complexity
Complex temporal and spatial sequences in the transformation of an object can also be used as a means of design. By way of example, the Aero X concept car employs a succession of simple but different movements that together turn the opening of the car doors into a sequential experience. The carefully choreographed serial addition of movements creates a quite fascinating motion sequence.

Weight
The perceived weight of an element has important implications for its formal appearance, all the more so when the construction, or parts thereof, are intended to be movable. The lens-shaped inflatable cushion that covers the roof of the bullring at the Palacio Vista Alegre in Madrid (structural engineer:

Schlaich Bergermann und Partner), for example, appears almost to float when open. By contrast, the slow, ponderous opening sequence of a massive steel door tells of the great effort required to shift its mass.

Balance
The optical disposition of mass can likewise be a design theme for mobile building elements. While the cantilever of a folding bridge can on its own appear quite daring, the balance and poise of Gateshead Millennium Bridge in Newcastle upon Tyne (architects: Wilkinson Eyre) as it pivots on its springing points is both visually expressive and spectacular. Its shape and design displays the structural forces at play.

Mystery
Some movements generate interest precisely because one cannot see where they come from or how they work. Many of Bang & Olufsen's hi-fi and entertainment consoles play on this sensation, the CD-player opening as if by magic as soon as one

approaches it with CD in hand. The mechanism, sensor and controls remain entirely concealed, its operation ostensibly a mystery.

Interaction
The above example also embodies a further element of kinematic design: the console's direct response to human movement links the movement of the CD-player to that of its user. The interactive interplay between the two heightens our appreciation of its movement.

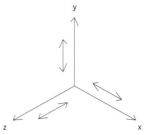

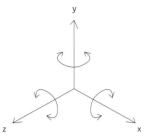

Three degrees of freedom of
translation

Three degrees of freedom of
rotation

■ 2.2 The principles of mechanics

In architecture, mobile building elements are typically employed in order to respond to changing functional requirements. Design tasks are influenced by the field of engineering mechanics, and the mechanics of solids in particular, as the built environment is defined primarily by solid matter as opposed to fluid or gaseous substances. Solid bodies can be categorised as rigid, elastic or plastic depending on which behavioural characteristic dominates in their use and dimensions. In architecture, rigid bodies are most common and are usually connected by hinged joints to form movable elements. Elastic bodies are also employed in movable elements at a small scale, for example in the form of steel springs or rubber dampers. At a larger scale,

and therefore in a loadbearing capacity, the use of elastic bodies is relatively rare, with the exception of flexible membrane structures.

Rope-like materials represent a special case within this categorisation. These very long and slender materials behave very differently depending on the direction of loading. Individual fibres of essentially rigid material can be spun or twisted to form threads and ropes that are extremely flexible in the lateral dimension but can resist tension longitudinally. Using additive techniques, such as weaving or meshing, sheets of fabric can be created that serve a wide variety of uses in architecture as highly flexible, two-dimensional building elements.

Kinematics and kinetics

The motion of rigid bodies can be described at two levels. Kinematics refers exclusively to the temporal process of motion and involves recording the geometric displacement of one or more bodies over time. This makes it possible to determine, alongside the distance travelled, other key parameters of movement such as the duration, velocity or acceleration. As the movement of a body is always caused by external forces, these forces and the corresponding motion they produce are described using methods of analytical dynamics. A subdivision of the study of dynamics with which architects are already familiar is statics, which describes the situation when all forces at play are in equilibrium. If, how-

One degree of freedom

Three degrees of freedom

Six degrees of freedom

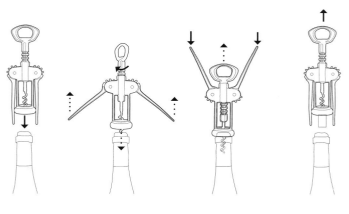

Combination of translation and rotation in a corkscrew

ever, one of the external forces exceeds the others, movement results. A static system becomes a kinetic system.

Translation and rotation

One can differentiate between two different kinds of movement: in the case of linear movement, so-called translation, the position of an object in space moves parallel to the coordinate axes; in the case of rotation, the object changes its orientation in space by rotating about the coordinate axes. For each of these kinds of movement, one can identify three degrees of freedom, depending on how the position or orientation of an object changes with respect to one, two or three coordinate axes. The ability of an object to move around in space is therefore defined by a maximum of six degrees of freedom. Geometric constraints can be applied to limit an object's degree of freedom. A door leaf, for example, has precisely one degree of freedom of rotation – the position and direction of the door can be defined unambiguously by one single coordinate: the angle at which it stands. The notion of degrees of freedom can be applied to several objects at once, where these are linked to one another by a connector of a fixed length. Similarly, the hinged arm of a door closer attached to the door also has one degree of freedom. Although it follows a much more complex pattern of movement than the door itself, the planar position of both arms of the clos-er can be determined by the angle at which the door stands.

Simple machines

Mechanical devices that are able to change either the magnitude, the point of application or the direction of an applied force are known as machines. The basic principles of machines date back to antiquity and were put to use in the form of "simple machines". There are four main types of machines: the first of these allows rigid objects to be pushed or pulled using a bar and rope, applying the same force in the same direction but at a different point to where it was exerted. If the rope is then passed around a pulley, the direction of the force can also

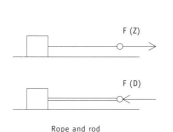

Rope and rod

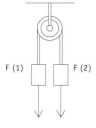

Rope and pulley

Lever

$$F(Z) = F(G) \times \sin \alpha$$

Inclined plane

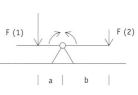

Simple machines

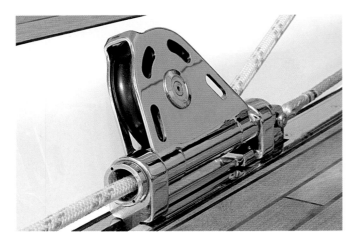

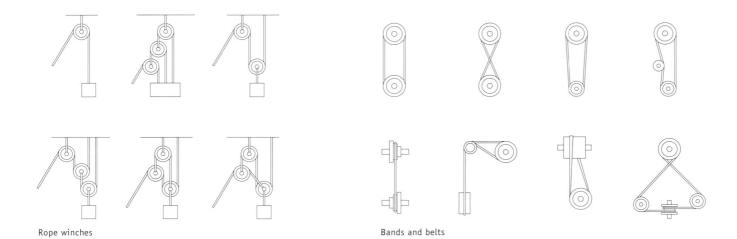

Rope winches

Bands and belts

be changed. A third machine from antiquity, the lever, allows one to change the magnitude of force. This device connects two forces by a stiff bar and has a fixed point of rotation, the fulcrum. The distance between the point of effort and the fulcrum is known as the lever arm. When a lever is balanced, the resulting product of effort and lever arm (the moment) on one side is equal to the force exerted on the other. The longer the lever arm, the smaller the amount of effort required to produce the same level of moment. The fourth principle involves the use of an inclined plane to change the magnitude of force required. The relationship is a function of the angle: the flatter the surface, the smaller the magnitude of force required to increase its eleva-

tion but the longer the distance it has to move along this plane to raise it to a particular height.

Compound machines

By combining and extending these simple basic principles it is possible to create more complex compound machines. The aim is always to convert the effort applied as efficiently and targeted as possible through the function of the machine. For example, a winch combines the principle of the lever with that of the rope and axle. Human muscle power is magnified by the lever of the crank and transferred to the rope. The point of application of the force is also changed: the rotational movement of the drum is converted into a continuous vertical

translation of the end of the rope. Other mechanical elements such as the screw can likewise be reduced to the fundamental principles of simple machines: the form of a screw is in essence an inclined plane wrapped around a shaft, which can convert the rotary torque of the screwdriver into a linear thrust and amplify it through the angle of incline of the thread.

Multiplication effects through gearing

Gears

Rod systems

■ 2.3 Scale and complexity of systems

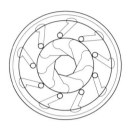

Photographic diaphragm shutter

Stadium roof

Movement has been and will continue to be integrated into architecture at all scales and orders of magnitude. In 1963, Peter Cook and Archigram envisioned entire moving cities and although this particular expression of ultimate mobility has remained a utopian ideal, there are numerous examples throughout the history of architecture of individual buildings that are transportable. Typically these buildings stand in the tradition of flexible shelters for nomadic living that are able to adapt to their respective changing environments. But as building

technology becomes increasingly advanced, movement also begins to play a larger role in stationary buildings.

In extreme cases, entire buildings are able to move as a whole, turning, for example, on their axis to follow the position of the sun. Sometimes individual rooms are made movable, whether within the confines of an external envelope or to extend the size of a room outwards. In other cases, individual surfaces or elements that enclose a room are made to move, as epitomised by the masterly drama of

Mies van der Rohe's lowerable glass wall in the Villa Tugendhat. But by far the most common use of movement in architecture is in the form of individual moving elements: opening doors, windows and gates which have long been part of the basic architectural repertoire. To improve the adaptability of buildings, individual components within an element can also be made movable. Lamellae and other manipulators, for example, are made to respond to changing environmental conditions. And at the far end of the scale of movement, this func-

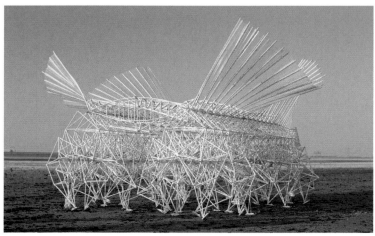

Strandbeest, Theo Jansen

Rhinoceros, Theo Jansen

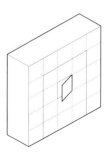

Olympic Tennis Centre, Dominique Perrault, Madrid, 2009

Boat deck hatch

tion is fulfilled in its simplest form by changes and movements within the material itself.

System scale and ease of realisation

The scale of the movable element – its order of magnitude in relation to the scale of the human being – has a determining effect on the complexity of the technical realisation of movement. Much of the construction process continues to be dominated by manual, hand-made production. In response to this means of manufacture, many building materials and elements are of a size that can be easily handled. Constructions that depart significantly from this familiar scale are more difficult to realise both in terms of cost and quality. This applies equally to small-scale constructions that require high-precision execution as well as to large-scale constructions, which have major implications for the structural framework of rigid building elements, as well as for coordinating construction work on site. As a result, two key strategies have evolved for handling movable elements in the building sector: on the one hand, smaller components such as hinges and window fittings are almost exclusively mass-produced and are available as prefabricated industrial products on the market. The ability to shape or personalise such products is very limited compared to non-movable building products. On the other hand, large building elements are usually conceived for a single, clearly defined type of movement and are optimised in the planning phase and then delivered to site either as a single large element or as a series of identical, repeating building elements. This last op-

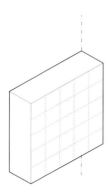

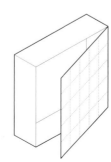

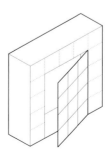

Scale of movement

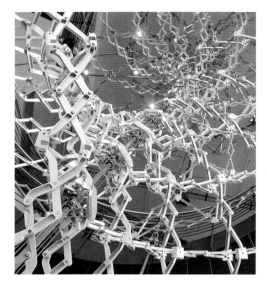 

Expanding Helicoid, Hoberman Associates, Milwaukee, Wisconsin, 2006

tion in particular offers greater design flexibility as more complex sequences of movements can be realised through the combination of essentially simple moving building elements.

System depth

The system depth describes the sum and complexity of the individual interacting movements needed to effect a larger movement. The system depth required to set a movable building element in motion can vary in practice considerably, depending on the application. One can identify three functional factors: the size of the moving element, its position in relation to the building envelope (internal, part of the skin, external) and the safety requirements necessary to protect people from harm when the element moves. The functional safety requirements for the doors of an aircraft hangar are in all respects greater than that of a set of sliding kitchen doors. The safety mechanism is usually part of the equipment used to move the main movable element: for example, a door may be secured with a motorised latch or the movement of a gate halted by a foot-operated bolt.

To achieve the required system depth, individual movements can be combined either mechanically (by a kinematic chain) or electronically (by a control unit).

Geometric complexity

Kinematics describes how the geometric disposition of mobile elements changes over time. For the most part, such movement is three-dimensional; solely two-dimensional movements, such as that of a pair of scissors, are comparatively rare in architecture. In most cases, systems are employed in which a change in the depth of a building component produces a three-dimensional effect but whose actual movement can be represented in a two-dimensional sectional view. Like their counterparts in CAD systems, these are known as two-and-a-half dimensional systems. The geometric complexity increases considerably when the movement itself is three-dimensional. With two-and-a-half dimensional systems, it is fairly straightforward to check for collisions in a single plane. Three-dimensional systems, by contrast, can require complex computer-aided models and simulation.

Similarly, the combination of individual movements into a kinematic chain increases the geometric complexity of movements. The chain of movements follow a hierarchical pattern in that the movements of a subordinate element (the child) are determined geometrically by the superordinate element (the parent). The addition of two of more individual movements in a kinematic chain already increases the complexity of the overall movement considerably. Likewise small changes to the initial configuration can have a comparatively large effect on the overall result.

The principle of linear kinematic chains can be extended through the additive combination of similar chains to create two or three-dimensional transforming structures. The overall shape is commonly a simple figure such as a ring or rectangular area, but three-dimensional lattices and complex geometric figures can also be realised in this manner as mobile mechanisms. Hoberman Associates, for example, developed an expanding helicoid made of innumerable cross-linked scissor arms for Discovery World in Milwaukee. A limiting factor by structures of this kind, and vitally important for the geometric configuration and detailed construction of the hinges, is the need for the elements to pack together tightly when closed. This is all the more relevant when, unlike the bar-shaped structural elements in the aforementioned example, solid planar elements are employed.

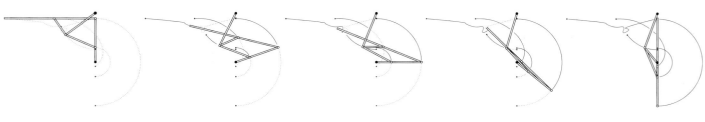

Sequence of movement of a trackless garage door

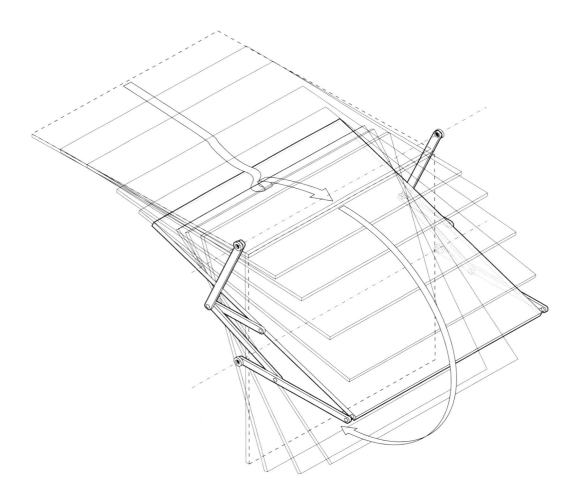

In contrast to conventional systems, the movement of the door panel is achieved using pivot hinges alone.

Storefront for Art and Architecture, Steven Holl, New York, 1993

■ 2.4 Typologies of movement

The movement of rigid materials

Mechanical movements can always be reduced to two basic types of movement: rotation and translation, or a combination of the two. This classification is used regardless of where the hinge or joint is located and without considering gravity. Both of these, however, have major implications for the design, the construction assembly and the means of making the architectural element move. For architectural applications, therefore, a further systematisation of movement types is more useful.

In many cases the way in which an architectural element moves as a whole at a large-scale differs from the sequential and geometric movements that occur at a detailed level. The simple rotation of a kitchen cupboard door at a macro level is achieved at a micro level by a complex hinge construction. This hinge effects a kinetic chain of movements in several rotational axes to first push the door outwards out of the plane of the unit and then turn it to one side. As we are concerned with movements at an architectural scale, the typologies discussed here always relate to the macro level relevant for their use. Here the function of the movement is considered rather than the precise mechanical or theoretical elaboration of a sequence of movements.

Rotation

Rotation causes the direction of a body in space to change while its position remains the same. In architecture, rotation usually occurs around a single axis, that is a single degree of freedom of rotation.

One differentiates between three architectonic types of rotation:

Where an element, for example a lamella, rotates back and forth around its centroidal axis, this is termed simple rotation. Typically the rotational movement is restricted by a stopper that prevents the element from rotating fully and holds the element in a resting position.

Revolving or spinning elements, by contrast, are able turn continually through more than 360°. A revolving door, for example, turns perpetually in the same direction and not in the opposite direction.

Where the rotational axis lies outside the element's centroidal axis, the element in question swings. In most cases the hinges or joints of a swinging architectural element are located on one of its edges. The use of swinging elements in architecture is widespread, for example as doors or windows. Due to the eccentric load distribution of swinging elements their angle of rotation is almost always limited; a separate examination of the typology of rotating swinging elements has therefore not been undertaken here.

Translation

Translations denotes a change of position of a body in space while its orientation remains the same. Here too, simple translations, that is movements along a single degree of freedom, are most common in architecture. Where objects themselves have a specific orientation, one differentiates between translation parallel to the orientation of the object and perpendicular to it. The latter case is consider-

ably more complex to realise as two rails or carriers are required to move the object.

Rotation and translation

More complex movements can be created through a combination of rotation and translation: the hinging of two or more building elements along their edges, for example, creates a folding element. Supporting these on rotating or mobile bearings opens up a variety of different areas of application. A characteristic aspect of folding elements is their capacity to change spatial configuration, often quite considerably. For example, an extensive surface area can be folded away into a relatively compact volume. The principle of a simple folding element can be extended through the addition of further rigid hinged elements to create a concertina-like folding arrangement. Although the basic movement of the mobile bearings remains the same, their reach is effectively doubled.

Effective direction of movement

The direction of movement in relation to the direction of gravity has a significant impact on the forces acting on the construction and with it the kinetic concept. Of key importance is the self-weight of the object and the height and lever arm in which it is moved. A flat, planar architectural element with appropriate bearings can be moved horizontally with relatively little technical means and only a small amount of energy input. To move the same element vertically requires either a system of counterweights linked by pulleys or a comparat-

Movement of rigid building elements

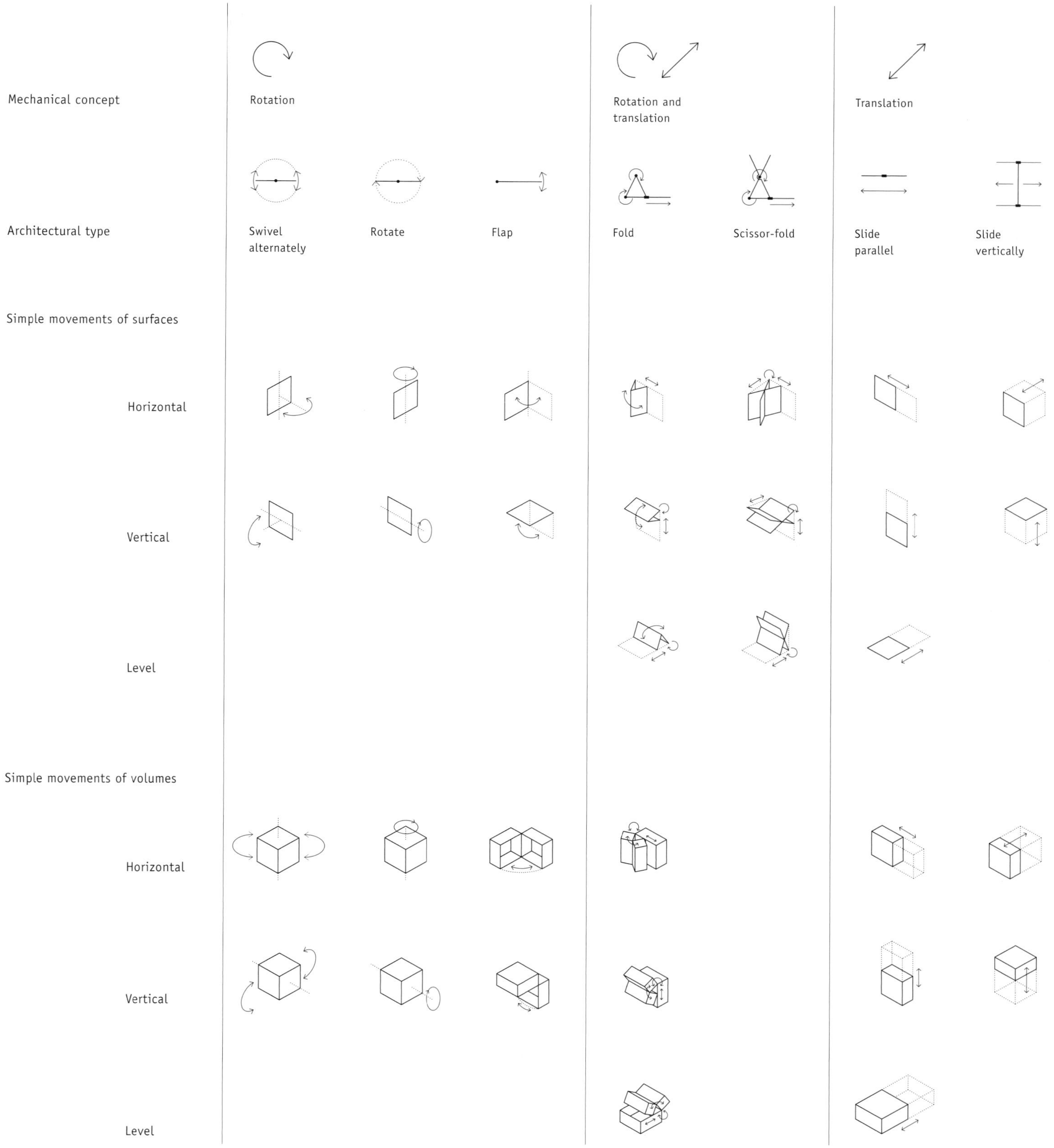

	Mechanical concept							
	Rotation			Rotation and translation		Translation		

Architectural type	Swivel alternately	Rotate	Flap	Fold	Scissor-fold	Slide parallel	Slide vertically

Simple movements of surfaces

Horizontal

Vertical

Level

Simple movements of volumes

Horizontal

Vertical

Level

A

2

Softwall + Softblock modular system, Molo Design, Vancouver, 2005

Movements of deformable building elements

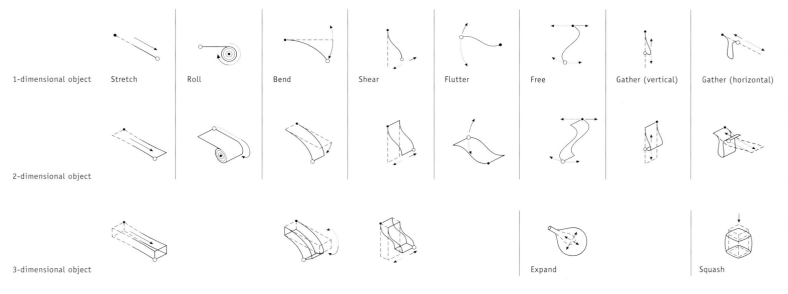

1-dimensional object	Stretch	Roll	Bend	Shear	Flutter	Free	Gather (vertical)	Gather (horizontal)

2-dimensional object

3-dimensional object · Expand · Squash

ively high level of energy input. Both cases require considerably more effort to effect this movement.

The directionality of material properties
A factor that determines the spectrum of possible movements is the spatial form of an architectural element. A linear element generally deforms differently to a planar or volumetric element of the same material. This allows us to derive a typology of possible patterns of movement for deformable architectural elements. The above illustration provides an overview of the most important typologies. Deformable elements used in architecture generally have extreme proportions and are, for example, long and slender or very flat. These materials often respond differently to the forces applied to them depending on whether these act parallel to or perpendicular to the axis of extension. This effect can be exploited by employing materials with strongly directional material properties, for example fibrous materials, or by combining different materials appropriately.

The movement of deformable architectural elements
Deformable architectural elements play an important role in small-scale movements in particular and in the flexible transformation of larger surfaces. In this case, formal and spatial transformations are not the product of different specific and temporal constellations of essentially rigid, unchanging building elements, as discussed above, but instead result from movement within the element or the material itself. Depending on the specific material properties

and combinations of the materials used, one differentiates between soft and flexible bodies and elastic bodies. Substances and plastic materials that deform irreversibly under force are rarely used in architecture. Shape memory alloys represent an exception, in that they are able to change between two different states.

The movement of soft and flexible materials
Flexible or supple materials are able to change shape permanently when external forces are applied without losing their overall formal consistency. Linear examples include fibres, cords or ropes, flat examples include textiles and woven or knitted fabrics. The behaviour of supple materials can also be imitated through the additive interlinking of many very small rigid elements. At a macro-scale a coat of chain mail behaves very similarly to a heavy textile material although at a micro-scale it consists of many hundreds of rigid steel links. Supple materials are used extensively in architecture, most commonly in the form of textiles. Textiles and membranes are extremely light and flexible in relation to the surface area they can cover. They are particularly well suited for creating strong visual and spatial divisions with a minimum amount of energy input and are used in combination with a whole vocabulary of hanging, rolling, gathering or pleating systems.

The movement of elastic materials
In contrast to flexible or supple materials, elastic materials are able to resume their original form after

deformation without the need for additional external force. In theory, elastic materials offer a wide variety of architectural applications, however most elastic materials are not available on the market at the necessary size, durability or visual quality. The use of this group of materials is therefore restricted to small-scale elements and less design-related functions, for example steel springs or rubber dampers.

Pneumatic forms
Flat deformable materials can be transformed into three-dimensional objects by inflating them with air under pressure. As with air balloons, both flexible as well as elastic materials can be used as the containing skin but, for the reasons explained above, only flexible materials are available at a sufficiently large scale and durability for actual use. As a result, pneumatic constructions are rarely able to oscillate elastically between two different forms of expansion but instead change between two different defined states: inflated and deflated. Deflated pneumatic forms occupy very little volume and can be stored away in a very small space and when sufficiently inflated, they acquire the desired spatial form.

■ 2.5 Choosing materials

JuCad CARBON Travel, electric caddy

Mobile constructions are particularly subject to different forms of stresses and strains, and the choice of appropriate materials for mobile building elements must accordingly be given special consideration. Heavy loads lead to material deformation and internal stresses, tribological stresses create friction, causing wear as well as material and energy loss, reactions with ambient substances lead to corrosion, temperature differences cause changes in length, while thermal extremes cause materials to soften when hot and become brittle when cold. Based on these conditions, a catalogue of material requirements can be drawn up which a building material needs to fulfil.

Furthermore, the fact that our available raw materials are finite along with the increasing cost of materials and energy has made it necessary to opti-mise material and energy usage, resulting in a trend towards lighter materials and structures. There is a constant struggle to achieve high strength and stability on the one hand and light weight on the other to minimise the energy required to move an element.

A historical example that epitomises how material choices and the sensible combination of materials and construction have proven the test of time over thousands of years are the sails of a windmill. They need to be able withstand sometimes quite considerable wind forces but also be light and mobile enough to be set in motion by the lightest possible wind. The use of canvas to cover the sails is an appropriate material both in terms of weight reduction as well as the ability to respond to changing environmental conditions. The ability to gather in sec-tions of the canvas to reduce the surface exposed to the wind also makes it possible to control the speed of rotation according to the particular prevailing conditions.

The poetry of weight

The choice of the "right" material can also influence the success of mobile architectural elements in another respect. The mass of a material and its execution and finish also contribute to the aesthetic expression of a building element. Alongside the economical and ecological use of materials, a further design strategy lies in emphasising and communicating the optical and haptic qualities of weight and solidity.

In the James Bond film *Goldfinger* the gold bullion is deposited in a strongroom in Fort Knox behind a

Blown chair, Stephen Newby

heavy, chrome-plated steel door. The metre-thick massive door, weighing many tons, opens very slowly, an impression heightened by the sound of a heavy mass being moved. Using cinematic means, the film communicates the extreme security requirements the armoured door must fulfil. The functional performance of the door is conveyed through the excessive use of materials, its detailing, haptic qualities and sound, and in this exaggerated portrayal acquires a certain poetic charm.

Such considerations and possibilities can also be applied in the real world to heighten the effect of movable elements. In the automotive industry, for example, the designers and construction studios focus not solely on the functionality of components such as car doors. The solidity communicated by a door as it is opened or closed, its material quality,

the way it is hung, how it mates with the car bodywork as well as the satisfying sound it makes as it falls shut are likewise design criteria. Many architectonic elements have a similar potential for optimisation in order to make the experience of using them on a daily basis more conscious and pleasant.

New contexts

In ideal cases, the function, form and material of a chosen solution are seamlessly interwoven. In general, one can differentiate between two principal approaches to the choice of material: either the functional requirements and formal expression determine which material is most suitable, or the material itself, and its aesthetic and technical properties, serve as inspiration for new products. During the design process, an ongoing dialogue takes place

between these two poles. Innovative production and bonding technologies and the availability of new materials open up new possibilities and new directions through the use of materials in other contexts or with a new aesthetic expression. An Austrian company, for example, has developed a lightweight, curtain-like element made of concrete, an intrinsically heavy material. The "concrete curtain" is designed to screen light, sound and views and can serve as a decorative room divider or as facade ornamentation. Using a metal, gridded mould similar to a waffle iron, the concrete is pressed into a form that resembles a textile surface with small, cushion-like rectangles. While the concrete textile is, of course, neither flexible nor soft, it does exhibit a certain flexibility along with a new aesthetic expression.

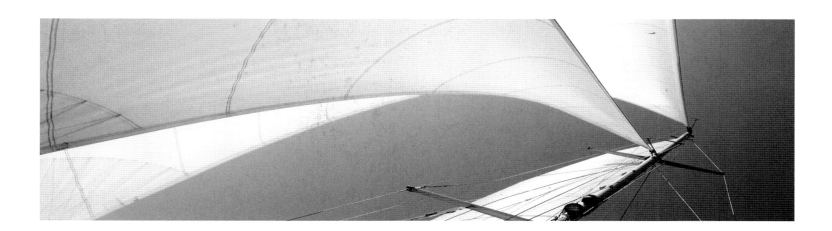

Concrete curtain

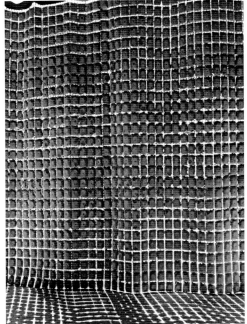

Concrete curtain, backlit

Curtain coated with stainless steel, Creation Baumann

A component-specific choice of materials

Complex building materials can be divided into three groups of components:

1. The movement mechanism
   (joints, bearings, drive, etc.)
2. The static loadbearing elements
   (cantilever, frame, etc.)
3. Planar surface elements
   (panels, lamellae, membranes, etc.)

Movement mechanism

For conventional articulated constructions, prefabricated products are commonly used for the mechanical elements. Track rails, hinges, rollers and other hardware are available on the market for many different purposes. For individual, heavyweight constructions, purpose-built solutions are required that necessitate mechanical engineering expertise. In most cases these elements are cast or extruded fittings made of aluminium, steel or steel alloys. Their weight relative to the weight of the entire building element is comparatively small. This is one reason – alongside the high cost – why high-performance materials such as magnesium alloys have as yet not been used more widely in architecture. In future, however, the trend towards high-strength materials resulting from modified material properties and manufacturing techniques will also make inroads into the building sector. One example is the thermomechanical treatment of steel, in which the raw steel material is rolled twice at high temperature lending it a very fine-grain structure that exhibits a much greater tensile strength.

Loadbearing elements

Loadbearing elements, by comparison, often contribute most to the overall weight of a building element. Systems and materials are required that are durable and strong enough to sustain high static and dynamic loads. Aluminium and steel, and to a certain extent also timber, remain the most proven materials. Here too it is worth examining the performance possibilities of high-tech materials. Glass and carbon fibre reinforced plastics and associated materials offer high performance at a low weight but are not widely available in the building sector and have to be 'imported' from other market areas and adapted to fit the respective needs

Planar surface elements

Infill materials represent the functional layer of mobile building elements. They protect against the weather, solar radiation, noise, fire and the like. They are transparent, translucent or opaque, made of a single homogenous material or of segments combined to form a whole. Planar infill elements used in mobile constructions can be generally classified into two groups:

1. Lightweight and stable: surfaces made of rigid, panel-like assemblies of elements that can be slid, folded or opened (roof segments, folding shutters, brise-soleils, etc.)
2. Soft and flexible: textiles and membranes that can be folded, gathered or rolled up.

Mobile building elements do not necessarily have to follow the above combination of mechanism, structure and infill material, and where they do, the different individual components and materials do not have to be distinct. For example, folding elements made of composite building materials serve through their stability both as a loadbearing material and as an infill material in one and the same component. Sandwich-panel elements such as "3F-board" or "foldtex" even address all three component categories with a single material. These are multi-ply panel materials that consist of two layers of conventional wood panels with a flexible core layer. Channels can be milled into the external layers of the panel to reveal the flexible inner layer which then serves as a hinge. By building in these "fold lines", spatial structures can be created by simply folding the material without the need for any additional hinges or fixtures.

Examples of the multifunctionality of the second group of planar materials include polymer strips and textile membranes. These can be gathered, rolled up or strung between elements, and they can sustain tensile stresses as well as form a flat layer.

The principle of a Freitag-bag: materials in a new context

The BMW GINA Light Visionary Model has a flexible outer skin made of a specially developed fabric based on Lycra. As a result its outer skin consists of just four parts.

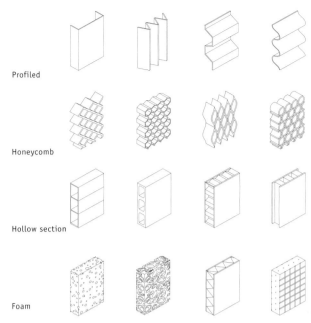

Profiled

Honeycomb

Hollow section

Foam

Lightweight and stable

■ 2.6 High-strength and flexible materials

The classification of a material as "lightweight and high-strength" or as "soft and flexible" can no longer be undertaken purely on the basis of its underlying chemical composition. Many materials are no longer employed in their "pure" form but consist of a combination of different materials. A major contributor to this shift is the development of new production and joining or bonding techniques. For example, metals in their raw form have a high bulk density and are heavier and more stable than natural materials such as wood; when folded in sheet form, however, the same metal can be lighter and can also support greater loads than equivalent timber panels. When woven as textiles, metals can be rolled up; conversely, woven textiles in combination with synthetic resins can also be formed into very rigid elements.

The following section examines selected material and product groups and provides an overview of the technological possibilities of materials development and the breadth of options available for material choices relevant for lightweight, flexible applications, in particular for movable components.

Materials
Metals
The basic properties of metal such as its weight, strength and formability have long been known. Today, the ability to precisely control the production process and to combine metals to form composite and hybrid materials provides the key to creating complex metallic structures and new high-performance materials. Magnesium alloys have made it possible to create thin but highly stable moulded articles such as those used in motor manufacturing. Composite materials with metallic and non-metallic constituents, such as plastics or ceramics, are used in rigid loadbearing panels and profiles. Aluminium can be foamed to form flat panels. Punched holes and perforations allow sheet materials to be lightweight and transparent. Metal threads and high-performance yarns (zylon) can be woven into fine, flexible textiles and netting. Metal wires can be woven into rigid mesh. The process of laser sintering allows powdered metals to be heated and formed into complex objects, for example for rapid prototyping directly from CAD files. Extrusion processes also use metal powders, compressing them to create extruded profiles with complex cross sections. On the other hand, the extensibility of metals also allows them to be "inflated" into cushion-like objects. By using embossing and moulding techniques – for example "hydroforming" which employs high-pressure fluids to shape sheet metal – metal sheeting panels can be made stiffer.

Clear PEP polycarbonate honeycomb panel

ALPORAS aluminium foam panel

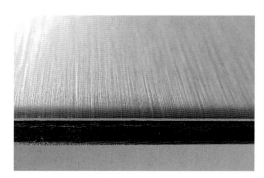

DIBOND sandwich panel

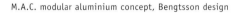

M.A.C. modular aluminium concept, Bengtsson design

Inflated metal, suspended screen, Stephen Newby

Polymers

Plastics are more versatile, lighter, softer, more durable, more colourful and cheaper than any other materials. In terms of their physical constitution, polymers can be divided into three groups:

1. Thermoplastics that become formable at a particular temperature range. The process is reversible: the plastic can be cooled and reheated, even to its molten state, as often as one wishes.

2. Elastomers have a predefined shape but can deform elastically. Under tension or compression they change shape elastically, returning to their original shape after pressure is released. Elastomers are used, for example, in tyres, elastic bands and rubber washers.

3. Thermosetting plastics once hardened can no longer be shaped. Thermosets are hard, glass-like polymers.

Most plastics that we use on an everyday basis are thermoplastics (ABS, polythene, polyethylene terephthalate, polystyrene, PVC, etc.). Thermoplastics can be deformed under tension only with difficulty and retain their shape once tension has been removed. Whether a thermoplastic is hard or soft at room temperature depends on the material's glass transition temperature. Above this temperature, it is soft and malleable, below this temperature hard and rigid. Independently of this, some plastics are mixed with a plasticizer that makes them soft and formable.

The particular quality of elastomers (synthetic rubber) is that its rubber-like elasticity lends it the state of being in equilibrium somewhere between being static and dynamic, between order and entropy. The elastomer does not store the tensile energy within the material but gives it off in the form of heat as it takes on a new internal arrangement. Like a muscle, therefore, it requires new energy to contract, which it draws from the ambient heat. At very cold temperatures, elastomers lose their strength and can freeze to a glass-hard state. A gentle increase in the temperature gives the material new energy and increases the elasticity of the elastomer.

Thermosetting plastics (polyester, epoxy resins, polyurethane, etc.) are much harder and more brittle than thermoplastics. They do not deform under tension, but eventually snap or break. Thermosets therefore have to be worked manually; in practice, however, this is seldom done as the product is usually manufactured directly in the desired form.

The spectrum of forming methods and finishing techniques for plastics is vast. All manner of fillers and additives made of different materials are possible and lend products new properties. Pigments can be added to make them shine and metal filaments allow synthetic textiles to conduct electricity. Polymers can also be foamed to different foam densities, hardness or softness. Other materials can be coated with elastomers to make them more resistant. Strong, weather-resistant and semi-transparent textiles and non-woven fabrics, composite materials consisting of fibres and drawn webs, are used for flexible,

weatherproof components that can be rolled up or gathered such as sails or membrane constructions.

Carbon fibre

Carbon in the form of diamonds or lonsdaleite (a stone formed by meteorite impact) is the hardest naturally-occurring material known to man. The same properties are exhibited by carbon fibres, which can be woven, braided or knitted into very strong textile-like matting. This industrially-produced material is often used in conjunction with other materials. By hardening these with synthetic resins (based on epoxy, polyester or polyurethane) they can be formed into cylinders, ropes, blocks or more complex forms that are extremely light and stable. Despite its high performance, carbon fibre is still in its infancy in product design. The material is expensive to produce in large quantities and a fully sustainable means of disposal or recycling has yet to be discovered.

Natural materials

Strips of natural materials such as bamboo, cotton, paper or leather can be woven into fabrics with different degrees of transparency and are particularly suitable for use in interiors. Recycled paper and card can be soaked in polyester or phenol resin to create stable and durable panels. Wood shavings, paper and other fibrous materials when combined with resin binders can be formed into spatially complex shapes. Soft woods can be pressure-impregnated with polymers to lend them a hardness akin to hard woods.

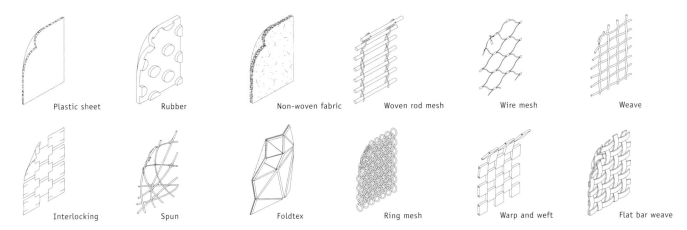

Plastic sheet   Rubber   Non-woven fabric   Woven rod mesh   Wire mesh   Weave

Interlocking   Spun   Foldtex   Ring mesh   Warp and weft   Flat bar weave

Soft and flexible

Bonding and joining methods
Sandwich materials

Of particular importance for stable and lightweight elements are so-called sandwich materials. These are laminated composite materials consisting of several layers or plies of materials laid on top of one another and bonded together. The most common manifestation is a three-ply sandwich panel with two identical outer plies that enclose an inner core material. The aim of sandwich panels is to combine the best qualities of different materials. New plastics and manufacturing technologies have made possible an increasing number of composite materials with different processing technologies. The spectrum of manufacturing methods ranges from simple bonding or laminated materials to materials with honeycomb cores or metal, polymer and ceramic foam fillings. Sandwich construction is usually employed to improve a panel's structural strength while keeping down the weight or price, as well as for thermal insulation or noise proofing. Soft core layers can be used to create articulated constructions: by milling channels in the outer rigid layers down to the soft core, a series of individual panels mounted on a soft inner layer can be created, resulting in a one-piece movable element. In recent years the layered structure of sandwich panels has acquired an aesthetic expression in design. In contrast to their original intention, designers have started expressing the structure of the material "honestly" by revealing the layered edges: what was once the "inferior quality" core has now become a design motif.

Foams

Foams exhibit a low density and lightweight cellular structure. The most common foams are plastics produced either chemically (foaming agent), physically (using a vacuum) or mechanically (aeration). These result in foams with different cell structures: closed-cell foams exhibits closed cell walls that prevent the uptake of water. Open-cell foams have an open pore structure and can absorb fluids like a sponge. Mixed-cell foams contain both kinds of cells. Integral-skin foams have a closed outer skin with successively less dense cells towards the centre.

Plastic foams are characterised by good insulation and good noise reduction properties but low strength. As a result they are commonly used as a lightweight core for rigid sandwich panels. Foamed glass and aluminium by contrast exhibit a high loading capacity. Foamed ceramics are non-combustible and can be used everywhere where effective fire protection is required.

Fibrous composites and fibre-reinforced materials

Fibrous composite materials consist of high-strength fibres made of glass, carbon, aramid (Kevlar) or natural fibres embedded in a matrix, usually a synthetic resin, elastomer or thermoplastic. The result is a material with advantageous stiffness and strength with respect to its weight. The fibres are typically embedded in the form of a fabric with different kinds of weaves. The type of weave affects the properties of the resulting composite. The matrix serves to hold the fibres in a set shape. The fibres and matrix distribute the tensile forces between them at the point of their transition.

Woven textiles

A textile is a flexible material that consists of a combination of fibres. The term textiles is used to denote fibres, yarns and textile surfaces such as cloth or knitted fabric as well as finished products. Both natural (animal, organic or mineral), synthetic or chemical fibres can be used. Weaving consists of the perpendicular intersection of two systems of threads (warp and weft) so that different kinds of connections result. The most important types of weave are taffeta, twill and satin weave. The distinctive appearance of satin weave is a product of the fact that the warp and weft do not form the upright loops (nap), which when cut open are known as pile. The principle of knitting is more akin to meshing techniques: to create the mesh the threads are shaped into loops that then interlock with one another. The term "technical textiles" refers to semi-finished products that are not destined for use as clothing or household textiles but primarily for non-aesthetic, technical purposes that utilise their special thermal, mechanical or chemical properties. To achieve this the properties of the underlying textile may be optimised or rendered with atypical properties.

Wire mesh

Wire mesh is created by weaving wires in a warp and weft, using special machines. The most common materials for meshes are steel and stainless steel.

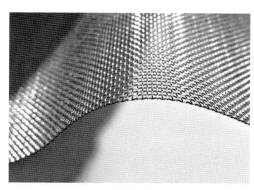

Copper wire mesh, Weisse & Eschrich

Scale mesh, proMesh

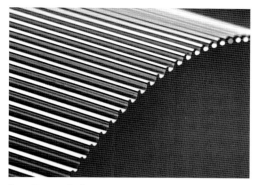

Aero, Forms + Surfaces

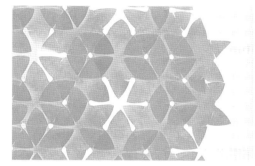

Flake, blind or room divider made of interlocking Tyvek pieces, Woodnotes

Ypsilon CS, room divider made of Trevira, nya nordiska

Wire mesh is also available made of brass, copper, bronze, aluminium, nickel, titanium or silver. As with cloth textiles, the wires can be arranged differently to create different weaves. Special weaves exist, some of them patented, that are specially tailored to a particular use or a particular aesthetic expression. In addition to the type of weave, the properties of the mesh are determined by the mesh size, shape and number, the diameter of the wire and the refinement they make possible.

Non-woven fabrics and felt

Non-woven fabrics are tissue-like sheets that do not exhibit any weave, knotting or other systematic linkage; the fibres lie loosely and uncontrolled on top of one another and are bound together by the attraction and entanglement of the fibres. Non-woven fabrics are differentiated according to the grade and kind of fibres, their means of manufacture and the fibre orientation. They are available made of glass fibres, mineral wool, silk, wool, cotton or synthetic chemical fibres. The compaction methods used to make non-woven fabrics include needling or carding, hydraulic compaction, spray bonding or thermal processes. Felt is made in the same way: although more densely compacted than most non-woven fabrics, it can be regarded as a subcategory of non-woven materials and is available as needled felt or wool or rag felt.

Scrims

Laid scrims are delicate yarn constructions that strengthen, reinforce and stabilise products. Unlike woven materials they consist of diagonally crossing threads that are neither woven nor knitted at the crossing points, but are laid and fixed with binders. The yarns of laid scrims are arranged in between 6 to 10 different directions and can accordingly sustain heavy loads. Its tensile strength derives from the star-shaped structure of the laid yarn, which offers a unique advantage compared to rectangular constructions. Scrims are used where woven fabrics are oversized and knitted constructions are too malleable due to their mesh-structure.

Banded materials

These are strips of textile materials, plastics, natural materials as well as metal sheeting that are woven together to form a web material. The lateral and vertical dimensions of the individual bands can be varied to lend the material a different structural directionality, for example so that it flexes in one direction. A subcategory of this construction are segmented belts of the kind more commonly used for watch straps: a band of metal segments loosely grip a cylindrical bar to form a kind of miniature joint. This principle extended laterally results in segmented textiles.

Chain-linked materials

Chain-link structures consist of rows of movable, loosely interconnected or hinged links. They are typically made of metal much like a historic coat of chain mail. The most interesting aspect of this means of joining materials is that it allows any conceivable material to be formed into flexible, more or less soft, fabric-like structures. Either the material elements are directly linked to one another, for example in the form of rings or scales, or they are joined by another connecting material, for example leather straps, which allow otherwise rigid materials such as metal plates to be connected to form a flat but flexible surface.

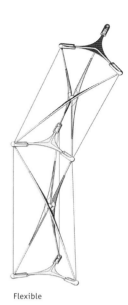

| Compact | Extended | Flexible |

Deployable cantilever structure, Zoran Novacki

■ 2.7 Movable loadbearing structures

Zoran Novacki, Andreas Kretzer

Convertible structures

Convertible structures are able to change both their form and mode of operation. As a structural system they serve as a loadbearing construction for the building; as a movable system they enable its form to change reversibly. Once the form of the structure has been changed, the movable elements of the system are fixed securely in place, signalling the transition from mechanism to loadbearing structure.

The distinctive formal language of structural systems is most visible when structures are required to span large distances or achieve great heights. It is not possible to change the dimensions of loadbearing structures without also changing the proportions of the structural elements. The correla-

tion between span length and bending slenderness of a structural beam is not linear but changes exponentially. To counteract this exceptionally material-intensive effect, structures are therefore typically broken down into a system of tension and compression members – as exemplified by a truss – to avoid the occurrence of bending moments.

A methodical analysis of basic structural systems, such as cantilevers for tower constructions, single-span beams for a bridge or biaxially-spanning slabs as flat structural elements, shows that a spectrum of intermediate forms exist between these basic systems. In particular the principle of the cantilever is one that recurs in the transitional states of convertible structures, for example before a folding bridge is fully lowered or a roof closed over.

Compact convertible cantilevers

Where transportability and mobility are central concerns, constructions have to be designed to be as compact as possible. Unlike transportable buildings that are reassembled from their constituent parts at each new location, a transformable structure must function structurally in each of its changing states. The transformation of a beam from a compact state to an extended state can be considered as a cantilever. This property is particularly apparent with telescopic systems such as mobile cranes. The optimised structure and form of cantilevered structures represent an ideal means of realising telescopic systems that can sustain bending moments, with the widest diameter at its point of fixation. The dimensions are, however, such that there is a limit to the

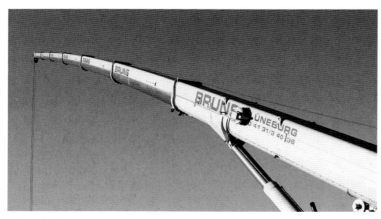

Telescopic principle, mobile crane

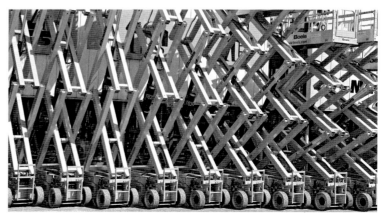

Scissor mechanism, scissor lift

Flexible movable crane, Frei Otto, 1963

Compact and flexible mobile structure, Zoran Novacki, 2009

number of individual telescopic elements that can be inserted inside one another. The system is therefore not modular.

Collapsible systems that employ a scissor extension mechanism can also be used for convertible constructions. They are most commonly used for elevated or working platforms. Unlike telescopic mechanisms, scissor mechanisms are modular and theoretically infinitely extendable. The loadbearing mechanism of a scissor system is, however, not optimal and the pivoting hinges experience bending moments that inevitably result in more sturdily-dimensioned structural components. To eliminate bending moments from a scissor system it would be necessary to "short-circuit" the forces between

every hinged connection of the individual scissor elements. It is also necessary to stabilise the overall structure, for example perpendicular to the plane of the scissor elements.

Flexible convertible cantilevers

Where systems do not have to be mobile and where their construction may also hinder accessibility, it may be necessary to develop a cantilever system that is itself flexible. The engineer and architect Frei Otto experimented in the 1960s and 70s with extendable constructions consisting of a series of vertebrae that could be controlled through a complex system of cables. The articulated boom could be moved in an S-shape much like controlling a puppet.

Flexible and compact cantilevers

A compact and simultaneously flexible construction can be achieved by combining the scissor-extension principle with telescopic elements, while stabilising the structural system using a truss-like geometric frame. This allows the modularity of the system to be maintained. Equipped with sensors and a control unit, such constructions can serve as adaptive systems and can be used, for example, as mobile bridges.

Movable bridge structures

Moving bridge structures are a further example of how the cantilever principle is employed for many different types of construction. This is the case, for

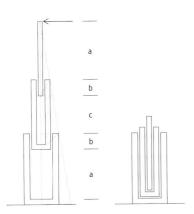

Telescopic shaft, horizontal loading, bending moment diagram

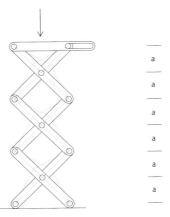

Scissor lift, vertical loading, without horizontal tensioning a bending moment results in the pivot joints

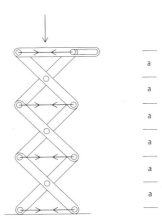

With horizontal tensioning no bending moment

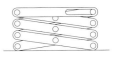

Puente de la mujer, Santiago Calatrava, Buenos Aires, 2001

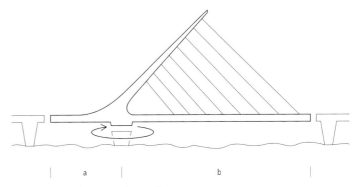

Structural principle, Puente de la mujer

example, with swing bridges and bascule bridges. Here, the cantilever system rotates around the point of support. In the case of bascule bridges, the stresses that arise at this point, which serves as the hinge, have to be counterpoised elsewhere so that the entire system balances. This is usually achieved by using a counterweight and the seesaw (bascule) principle: the further the counterweight is located from the pivot the smaller it needs to be to restore balance. Often these counterweights are visible as is the case, for example, with the folding bridge at Lindaunis in North Germany. As the cantilevered construction of the bridge rises, the rearward end of

the bridge section with the counterweight rolls downwards. The counterweight, a large reinforced concrete block, is clearly visible. The interplay of bridge and counterweight is also the theme of the Gateshead Millennium Bridge in Newcastle upon Tyne by the architects Wilkinson Eyre. In this case, however, the counterweight – which is the supporting arch for the bridge – is only fully effective as the bridge reaches the open position. As the arch tilts to one side, its centre of gravity travels further away from the axis of the pivot, increasing the tilting moment. Accordingly the energy required to tilt the bridge is not constant: more energy is required

to set the bridge in motion at the beginning of the tilting process than at the end. Hydraulic rams are used to help get the process underway, which leads to a comparatively high level of energy use. The resulting construction and operating costs should, however, be seen in relation to the high quality of the bridge's design and its urban integration. Swing bridges, by contrast, are more efficient in terms of energy use. As there is no need for heavy lifting, energy is only required to overcome the resistance of the construction to turning. Ideally swing bridges are symmetrically arranged so that the weight of the cantilevering arms balance one another. This is

Convertible umbrellas in the interior courtyard of the Mosque in Medina, Frei Otto and Bodo Rasch, Saudi Arabia, 1971

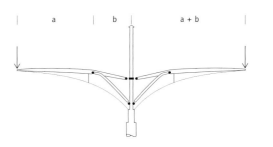

Functioning principle, convertible umbrellas

Top: closed. Moment load at the pivot point

Bottom: open. System is in balance

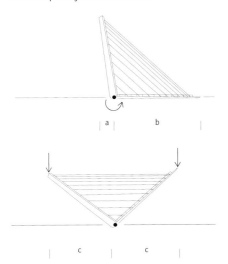

Structural principle, Gateshead Millennium Bridge

Gateshead Millennium Bridge, Wilkinson Eyre Architects, Newcastle upon Tyne, 2001

only possible, however, when a support can be placed in the river itself. Additionally sufficient space is required for the bridge to rotate. The El Ferdan Bridge spanning 340 m over the Suez Canal in Egypt is the longest swing bridge in the world.

Movable roof structures

Cantilevered structures are also used for roof constructions. Since antiquity, awnings, known as *vela*, have been used as a retractable means of shading spectators in theatres and arenas from the sun: sailcloth was fixed to permanently installed cantilevered rods and shifted to one side when no longer needed. To the present day, membrane constructions serve as an effective means of protecting against wind and rain: their low self-weight and the ability to gather them up means that they occupy little space when not in use. The cantilever principle is all the more apparent when the supporting construction also unfolds, such as with a parasol or projecting awning. Frei Otto and Bodo Rasch developed large, solar-powered inverted umbrellas for a mosque in Medina, Saudi Arabia, that received much admiration from the press and public alike. Where membrane roofs are not appropriate for thermal reasons, it is still possible to retract large sections of rigid roof constructions by shifting them to one side. In Shanghai, the segments of a retractable roof of a tennis stadium have been designed to open like an iris shutter. The separate sections are retracted simultaneously and follow the same pattern of movement to reveal an opening in the centre of the roof. A more conventional solution is to use a pair of single span beams that retract to each side along a single axis. The sports stadium of the University of Phoenix in Arizona, designed by the architect Peter Eisenman, functions according to this principle.

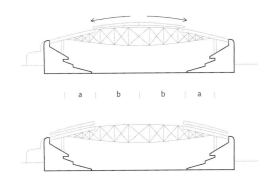

Functioning principle of sliding roof, University of Phoenix Stadium

University of Phoenix Stadium, Peter Eisenman, Arizona, 2006

Qi Zhong Tennis Centre, Mitsuru Senda and Environment Design Institute, Shanghai, 2006

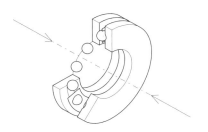

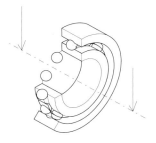

Thrust ball bearing

Radial ball bearing

■ 2.8 Movable connections

In classical structural design theory, the term *bearing* denotes the force-closed connection between two consecutive structural elements in the load-bearing hierarchy. The supporting element serves the loaded element as a bearing. One differentiates between fixed, pinned and free bearings. While the first allows no movement at all, pinned bearings allow rotational movements around the point of support and transmit horizontal and vertical forces. The third category of free bearings are able to translate and can therefore only support loads that are perpendicular to the plane of translation, typically gravitational forces from above. With the help of this mental model most immobile constructions can be broken down into structurally definable and explicitly calculable systems. In practice the final

construction attempts to approximate this idealised system as closely as possible. A pinned bearing is then not necessarily constructed as a hinge but is flexible enough to be able to accommodate possible rotational movements that may result from loads applied to the construction. It should be clear that for kinetic structures, bearings must be constructed quite differently to ensure the transfer of loads while simultaneously allowing the element to move.

To facilitate movable connections between two loadbearing elements, independent components, bearings or hinges are required. One differentiates between hinged connections that can accommodate rotation or translation, as well as a combination of both movements which can allow up to five degrees

of freedom. Depending on the construction of the hinge, the maximum degree of movement can be artificially restricted through the use of constraints (stoppers).

Sliding and roller bearings
Where two building elements are connected by a movable connection, the external forces result in friction at the points where the two elements touch. Sliding or roller bearings are used to reduce this undesirable effect to a minimum.

Lubricated sliding bearings employ a fluid to as far as possible separate both contact surfaces from one another. The material properties of the two surfaces and the lubricating film must be carefully chosen to function together. Lubricating agents include greas-

Recliner hinge fitting for a headrest

Flush-fitting filler cap

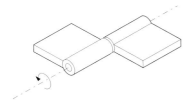

Turning around its axis

Sliding along its axis

Bending the axis

Screwing around its axis

es or oils that are replenished either from an appropriately located reservoir or by pressure-feed lubrication. Sliding bearings therefore require a higher degree of maintenance but are in turn able to support high loads and high speeds of revolution and are impact-resistant, noise-absorbent and highly durable. Due to the complexity of their construction, however, continuously lubricated sliding bearings are only rarely used in architecture. Low-maintenance, lubricant-free sliding bearings whose material properties allow one of the two contact surfaces to slide comparatively freely are more suitable for architectural applications. Such materials include plastics such as PTFE (also known as Teflon), which in combination with steel surfaces has a very low coefficient of friction.

Roller bearings, by contrast, use an intermediary element, such as ball or cylindrical bearings, to transfer forces from one contact surface to the other with as little friction as possible. Bearings of this kind require little lubrication and are comparatively low-maintenance, though susceptible to impact damage. Ball bearings and roller bearings are available in all manner of different industrially-produced forms and variants for immediate installation.

Whether sliding or rolling, both approaches to minimising friction losses are commonly used in a simplified form in architectural applications, as in most cases movable elements have a high self-weight and move at a comparatively slow speed. With the exception of rotors used in wind generators and high-traffic door systems, most building elements move only at certain times or very slowly but have to function reliably over the entire service life of the building. Special attention must be given to the appropriate choice of bearings for mobile elements: they should distribute loads effectively, also when the element is stationary, be hard-wearing and require little maintenance.

For particular applications, special technical solutions have been devised to facilitate the low-friction movement of large objects. Floating bearings have been conceived that employ water baths, electromagnetic forces, air cushions or air film systems. For example, the entire football turf in the Sapporo dome football arena in Japan can be raised with help of air cushions for removal to a well-sunlit forecourt outside the arena.

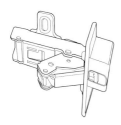

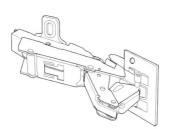

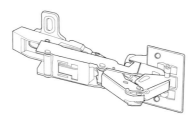

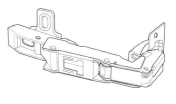

Complex movement in details: door cup hinge

Left: traditional sliding door fitting for a wooden door, Summer House, Hanne Dalsgaard and Henrik Jeppesen, Ordrup Næs, Denmark, 2005

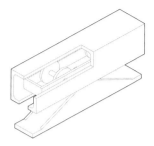 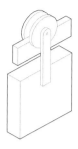  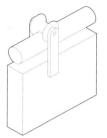 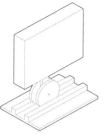

Types of rail and track systems for linear-sliding panel elements

Typical connections for hinged elements

In the simplest of cases, swivelling hinges take the form of sliding bushes with a single degree of freedom of rotation and are used to connect flat building elements along one edge so that they can swing. Such hinges are commonly used for furniture, doors, windows and gates and must be able to sustain strong loads resulting from the cantilevered self-weight of the hinged element as well as from regular continual use.

Hinged metal joints usually require regular lubrication to ensure smooth and noise-free operation, although maintenance-free bearings are also available, for example with Teflon-coated plastics. One generally differentiates between hinges that are inseparably connected by a pin that runs the entire length of the hinge, and hinges that are separable, for example, to allow one to remove a door, literally to "unhinge" it.

Hinged elements and flaps are mostly used to close an opening entirely. The thickness of the hinged element also plays a particular role: for reasons of structural stability and construction, door leaves are often thicker than the diameter or depth of the actual hinge. Where simple hinges are used with a single rotational axis, this axis must be located on one of the outside edges of the hinged element. As a result, although the element can turn fully towards the side with the hinge through a maximum of 180°, it is geometrically impossible for it to fully open in the opposite direction.

More complex hinges are required to be able to open a pivoting element to the same degree in both directions. Shifting the axis of rotation slightly towards the centre of the hinged element can create the necessary geometric freedom of movement. A glass swing door with pivot hinges illustrates the limitations of this solution: the door can only be held at the top and bottom of its axis of rotation which means that the entire self-weight of the door is borne by the conical seat of the pivot at the bottom. Additionally, it is not possible to achieve a seal (water, heat, noise) through contact pressure against a frame, and the narrow gap between the axis of rotation and the door frame could potentially cause injury. An alternative would be to use hinges that feature two rotational axes, one on each side of the hinged element.

It is sometimes desirable to make the hinge disappear from view and to integrate it into the door frame and the door leaf. Concealed hinges are available for both metal frame as well as wood frame doors. In addition a broad spectrum of highly-developed furniture and building hinges are available for specific applications. There are a vast number of recessed hinges for the flush mounting of cupboard doors where the hinge is not visible from outside.

 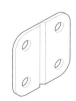  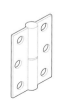    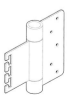

Examples of different interior door, window and cabinet hinges

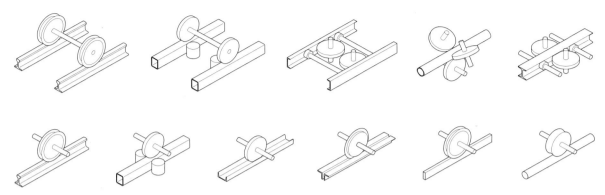

Different types of wheel-rail systems

Different hinges cater for different door-to-unit configurations depending on the respective situation. More complex patterns of movements such as the folding-out of furniture door elements can now also be realised using standardised hinges. Additional functions such as defined open-closed positions or self-closing mechanisms can be directly integrated into the hinge.

Common roller bearings for rotational movements
For larger building elements with a correspondingly large self-weight, pre-mounted roller bearings are used to distribute the load in hinged connections with as little friction as possible. One distinguishes between radial and axial thrust bearings depending on whether the load distribution is perpendicular or parallel to the axis of rotation. Numerous types of bearings are available for different loading conditions in standard product sizes, with diameters ranging from approximately 10 mm (needle bearings) to around 4 m (industrial bearings for cranes). Large-scale rotational movements, for example the rotation of a restaurant, require a rotary bearing with a sufficiently large radius. Due to the low curvature of the perimeter bearing ring in relation to the mechanical construction, the technical realisation of such bearings is similar to that of linear translation bearings.

Common translation bearings
With the exception of simple, lightweight drawers, translation bearings are almost exclusively realised as roller bearings of some kind. The basic principle follows that of a wheel and rail. Depending on the direction of the external forces, each bearing point may have one, two or three rollers in different directions to transfer the load effectively to the profile of the rail. Plastic or rubber rollers are quieter but less durable than steel or brass rollers. To prevent horizontal displacement, either the rail and roller are given corresponding interlocking profiles or a parallel roller is arranged at right angles to the load direction. In both standing as well as hanging configurations, the self-weight of the mobile element is in many cases sufficient to prevent vertical displacement that would result in unhooking and derailment. A particularly elegant solution is available for hanging systems: the parallel arrangement of a pair of roller bearings mounted in a U-shaped rail makes derailment impossible and also transfers the

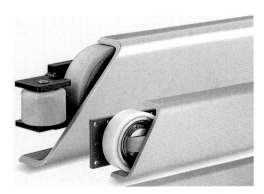

Low-noise combined roller bearings

Combined roller bearings made of case-hardened steel

Rolling gear for a rollercoaster

Rail system for the entrance doors of the CargoLifter dockyard, SIAT Architektur + Technik, Brand, Germany, 2000

Pivot hinge at the top of the doors

weight of the element optimally into the symmetrical axis of the rail.

Complex hinges

The aforementioned functional principles can be combined to construct hinges with two to five degrees of freedom of rotation and translation. This is required, for example, to open an umbrella: a collar is slid along a pole causing the supporting struts fixed to the collar to open outwards radially. By chaining a sequence of several hinges, systems can be built that have more than just one degree of freedom. The position of all the elements of an umbrella in space can be determined precisely by a single variable: the position of the sliding collar.

In addition, specially developed hinges are available whose construction affords a particular combi-

nation of degrees of freedom and constraints. A ball joint, for example, allows an element to turn on an axis as well as to tilt this axis in all directions by up to 90°. A universal joint also enables the axis of movement to change angle but can also transfer the rotational force around its axis through the hinged joint.

Tape-spring rolling hinges represent a special case. In this case the rotational movement does not occur around an axis but is achieved by two semicircular hinging pieces that roll against each other. The two parts of the hinge are held in place by fixing them to one another crosswise with flexible bands.

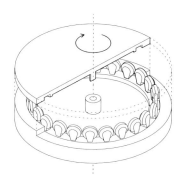

Turntable with fixed rollers

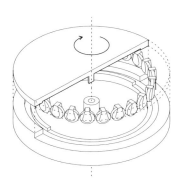

Turntable with mobile rollers

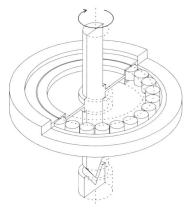

Rotating insert

Azimuth gear

■ 2.9 Actuators

Actuator technology encompasses the entire constellation of mechanical elements required to set a body in motion. The core of this system consists of a power or drive mechanism that converts energy into mechanical work. For mobile systems, internal combustion engines are most commonly used; they provide good performance but need to be supplied with fluid or gaseous fuels and emit noise and exhaust gases at the place of use. Both are sub-optimal for stationary operation and for this reason electrically powered engines are more commonly used in buildings. Alongside these, wind or water-powered systems are also used which draw energy directly from regenerative natural energy sources. Modes of action

Numerous different approaches can be used for transmitting the power provided by an engine. For architectural applications, systems that are able to transmit comparatively high forces over sufficiently long distances are of most interest; the speed of transmission can be slower and may indeed be required to be so for safety reasons. Compact systems that are able to transmit power without the need for bulky conversion mechanisms such as gearboxes are most desirable. As most architectural applications do not require a high degree of technical innovation, conventional commercially-available products can be used. This reduces the choice of appropriate sources of power to electromotive motors and pumps in combination with hydraulic or

pneumatic systems. In the following section these systems are described in greater detail together with a review of innovative transmission systems that have as yet not been used widely in the building sector.

Parameters

The capacity of an engine is described using a series of typical parameters. The efficiency of an engine denotes the proportion of power transmitted with respect to the power intake required, that is the percentage of the energy input actually converted in motion. The maximum output of a motor is then broken down further according to the basic mode of movement. Translation drive mechanisms are de-

Toothed rack

Cogged belt

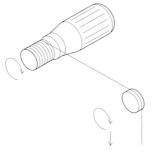

Winch

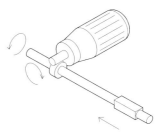

Thrust gear

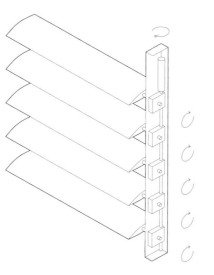

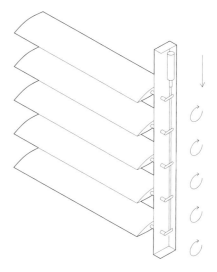

Sunscreen louvres powered by worm gear

Sunscreen louvres powered by push rod

scribed by their actuating force (in newtons) and actuating speed in (metres per second). For linear operations with limited travel, the actuating path (in metres) is also relevant. Rotation drive mechanisms are described by their torque (force × lever arm in newton metres) and rotational speed (revolutions per minute).

To compare these parameters in relation to one another, they can be portrayed in the form of a performance or characteristic curve. This representation allows one to ascertain the rotational speed at which a motor provides maximum torque. The product of the rotational speed and torque describes the mechanical capacity of the drive mechanism; for electric motors this is typically termed the power

rating or nominal output, the actual usable power of the engine under load, and is stated over a wide speed range.

Gears and transmission

Engines provide mechanical power in the form of translation or rotation movement. This is used to move further functional components of the system – the machine. Gears can be employed between the drive mechanism and the machine to adapt the power and capacity of the engine to the needs of the machine. This can be used, for example, to translate the high speed of a comparatively small electric motor to the slower, more powerful rotation required for a cable winch. In addition to adjusting the

amount of power, gearing can also be used to change the direction of the applied force to fit the respective requirements. A flywheel arrangement makes it possible to convert rotation into translation or vice versa; likewise the direction of rotation or the axis of rotation can also be changed. By using a threaded rod, for example, a single motor can be used to operate numerous blinds simultaneously, although one is not able to adjust blinds individually.

Switching gears represents a special case: by switching between different gear ratios a single motor can be used to provide different performance curves. While this principle is commonly used in household power drills, it is rarely used in architectural applications due to the complexity of having to manu-

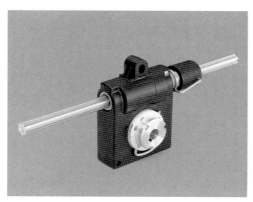

Angle gear for adjusting facade systems

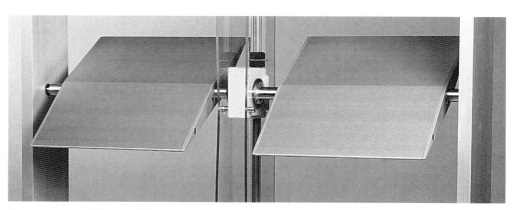

Angle gear in use with horizontal louvres

Chain actuator

Swing door opener

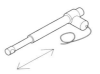

Roller drive

Linear actuator

Rack and pinion drive

Sliding door opener

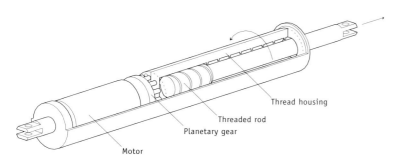

Thread housing

Threaded rod

Planetary gear

Motor

Left and above: Linear actuator for external use

ally switch gears. Usually, it is sufficient to be able to control the speed of an electric motor by applying a different electric voltage. For this, the speed, power and temperature range of an electric motor needs to be dimensioned to correspond to the required speed profile.

Electromechanical actuators

An electric motor consists of at least one moving and one fixed electromechanical element. There are numerous different kinds of constructions but all share the principle of physical deflection caused by a current-carrying conductor in a magnetic field. The arrangement and articulation of the fixed (stator) and moving parts (rotor or armature) varies, enabling different kinds of movement – translation or rotation – to be produced. The energy input is usually standardised and matches the voltage provided by the local electricity provider or an energy carrier. Typically these vary between 12 – 24 V (starter battery), 230 V (domestic electricity) and 400 V (three phase alternating current) to 690 V (maximum permissible voltage for socket connections according to DIN EN 60309).

Electric linear motors create a translation movement by moving the rotor element with respect to the stationary stator. Due to their high acceleration and precision, such motors are typically used in indus-

trial mechanical engineering and are optimised for specific purposes. The maximum thrust provided by these highly dynamic motors typically lies in the lower double-digit kN region and is therefore much lower than hydraulic linear drive systems.

As the stationary elements of such linear motors can in theory be extended indefinitely, they are ideally suited for rail-bound means of transport. The German Transrapid magnetic levitation railway employs this principle: a magnetic field travels along the surface of the rail pulling the train, while further electromagnets are used to levitate the vehicle so that it can move frictionlessly over the rails. Here the rails themselves function as the stator that sets the train, the rotor, in motion.

Electric rotary motors, which turn around the rotation axis of the rotor, are widely available, cheap and universally applicable. Sizes can vary from microscopic motors measuring just a few millimetres to heavy-duty motors for operating lifts and cranes. In conjunction with toothed belts, rack and pinions, push rods or chains, the rotation of the motor can easily be translated into linear movement. In the building sector, specialised drive units are commonly used consisting of a combination of electric motor and gearing for particular applications such as to open and close doors or to roll up or unfurl hanging elements.

Hydraulic and pneumatic actuators

Fluid-based actuators are characterised by a very high power output in relation to their size. Due to the flow-resistances in the system, however, they are relatively inefficient and therefore require greater energy input. The basis is formed by a motorised pump that serves as the engine required to build up the necessary pressure using blades, gears, screws or pistons. A volumetric flow results that is transferred through pressure lines to a pressure cylinder or jack (translation movement) or a hydraulic or pneumatic motor (rotation movement). This power output element can be made relatively compact in relation to the power it produces (high power density). All other bulkier parts of the system such as the pump and, depending on the system, the pressure accumulator or fluid reservoir, can be placed elsewhere and connected to the machine by flexible pressure lines. The corresponding reduction in noise emissions is an advantage for architectural applications. The maximum transfer distance is around 1000 m for pneumatic systems, 100 m for hydraulic systems.

Hydraulic systems employ low-compression oils as their pressure medium. With a system pressure of up to 600 bar and maximum power output of 3000 kN, they are much more powerful than air-based pneumatic systems which for safety reasons (compressed

Facing page: glass roof of Stuttgart stock exchange

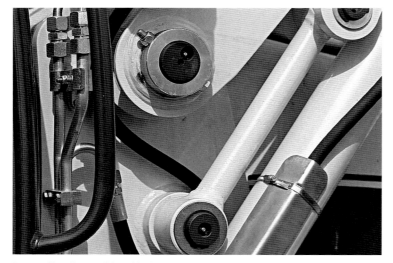

Pressure lines for an oil-based hydraulic system

Crane boom hydraulic pistons

air can store energy) are designed for an operating pressure of 6 bar and can develop a maximum power output of 30 N. On the other hand, pneumatic actuators are much less complex to realise and therefore much more cost-effective: they can do without return lines, as the pressure medium (air) can be released into the surroundings (open cycle) and because the retention of pressurised air for later use is relatively straightforward. Hydraulic fluids, by comparison, are almost always contained in closed cycles, making it necessary to provide pressure lines, reservoirs and filter units. In addition environmental protection guidelines are more strict.

In buildings, linear cylinders are most commonly used when high loads are involved. There are two different types: simple unidirectional piston drives where the flow pressure causes them to move in a single direction and a spring or gravity is used to return them to their waiting state, and bidirectional cylinders which can move actively in both directions.

The advantages of fluid-powered rotation motors (overload protection, insusceptibility to dust, compact construction) over electric motors are rarely utilised in buildings. Typically a project may require a large number of rotation drives in different arrangements, resulting in a need for specially created

hydraulic or pneumatic supply connections. Such systems are relatively complex and inflexible. In this case electric motors are more economical.

A special case in the field of pneumatic actuators are pressurised cushions for creating compression forces and artificial muscles for creating tensile forces. The former are used, for example, as transportable lifting bags for rescue services, the latter, due to their frictionless construction, are ideal for precision positioning work in mechanical engineering. Unlike pneumatically pre-stressed membrane cushions, which ascertain a stationary state with the help of air pressure, both of these systems make use of changes in volume within a soft enclosure. As such they do not employ enclosed pistons but offer a single simple mode of operation. Pneumatic muscles are tubular. By increasing the inner air pressure, the diameter of the membrane expands, causing the muscle to shorten or contract. Commercially available and economically viable systems shorten their nominal length by around 15 % at a maximum contraction of 25 % and a lifting capacity of 6000 kN.

Microactuators

Numerous other modes of operation for actuators employing thermal, chemical or electrical principles can be found in industrial applications. In most cases the actuating path of these systems extends

only a few millimetres but can provide an extremely large actuating force. By using translation methods to extend the actuating path, they can also be employed in other areas of applications. Electromagnetic actuators, such as those used in plunger coils in loudspeakers, have a slightly longer actuating path and are used, for example, in clamping lock cylinders. The advantage of these modes of action lies in the reduction of the number of components resulting from their somewhat simplified construction. The actuating technology can therefore be integrated directly within the moving element and, through the additive use of several microactuators, can be used to create complex patterns of movement. Future application areas include vibration dampening as well as the fine control of small-scale facade elements, for example to adapt the building envelope to changing climatic conditions.

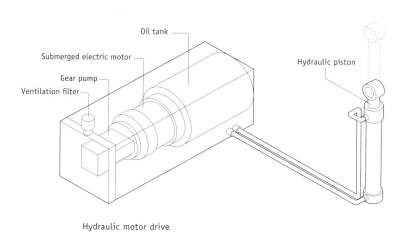

In-ground hydraulic vehicle lift

Hydraulic motor drive

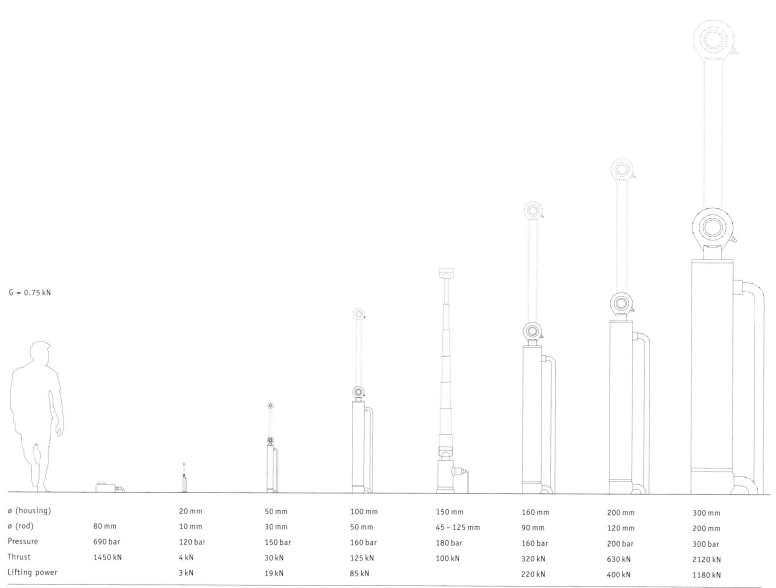

G = 0.75 kN

ø (housing)		20 mm	50 mm	100 mm	150 mm	160 mm	200 mm	300 mm
ø (rod)	80 mm	10 mm	30 mm	50 mm	45 – 125 mm	90 mm	120 mm	200 mm
Pressure	690 bar	120 bar	150 bar	160 bar	180 bar	160 bar	200 bar	300 bar
Thrust	1450 kN	4 kN	30 kN	125 kN	100 kN	320 kN	630 kN	2120 kN
Lifting power		3 kN	19 kN	85 kN		220 kN	400 kN	1180 kN

Comparison of different hydraulic piston systems, 1:50

■ 2.10 Measuring, controlling, regulating

Mechatronics system

Martin Becker

The term automatic has its roots in the Greek word *automatos*, which is composed of *autos* meaning "self" and *matos* meaning "moving by itself". In today's time automation means that the speed, direction, efficiency, etc. of dynamic processes is ascertained (measured) and influenced (controlled) so that these processes fulfil a given task or function on their own. Automation is thus synonymous with the current state of modern technological developments as characterised by the now widespread use of largely unattended systems. The degree to which such systems can act independently is described by the level of automation, for example manually-operated, semi-automated or fully-automated.

Furthermore automation today is inseparably connected with modern information and communication technology as not only the regulating devices but increasingly also sensors and actuators are now available as electronic systems with integrated microcomputers and data interfaces. This has led to the networking of sensors, actuators and regulating devices by cables or wireless devices that facilitate information transfer for better control and regulation of systems as well as for monitoring and diagnostic purposes. This in turn has extended the primary purpose of measuring and control equipment to encompass more comprehensive and extensive automation functions.

When employed correctly, automation allows one to direct and control the flow of information and energy. For this it is necessary to acquire the information required to achieve this task by using sensors to capture data from the real world and then, using

an appropriate actuator (regulating device), to intervene in the process (for example to move a section of the facade, to close a fire safety vent or a gate, to start an escalator or lift) to the right degree at the right moment in time and the right place. The information captured by the sensors is processed and the resulting instructions passed to the appropriate point of intervention for putting into effect. This process is the task of regulators or controllers.

Sensor technology

In rooms, building envelopes, facade systems as well as in plant and conveyor technology, many different sensors gather numerous different kinds of data on both direct physical parameters (e. g. temperature) as well as indirect quantities (e. g. comfort levels). These can include air temperature, relative humidity, air quality, light intensity, window and door contacts, movement sensors, fire alarms, burglar alarms, buttons and switches for manual controls, load and end terminals for motorised drive systems, wind and rain measurements, solar irradiation, pressure, force, revolutions per minute, torque, air speed, mass and volume flow, power consumption, energy consumption, mechanical and electrical efficiency to name just a few.

The following criteria should be taken into account when choosing sensors:

– Kind of power supply (e. g. separate 24 V DC or powered by the bus system)
– Direct wired connection or communication through the bus system

– Kind of mounting and correct positioning of the sensor
– Space requirement and installation size
– Kind and routing of cabling (for example for connector placement)
– Self-heating
– Static and dynamic transfer characteristics
– Sensor tolerance and degree of measurement uncertainty for sensors and for the entire system
– Measuring errors resulting from component aging, electromagnetic interference and environmental conditions
– Necessary maintenance and calibration
– The cost of the different means of measurement

The effectiveness of a controlled or self-regulating system depends on the choice of appropriate measuring and sensor technology. Of crucial importance is the level of measurement accuracy across the entire system, from the sensor element to the data processing to the assessment of the measurement data. As a guiding principle, measurements should be as imprecise as possible and as precise as necessary.

In addition to choosing sensors with the correct technical properties, the correct placement of sensors is also important. Time and again, practice shows that despite clear manufacturer recommendations, sensors are placed in the wrong or in unfavourable positions; for example external temperature sensors are not placed on the north side of the building or are partially exposed to direct sunlight.

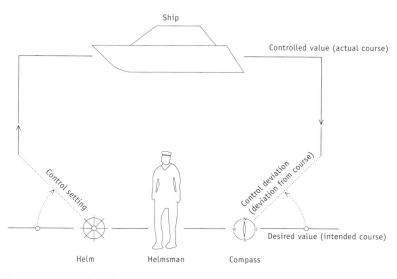

Cybernetics: the art of steering

This results in regulation and control systems that are at best inefficient and at worst ineffective. While such installation errors do not necessarily lead to a system breakdown, they often result in an unnecessarily high level of energy consumption or reduced functionality, which is not immediately detected and may only be discovered later during operation when the building systems do not function as desired.

A further cause of false measurements results when sensors for measuring room temperature are placed in what may be visually attractive but thermally enclosed housings, or are "concealed" in the wall or ceiling construction. This results in the sensor returning the temperature of the building construction (either the temperature of the wall surface or the sensor housing) rather than a representative temperature of the room. This in turn then serves as an incorrect basis for regulating the heating system.

In addition to the different sensors used for measuring direct and indirect physical parameters, rooms may also contain control units with which the user can access and control the building's technical installations as well as the sensors. The simplest of these are conventional switches or buttons which allow the user to turn on or dim lights, to adjust the position of window blinds or shutters or to open or close motorised skylights.

Increasingly these units serve not only as control devices but also as a display or means of visualizing the system directly in the room. Modern communication devices such as mobile phones, PDAs and iPhones are now also used as operating and display devices.

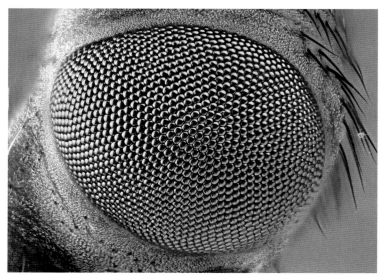

Compound eye of an insect

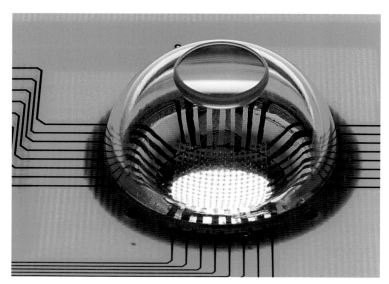

Technical realisation of an insect eye for measuring visual stimuli

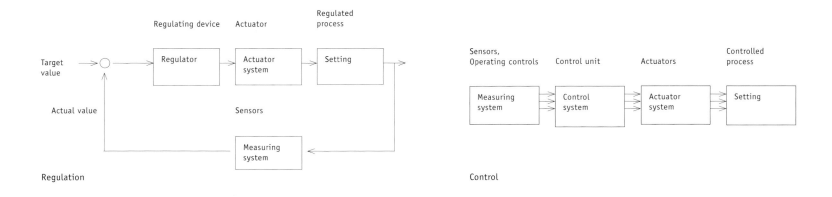

Regulating device   Actuator   Regulated process

Target value → ○ → Regulator → Actuator system → Setting →

Actual value   Sensors

Measuring system

Regulation

Sensors, Operating controls   Control unit   Actuators   Controlled process

Measuring system → Control system → Actuator system → Setting

Control

Control and regulating technology

The kind and scope of a control or regulating system depends to a large degree on the specific requirements of the process to be automated. For this reason we will discuss the use of control and regulating technology using the example of automation within a room. Numerous control and regulation tasks can apply to a room, some of which can be coupled with one another, for example the regulation of constant light levels and daylight maximisation by controllable louvres and motorised window openers used for ventilation purposes.

The conception and realisation of such systems can vary considerably depending on the kind and struc-

ture of the automation concept (centrally controlled by an automation station, by a bus system with decentralised control and regulation units, hybrid variants and so on).

In all cases, control and regulation devices (whether centrally controlled or decentralised) aim to allow a process or system to take place autonomously. In the field of automation technology one differentiates between control and regulation systems.

For example, a light control system will switch a light on or off at a particular light level (threshold value). A light regulation system, by contrast, will continuously adjust or dim the lighting to maintain a particular level of illumination (target value). For

this it is necessary to measure the actual light level at a representative point and to compare this with the target value.

A typical characteristic of control systems is the ability to set preset values for many different input parameters using a programmable control device (for example a programmable logic controller or PLC) that is then used to control the relevant actuators, which in turn influence the process to be controlled (e.g. to switch a light on or off). In addition to being able to process input values obtained from the sensors, it should be possible for the user to intervene manually to set a particular input value using a switch, button or other kind of console.

Infrared rain sensor   Wind vane   Air pressure and temperature

Capacitive rain sensor   Wind speed   Light sensor

Measuring devices

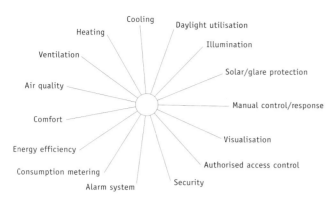

Room automation functions

Room automation central control unit, touch screen

Typical examples of controlled processes include the control of lifts, escalators, gates, blinds and roller shutters.

Regulating systems or loops on the other hand, are characterised by a continuous comparison of the desired situation (target value) with the actual situation (actual value) and a corresponding adjustment of the system using actuators. The aim of regulating systems is to minimise the difference between the target and the actual value, ideally to zero. The process to be regulated (for example, a room or ventilation duct) is described as a controlled process loop. Unlike control systems, regulating systems make it possible to continually adapt the controlled process loop to changing boundary conditions, for example internal loads and environmental conditions. Regulating devices therefore ensure that the effects of so-called disturbance variables such as fluctuations in outdoor temperature, solar irradiation or internal heat loads can be compensated for as quickly as possible. Typical examples of regulated systems include room temperature regulation, constant light illumination levels or air change rates.

One differentiates generally between two different types of regulating devices: discontinuous or intermittent control devices that can be switched either on or off (for example, the closure or opening of a smoke exhaust vent) and continuous control devices which use an actuator (for example, the adjustment range of an elevating spindle motor) with which to predefine a particular value between 0 and 100 % of the possible range.

The technical requirements of regulation systems, such as the necessary speed of regulation or the accuracy required, determine the appropriate regulation concept along with the kind of process to be regulated and the choice of sensor and actuator technology.

Mechatronic systems for integrated building control systems

In addition to the primary tasks of measuring, controlling, regulating and monitoring, contemporary automation technology is also able to exploit a variety of means of optimising the potential of interactions between all the different systems in an overall energy and building management system.

A clear trend is emerging towards the development of integrated ready-built component systems that feature compatible subcomponents. An example of such a system is the availability of all-in-one heat pump units with an integrated hydraulic assembly and measuring and control equipment. This trend will in future extend to facade and building envelope technology. The first integrated facade systems are now available on the market and incorporate local ventilation devices, sun blinds as well as illumination systems and even photovoltaic modules for generating energy. By employing motorised window and facade panel openers, such facade systems can also link into a building's controlled natural ventilation strategies. The individual systems are connected by an integral facade controller unit and are optimised to work together as effectively as possible. The facade controller is in turn linked by

a standardised bus protocol to the room and building automation system so that the entire operation of the building can be optimised with regard to patterns of use and energy efficiency. Here the window, or in this case the facade, is no longer a purely passive element and has become an active technological element of the building. In this context we can speak of a mechatronic facade system which links together mechanical, electromechanical/electronic and information technology components to form a new, higher-order, all-embracing control system.

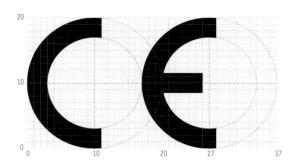

The CE-marking symbol for product conformity has to be constructed according to predetermined geometric rules

■ 2.11 Planning guidelines and legal frameworks

Kurt-Patrik Beckmann

Planning guidelines

Buildings are, generally speaking, immobile. The rules and regulations set out in planning regulations and building codes therefore refer to static building elements, to selected movable elements such as windows, doors and gates as well as to conveyor systems for people and goods within or on buildings. The regulation of other kinds of moving structures and building elements is documented only sparingly in the general building codes and regulations.

The codes that govern moving structures and elements derive from rules and regulations from the realm of mechanical engineering and follow a somewhat different arrangement to the building regulations with regard to planning and execution. This is due not least to the fact that, unlike architecture, elements in mechanical engineering are generally serially produced and do not have any specific relationship to place.

Background

For a better understanding of the planning steps described below, it is useful to have a brief overview of the current building regulations situation in Germany.

The building regulations follow from the requirements of the German constitution and the laws set down within the European Union. The EU laws can be regarded as an independent legal framework that exists outside and takes priority over the member states' legislation. The intention of both legal systems is to uphold and protect the rights of the individual and of the community.

Today, each federal German state has its own individual building regulations, a product of the division of power in the German federalist structure. A model building code, the Musterbauordnung (MBO, 8 November 2002) ratified by the conference of building ministers in November 2008, lays down the basic standards or minimum requirements, although each federal state may deviate from this.

EU guidelines have been put in place that aim to ensure that a product can be used throughout the European Union. Each EU member state may determine how these guidelines are put into effect.

The EU directive governing this is the "Directive 98/37/EC of the European Parliament and of the Council of 22 June 1998 on the harmonisation of the laws of the Member States relating to machinery". This is valid until 28 December 2009 whereupon it will be replaced by the new "Directive 2006/42/EC of the European Parliament and of the Council of 17 May 2006 on machinery, and amending Directive 95/16/EC (revised)".

In Germany the implementation of the EU directive is effected by the "Equipment and Product Safety Act" (Geräte- und Produktsicherheitsgesetz, GPSG) and the "Ninth Ordinance to the Equipment and Product Safety Act (Maschinenverordnung, 9. GPSGV) of 12 May 1993, last amended on 6 January 2004". This ordinance concerns the distribution (sale and use) of machinery, equipment or building elements of which at least one part is movable. On the one hand, the Equipment and Product Safety Act aims to ensure the rights and safety of the individual and the community, on the other it offers the designer

and builder the necessary legal security that in the event of an accident, they have done everything in their means during the planning and building process to ensure that the product or building element should not be the cause of an accident.

The conformity of a building product to the technical regulations and guidelines is documented according to EU law by a CE-marking on the item itself. The CE-marking is a symbol that the manufacturer or creator should affix to the product to denote that it falls within the respective guidelines in its area of use, and secondly that the product conforms to safety guidelines set out in the regulations. This assessment must be underpinned by a written declaration of conformity and only this has a legally binding effect. In general, however, not all guidelines oblige manufacturers to provide such a declaration. As a rule, a declaration of conformity must be provided to official authorities and where products fall under the machinery directive.

When a movable building element is employed for the first time in or on a building, the building control authorities will usually require that the element undergo safety assessment before it can be installed or put into use. This can be undertaken in advance by a certified accreditation body. These centres assess the submitted documentation to ascertain whether a product fulfils the regulations in each specific case and provide corresponding certification to the manufacturer or designer. Similarly the submitted documentation can also be assessed with respect to the technical documentation requirements for EC type examination.

Standard emergency stop buttons

Safety systems on a production floor

Planning steps

To ensure that a building element is in line with the relevant guidelines and standards, the following steps are advisable in planning the execution of the design. As both the planning and building approval steps depend on the design itself, the criteria for decisions within the planning process depend on the respective task or intention. The following points should be clarified during the decision-making process:

1. What is the proposed use?
2. Who are the users?
3. What purpose does it serve?
4. To what category does the building belong in which the building element is to be implemented?
5. Is the movement perceived only visually or is the construction or building element actually set in motion?
6. How is the movement realised – is it powered or hand-operated?
7. Does the movement start automatically or have to be started manually?
8. Does the design make use of existing certified components?
9. Do components need to be specially developed for the construction?

Different planning and implementation scenarios can be derived from the aforementioned criteria, and variants thereof. The individual guidelines provide a definition of the equipment they cover while also leaving room for exceptions. When in doubt, one can consult an accrediting body for clarification.

1. Purpose and usage:

First and foremost, it is important to clarify what the moving element or product does. In short, the function, purpose or use it serves.

2. Relevant directives:

The above, along with the types of component assemblies used, determines which guidelines are to be applied. The following categorisation provides a simplified overview of existing guidelines:

2.1. General EU directives:

The EU Machinery Directive together with the EU Noise at Work Directive 2003/10/EC, and two further directives concerning:
– Lifts in the EU Lifts Directive 95/16/EC, and
– Cableway installations in the EU Directive 2000/9/EC on cableway installations designed to carry persons.

2.2. Pressure vessels:

– Pressure Equipment Directive, for example for pneumatic or hydraulically-powered components.
– Simple Pressure Vessels Directive (this covers a slightly different area to the Pressure Equipment Directive).

2.3. Explosion protection:

If the product or installation is to be used in potentially explosive atmospheres: EU Directive 94/9/EC (see also, ATEX 95, the VDMA / German Engineering Federation recommendations for explosion protection for machinery).

2.5. Electrical equipment:

Electrical equipment, for example for control systems, are subject to the following directives:
– Electromagnetic compatibility, given in the EU EMC Directive
– Low Voltage Directive
– R&TTE, Radio & Telecom Terminal Equipment Directive
– The German Electrical and Electronic Equipment Act (ElektroG) manages the distribution, recovery and recycling of electrical and electronic equipment in Germany, dated 16 March 2005.
– The ElektroG implements the RoHS, Restriction of certain Hazardous Substances, (EU Directive 2002/95/EC). The RoHS guideline is not part of CE certification and came into effect on 1 June 2006. This defines maximum permissible levels and restrictions with regard to the use of hazardous substances such as lead, mercury, cadmium and polybrominated biphenyl flame retardants.
– The WEEE, Waste Electrical and Electronic Equipment Directive, is likewise not part of CE certification and determines the safe disposal of electrical and electronic goods. It applies, for example, where electronic control devices are used.

2.6. Building products:

Assessed according to the EU Construction Products Directive 89/106/EEC which has been implemented

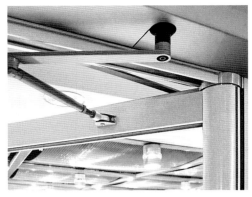

Finger protection door according to DIN 18650: an 8 mm gap between the door frame and leaf prevents fingers from getting trapped in the hinge

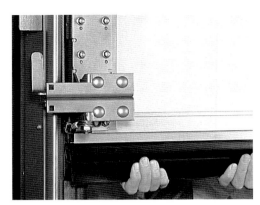

Contact strip: conductive switch with copper braid

Broken beam switch

Multi-beam light barrier

One-way light barrier

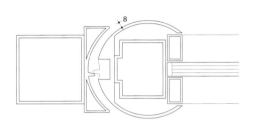

Planning principles for safety systems:

Design solution: for example, finger guard at hinge between door frame and leaf

In-built safety shut-off: for example, a pressure-sensitive floor-mounted shut-off for a vertical roller door

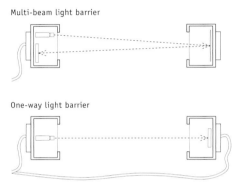

Room monitoring system: for example, safety shut-off mechanism using laser beams that monitor the space in front of a door

in the German Construction Products Act (Bauproduktegesetz, BauPG).

2.7. Consumption of energy and resources:

The EuP directive 2005/32/EC – EuP stands for "Energy-using Products". This directive serves presently only as a framework and is not yet binding. It establishes a framework for the ecodesign requirements of energy-using products. In Germany it is implemented in the Energiebetriebene-Produkte-Gesetz (EBPG) of 7 March 2008.

2.8. Further directives:

Personal protective equipment. In Germany this is implemented in the Eighth Ordinance to the Equipment and Product Safety Act (8. GPSG).
– Toy safety,
– Medical equipment

3. Reference standards:

The norms that are applicable with respect to a particular guideline are dealt with in greater detail in the regulations given in the basic directives listed under point 2.

4. Risk assessment:

The standards and directives outline the necessary steps to be taken in a risk analysis or assessment (sometimes known as hazards analysis). These aspects of risk analysis need to be examined in turn and collated for the respective product.

5. Inspection and adaptation of a building element or product with regard to required safety standards:

The building element or product needs to be assessed according to the individual risk assessment criteria drawn up in the previous step. When the product is able to fulfil all the requirements, the product can be regarded as safe with regard to the requirements and can be accorded CE certification.

Where elements are installed in fire escape routes or fire safety areas or when the product itself has potential fire safety implications, permission will also have to be sought from the certifying authority and the fire safety authorities. In most cases the authorities will request that a fire safety assessment is undertaken for the envisaged usage scenario.

6. Technical documentation:

Technical documentation should include all information regarding its use and operation, as detailed in the applicable directives, possibly optimised with regard to the prior risk assessment. In addition to operating and maintenance instructions and a list of replacement parts, this must also include warnings about potential hazards as well as technical documentation, plans, circuit plans and so on.

7. Translation:

Should a directive require that a translation of the "original operating instructions" be produced, or where its field of application makes it necessary (for example, in buildings for transport such as airports), translations of the operating and maintenance instructions will need to be provided.

8. Compiling documentation:

Alongside the aforementioned documentation, a list of the relevant standards, directives and ordinances should be compiled and signed by a relevant authorised signatory (designer/manufacturer) with date and time.

Basis for the design		
Pre-existing complete system Manufacturer's system, product already proven in use	**Use or new combination of existing components or assembly** Manufacturers offer prefabricated assemblies (new combinations of existing components)	**New system or partial use of existing component assemblies** Manufacturers offer prefabricated assemblies (new combinations of existing components)
Geometry within the approved tolerance limit for adaptation to local situation		
	Geometry outside the approved tolerance limits	
Application falls within the approved usage scenarios		
	Change of use	
		Entirely new application
Utilisation of an existing approved combination of components/building elements		
	New untested combination of existing component assemblies	
		New component assembly

9. Liability and assessment of documentation by an official accreditation body:

The signatory is responsible for meeting the standards set out in the declaration of conformity. From a liability perspective it is advisable to have one's declaration assessed by a certified accrediting body, indeed for planning permission applications and building control approval it is very often necessary as the assessment procedure of an installation, its construction and respective safety requirements requires a high level of technical expertise and interdisciplinary engineering knowledge.

The planning and approval procedure discussed here shows that it is advisable to include the manufacturer, builder or installation company at an early stage in the process in order to ascertain that the construction can be built and establish a realistic cost assessment. Should this not be possible, for example due to tendering legislation, it may be advisable to commission an engineering office specialising in machinery or plant technology or a manufacturer of similar constructions or products to undertake advance planning work.

Planning movable elements in the context of the building project:

The planning steps discussed above focus primarily on fulfilling existing regulations and approval requirements with a view to acquiring construction consent for a building with moving elements.

They do not replace the general planning permission requirements of the respective state or country but are a prerequisite to obtaining higher-level planning permission.

In most cases, the respective planning authority will either require a declaration of conformity to the CE Machinery Directive as a condition of planning approval or at the very latest will request it as part of the final building inspection. The building inspection authority does not assess the component, machinery or equipment itself but its function in the context of the building and its usage.

Where the component, equipment or machinery is connected with the safety or evacuation of people or contained items (for example, fire escape routes, fire prevention), the planning authorities will consult other assessors or authorities for detailed assessment.

For the final building control inspection, the inspection authority will typically call in an external assessor to assess the safety and operability of machinery or equipment.

Rule of thumb:

– The more well-known and established the system employed in the building project is, the simpler it is to obtain planning permission and building control approval.
– If, however, the system employed is new and untested, the planning and approval process will be correspondingly longer and more complex.

Planning approval stages for a pre-existing complete system	Planning approval stages for a system made with different prefabricated components		Planning approval stages for an entirely new system or partial use of existing components

Classic approach:	All major components made by the **same** manufacturer:	Major components made by **different** manufacturers:	Major components to be developed, subcomponents from **different** manufacturers:
– Agree necessary dimensioning of general technical services with specialist design engineers	– Agree necessary dimensioning of general technical services with specialist design engineers	– Agree necessary dimensioning of general technical services with specialist design engineers	– Agree necessary dimensioning of general technical services with specialist design engineers
– Specification of system together with the manufacturer	– Proposal developed by the system manufacturer	– Proposal developed by specialist design engineer or with one of the manufacturers	– Proposal developed together with specialist design engineer or with one of the manufacturers
			– Risk assessment, collation of applicable norms and guidelines – Adaptation of the construction
	– Negotiation with the building control authorities, trade association, health and safety control, insurance, etc. where relevant	– Negotiation with the building control authorities, trade association, health and safety control, insurance, etc. where relevant	– Negotiation with the building control authorities, trade association, health and safety control, insurance, etc. where relevant
	– Incorporation of additional requirements from the authorities/client together with the system manufacturer	– Incorporation of additional requirements from the authorities/client together with the specialist design engineer or system manufacturer	– Incorporation of additional requirements from the authorities/client together with the specialist design engineer or system manufacturer
			– Assessment of documents and construction with regard to conformity with guidelines by an official accreditation agency
– Tendering – Contract award – Works planning by the contractor	– Tendering – Contract award – Works planning by the contractor	– Tendering – Contract award – Works planning by the contractor	– Tendering – Contract award – Works planning by the contractor
		– Where necessary apply for technical approval (individual case) drawn up by contractor and design engineer (include proofs of conformity for all approved components used)	– In most cases, apply for technical approval (individual case) drawn up by contractor and design engineer – The planning authorities will generally require proof of conformity for their assessment
– Manufacture, delivery and – Installation – Functionality and safety assessment by the contractor	– Manufacture, delivery and – Installation – Functionality and safety assessment by the contractor	– Manufacture, delivery and – Installation – Functionality and safety assessment by the contractor	– Manufacture, delivery and – Installation – Functionality and safety assessment by the contractor
		– Assessment of agreed standards by an external assessor reporting to the building control authorities and/or planning authorities – Approval of fitness for function and safety	– Assessment of agreed standards by an external assessor reporting to the building control authorities and/or planning authorities – Approval of fitness for function and safety
– Documentation and briefing by the contractor on handover – Inspection by the design engineer, building control authorities and client	– Documentation and briefing by the contractor on handover – Inspection by the design engineer, building control authorities and client	– Documentation and briefing by the contractor on handover – Inspection by the design engineer, building control authorities and client	– Documentation and briefing by the contractor on handover – Inspection by the design engineer, building control authorities and client

Movement and construction principles

A

2

Facing page: Zollverein Coal Mine Industrial Complex, Shaft XII, consortium Office for Metropolitan Architecture, Heinrich Böll, Hans Krabel, Essen, 2006

A

Theory and planning

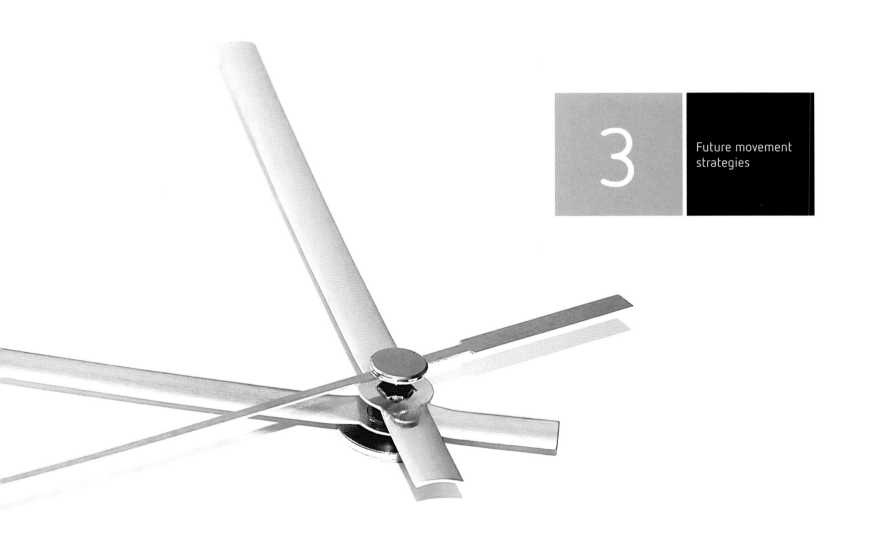

As the temperature rises, particle movement increases ⟶

	Solid	Liquid	Gaseous
Solid	Alloy, conglomerate	Suspension, suspended solids, mud, colloid	Smoke, aerosol
Fluid	Gel, wet sponge	Emulsion, dispersion	Fog, aerosol
Gaseous	Rigid foam	Foam	Gas mixture

Mixed states of aggregation

■ 3.1 Making use of changing states of matter

Depending on prevailing external conditions, any substance can take the form of a solid, liquid or gas. These three physical states are known as states of aggregation or phases of the material.

Solid

Solid materials exhibit cohesive properties, that is the molecular forces of attraction and repulsion are in equilibrium, holding together the atoms or molecules. The molecules form a molecular lattice and each particle vibrates only around its position of equilibrium. The material has a stable, definite shape and volume.

Liquid

Liquids represents a transitional phase between solid and gas. The intermolecular cohesive forces are still present but very much weaker so that the individual particles are free to move around. The particles have a higher kinetic energy and are no longer bound in a lattice structure but can move around. Particles can squeeze between gaps between neighbouring particles. The material maintains its volume but is unstable and changes its shape to fill the available space.

Gas

In gases, cohesive forces are almost non-existent and one can consider the moving particles independently. Their kinetic energy is so large that any remaining cohesive forces have no effect. The particles move around freely, colliding with one an-

other. The material has no definite shape or volume and expands to fill the bounding container.

Plasma

Plasmas are highly-ionised gases, a gaseous form with high levels of 'free' electrons and ionised atoms, and are occasionally termed the fourth state of aggregation. The plasma phase occurs at very high temperatures (thermal decomposition) and can also be brought about by very strong electric fields (lightning, gas discharge lamp). At extreme temperatures ($\approx 5000\,K$) gases decompose almost completely to plasma. In some solids and liquids, free electrons and ionised atoms are also present at lower temperatures, but in principle plasma behaves like a gas with electrons, cations and atomic nuclei as its smallest particles. Plasmas are accordingly very good conductors. Plasmas are known for their luminescent qualities caused by the radiant emissions of excited gas atoms, ions or molecules.

Hybrid states of aggregation

Some materials occur in a state that cannot be clearly attributed to a particular phase. Gels, for example, are neither pure liquids nor pure solids. They consist of larger, suspended solid particles (dispersed phase) in a solvent solution (dispersion medium). Because its particles are larger, it cannot diffuse through a membrane in the same way that a solution can, for example salt water. As such, they are known as colloidal solutions or colloids for short. Foams are also colloidal as they consist of a gas

(dispersed phase) suspended in a liquid suspension medium (dispersion medium).

Phase transitions

The state of aggregation of a material is dependent on ambient pressure and temperature. A material may be solid at a low temperature, turning liquid as the temperature rises before finally turning gaseous. The transition from one state of aggregation to the next is known as the phase transition or phase change. For each phase change a particular amount of energy in the form of heat is absorbed or given off. Temperature changes the kinetic energy of particles: the higher the temperature the greater the activity of the particles. The temperature thresholds that mark the transition from one state of aggregation to the next (at normal pressure) are known as the condensation point, boiling point, freezing point or melting point. Warming a material causes its particles to acquire ever greater kinetic energy. Particles in a solid state begin to vibrate more strongly within the lattice and in liquids and gases gain velocity. Above a certain temperature, the energy of the vibrations becomes so great that it exceeds the molecular force of attraction, causing the structure of a solid material to break down so that it melts and turns into a fluid. In reverse, when a fluid cools, the molecular forces of attraction exceed the kinetic energy of the particles causing the fluid to solidify. The excess energy is given off as heat. The melting point of many materials can be lowered by increasing the pressure. Under pressure, ice, for

Ice hotel, Jukkasjärvi, Swedish Lapland

example, can become liquid at 0 °C. If one reduces the pressure, ice will form again. This process is known as regulation and is responsible, for example, for glacier flow. Scientists at the Max Planck Institute for Metals Research in Stuttgart have observed that glacial ice passing over a mineral such as silica begins to melt at a temperature as low as -17 °C, far below the freezing point. This thin layer of highly compressed water (approx. 1.2 g/cm³) is only a few nanometres thick and 20 % more compact than normal water. This only recently discovered property could contribute to a better understanding of the phenomenon of glaciation.

Buildings made of ice

In December 2008, a house made of snow and ice was built in the small village of Jukkasjärvi in Sweden, 200 km north of the arctic circle. It was the 18th time that the ice hotel had been built. During the Nordic winter, snow is applied to a temporary supporting shell or sprayed as water from a snow cannon. After it freezes, the supporting structure is removed to leave a slightly translucent shell of ice. A second method also employed resembles the building of an igloo, using blocks of ice cut out of rivers. Clear water in combination with a strong current produces especially clear ice that allows light

to pass through it particularly well and can be used in place of glass. The hotel encompasses a total area of around 4000 m² and provides over 60 rooms and suites. The indoor temperature never exceeds 5 °C so that almost all the furniture and wall decorations can also be made of ice. The translucent quality of the material is exploited by illuminating it with artificial light to create specific atmospheric lighting. In summer the building changes its state of aggregation – and melts: a transient structure made of locally available materials and in tune with the rhythm of nature.

Structures made of fog

An example for the potential and new atmospheric possibilities of designing with states of aggregation, and the medium of water in particular, is the Blur Building designed by the New York architectural office of Elizabeth Diller and Ricardo Scofidio for the Swiss Expo 2002 in Yverdon. It consists of an artificial cloud. Water is pumped through a system of pipes with microscopic spray nozzles to create a white world out of finely atomised water particles. Diller and Scofidio succeed in giving structure, facade and space an entirely new visual, acoustic and haptic dimension. The building has no clear form or extents. The views out change con-

stantly and one loses all sense of dimension. Bridges and walkways allow one to pass through the cloud which is additionally illuminated with a diffuse blue light. The boundaries between inside and outside, between nature and architecture blur. A finely calibrated system of sensors measures climatic conditions such as temperature, wind and air humidity and adjusts the consistency of the fog accordingly. Depending on the weather, the cloud changes its form and with it the microclimate of the building.

Harnessing energy exchanging effects

The absorption or emission of energy that occurs during phase changes can be exploited for certain applications: latent-heat storage tanks are used as cooling accumulators, heating pads or as thermal retention tanks for solar-powered systems. These exploit the kinetic change of state of a storage medium during the phase change. Phase change materials, or PCMs as they are commonly known, usually utilise the energy produced in the change from solid to liquid states. Materials are chosen that undergo phase changes in temperature ranges favourable for the intended application. Typically thermal storage materials are made of special salts or paraffins that absorb large amounts of thermal energy as

Blur Building, Pavilion for the Swiss Expo, Diller Scofidio + Renfro, Yverdon, 2002

they melt, the so-called melting heat. As this process is reversible, the PCM gives off precisely the same amount of heat when it solidifies. Thermal pads employ a related principle: a fill material made of sodium acetate trihydrate melts when heated to a temperature of 58 °C. As it cools, however, it undergoes a process known as supercooling, maintaining its fluid state. The process of crystallisation is triggered by applying pressure to the pad, causing the material to solidify to a temperature of 58 °C. Latent-heat storage tanks can also be employed in other temperature ranges; one need only find a material with a phase change temperature appropriate to the intended application.

The clothing industry also employs PCMs to enable an item of clothing to protect against both extreme cold and heat. The clothing incorporates coated fabric or viscous fibres that contain millions of microscopically small PCM capsules, each filled with paraffin wax that melts in a temperature range between 26 °C and 34 °C. These absorb any excess body heat and store the heat in the fabric. As soon as the temperature drops, the capsules crystallise, emitting the stored energy again as heat. Microencapsulated paraffins are also used as a PCM in building materials, for example in plasters, mortars and dry lining products, to provide a means of passive cooling. During the phase change, heat is stored latently – the temperature of the PCM remains almost constant. As a result, PCMs can be used to increase the thermal retention properties of buildings without sacrificing the advantages of lightweight construction methods. During the day the

PCM stores excess heat, emitting it at night through vents or windows. PCM-based building materials are not conceived of as a replacement for conventional thermal insulation methods such as shading but as the final link in a chain of thermal protection measures aimed at avoiding overheating. Provided that sufficient night-time ventilation is ensured, PCM plaster can reduce the temperature by up to 4 K, creating a much more comfortable indoor climate without the need for active air conditioning. Other PCM-based building materials achieve similar results.

Passive systems, and with them PCM-based passive cooling, are dependent on cool evening air. If the overnight temperature remains high for several days in a row, the PCM cannot effectively release its energy. With each successive day its retention capacity is reduced and the building is liable to overheat more rapidly.

In a further development, research is being conducted at the Frauenhofer Institute for Solar Energy Systems into phase change fluids (suspensions and emulsions) that have a much greater thermal retention capacity at their melting point than water and are just as straightforward to use. The aim is that such materials can be employed in conventional technical installations with as little modifications as necessary.

Phase change fluids are able to store large quantities of thermal energy in comparatively small temperature intervals. A comparison between water and a 30 % phase change suspension illustrates the potential they hold: to store 60 kJ/kg thermal energy,

water needs to be warmed by 14.3 K; a phase change fluid is able to store the same amount of energy in only 6.5 K.

Plasma emissions

The luminescent qualities typical of plasmas are also utilised in lighting technology. Collisions between fast-moving electrons and gas atoms or molecules cause energy to be passed to the electrons that surround the respective particle. This energy is then emitted later as radiant light. The spectrum of this light depends mainly on the gases involved, the pressure and the mean energy of the electrons. In some cases the emitted light can be used directly, for example in metal vapour high-pressure lamps, such as mercury and sodium-based street lamps, or in certain noble gas high-pressure discharge lamps, such as xenon lamps. In other cases, where the spectrum of emissions lies predominantly in the UV range, the electromagnetic radiation must first be converted into a spectral region that humans can see. This is usually achieved using fluorescent materials that are most often applied to the inner walls of the discharge lamp. The ultraviolet radiation is absorbed by the fluorescent material which radiates this energy as visible light. Examples of these kinds of lamps include fluorescent light bulbs and energy-saving lamps often used to illuminate interiors.

Adiabatic air conditioning

The principle of this cooling method is very straightforward: as water evaporates, it absorbs energy from

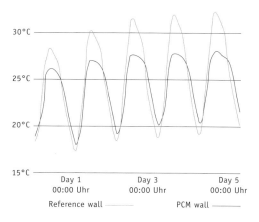

Temperature differences in a room with PCM insulation (black) and with conventional insulation (grey)

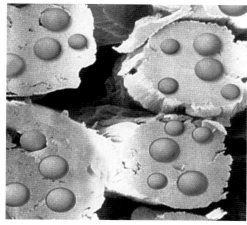

Microscopic view of polyacrylic fibres with embedded PCM microcapsules

A

3

the air around it, causing the air to cool down. This principle of physics is something we experience all the time: in summer, the body begins to sweat; perspiration (water) comes into contact with air causing the body to cool down.

The most commonly employed architectural use of adiabatic or evaporative cooling is a process that involves humidifying the air that is expelled from the building. The evaporation of the water causes energy to be drawn out of the exhaust air, lowering its temperature. By using a heat exchanger, which serves as a heat recovery system, the cool temperature of the exhaust air is passed to the incoming air entering the building. This kind of cooling can re-duce the temperature of the fresh air intake by 10 °C without the outgoing stale air and incoming fresh air mixing and without having to humidify the incoming air. As water and air are the only sources for this latent heat of evaporation, a well-designed adiabatic cooling system is often beneficial. External energy is only required to operate the heat exchanger and humidifier. 1 m³ of water is sufficient to cool 1000 m² of office space per day.

Solar air conditioning

This cooling method removes the heat from the air using especially sorbent materials, such as silica gel, that draw moisture out of the air in a process known as adsorption. The latent heat of evaporation causes the air to cool down. For the sorbent to be able to take up more moisture, it has to be dried using heat provided by a solar collector. As the sun is both the cause of high daytime temperatures as well as the energy source for driving the cooling system, one can always be sure that there will be sufficient sun to drive the air conditioning when it is needed. Solar cooling methods, therefore, do not need thermal retention methods.

Product name	Product type	Melting point, approx.	Application	Storage capacity, approx.	Solids content	Density	Viscosity
DS 5000	Dispersion	26 °C	Prevention of summer overheating	59 kJ/kg	~ 42 %	~ 0.98	~ 200 – 600 mPas
DS 5007	Dispersion	23 °C	Stabilisation of room temperature	55 kJ/kg	~ 42 %	~ 0.98	~ 200 – 600 mPas
DS 5030	Dispersion	21 °C	Panel cooling systems	51 kJ/kg	~ 42 %	~ 0.98	~ 200 – 600 mPas
DS 5001	Powder	26 °C	Prevention of summer overheating	145 kJ/kg	powdered	~ 250 – 350 kg/m³	
DS 5008	Powder	23 °C	Stabilisation of room temperature	135 kJ/kg	powdered	~ 250 – 350 kg/m³	
DS 5029	Powder	21 °C	Panel cooling systems	125 kJ/kg	powdered	~ 250 – 350 kg/m³	

Phase Change Materials (PCM), product portfolio BASF Micronal®

■ 3.2 Changing colours, forms and properties

Steel, glass, concrete, and more recently artificial and composite materials, have led to new impulses in architecture. For the most part, these materials are monofunctional – they are employed for their specific properties, only becoming suitable for use in adaptable systems in combination with other components. Modern-day materials research goes a step further. Materials are now being developed directly at the molecular level, tailor-made to have explicitly defined properties and manipulated in such a way that they can adapt autonomously to their respective environmental conditions. Product developments will no longer be dictated by the properties of the most suitable material; the material will instead be invested with properties that are most appropriate for their use in the product. A new breed of "smart materials" is emerging: plastics that change shape, metals that change strength at the right moment or wafer-thin coatings that lend the underlying material certain additional properties. While the properties of so-called switchable materials can be changed externally by sensors or controllers, intelligent materials are able to regulate this process themselves, reacting without outside control. These adaptive materials will in future open up new application areas and make other architectural forms and technical constructions possible. A particular advantage lies in the potential to make constructions lighter, more slender and more comfortable. In addition, it will be possible to reduce the number of mechanical moving parts, in turn reducing the risk of failure. For many of these application areas, such transformations will take place predominantly at a micro- or even nano-scale. As a result, the sequence of movements may no longer be visible to the naked eye, but they will nevertheless have a significant impact on the appearance and impression of buildings as well as improve their functionality.

A reactive surface structure: changes in the ambient air humidity alter the geometry of the surface elements, Design Unit for form generation and materialisation, Academy of Art and Design, Achim Menges, Steffen Reichert, HfG Offenbach, 2005 – 2007

Continuously deformable aerofoil made of a shape memory alloy, Continuum Dynamics Inc./Lockheed Martin

Other industrial sectors are already a step ahead of the construction industry. It is instructive to take a closer look at parallel developments in order to elaborate visions for future moving elements in buildings.

Semi-smart materials and smart materials

Adaptive functional materials can be categorised according to their properties into two groups: "semi-smart materials" that can change their properties once or a few times only, and "smart materials" which have permanently reversible properties. These changes are triggered by external physical and chemical influences such as temperature, light, pressure, electrical, magnetic or chemical stimuli. The changes that result fall into a variety of different categories.

Materials that change form

Piezoelectric ceramics are able to convert mechanical impulses into electrical impulses and vice versa. In the latter direction, piezo technology functions much like a muscle: electrical impulses cause a material to contract and then to expand. One application area currently being developed in the construction sector is the use of piezoelectric ceramics for soundproofing windows. Double and triple glazing can absorb high-frequency sound, but to absorb low-frequency sounds, such as aircraft noise or deep bass tones in music, the panes have to be thick and heavy, which in turn presents problems for lightweight constructions or large facades. An accelerometer measures the vibrations that the sound causes in the pane. Piezoelectric fibres embedded in a polymer film or patch laminated to the glass or another element then create a vibration that cancels out the frequency of vibration caused by the sound, stiffening the building element.

In the above scenario, the piezos are controlled by sensors and are, therefore, strictly speaking not wholly smart materials.

Using the reverse principle, pressure applied to a piezo plate can be converted into an electric current. Light switches that employ this method produce a charge when pressed that is sufficient to send a wireless signal to a receiver (for example a light). As the switch does not require electricity, it can be placed wherever one needs it.

A further reactive material currently under development is electroactive polymers: plastic fibres and films that deform when a voltage is applied to them and can be used as actuators. Sandwich materials such as thermostatic bimetals consist of two different materials with different thermal expansion coefficients. The material with the larger coefficient of thermal expansion is termed the active element, the other the passive element. Typically metals such as zinc and steel, or bronze and steel, are fused together to form a bimetallic plate or band. Trials are being conducted for a solar shading system that employ bimetals to enable the lamella to adapt autonomously in response to temperature changes caused by solar irradiation. Besides metals, other self-controlling composite materials are also conceivable. At the Architectural Association School of Architecture in London a task group led by Achim Menges has developed a partition made of wooden scales that react to the level of ambient humidity, causing the scales to open and close like the feathers of a bird's plumage.

Materials that change volume

Fluids that exhibit thermal expansion are used, for example, in pressure control media and linear actuators as they expand continuously as the temperature rises. Thermometers, heating valves and thermostats in taps and sprinkler systems are well-known examples of devices that employ expanding materials. The material chosen is typically paraffin oil, paraffin wax or alcohol. As the temperature rises, the volume of the fluid expands, in turn pushing a piston. As the material cools, the piston is pressed back into the casing, usually assisted by a spring mechanism.

Materials that memorise shape

Plastics and metal alloys with shape memory properties are pressed, using a thermomechanical process, into a stable initial form that can sustain low levels of deformation and then revert back to its original form. In the case of shape memory metal alloys, a phase change takes place between two crystalline structures. Above a critical temperature, the structure exhibits a hard crystalline structure that changes to a structure that can sustain slight deformations as the temperature drops. Common metal compounds include gold-cadmium alloys, copper-zinc alloys and nickel-titanium alloys (nitinol). The additional introduction of further alloying elements allows one to influence the temperature of transformation, the extent of the effect as well as other properties. The spectrum of currently avail-

A wave of "memory foam" in the "Mute Room", Thom Faulders, San Francisco, 2001

able semi-finished products ranges from wires, rods and springs to panels, which are all employed in actuating and positioning gears, spring elements and woven textiles. In the field of medicine, minute metal and plastic stents are implanted into coronary blood vessels to reinforce them and reduce clogging and blockages. The stents are injected directly using minimal surgery into the artery and assume the desired form triggered by the temperature of the

body. Fibrous polymers are also used to close wounds in surgery. The temperature of the body causes the material to bunch up in the form in which it was applied, obviating the need for complex stitching. In addition, the fibres are biodegraded by the body. The automobile industry uses plastics for bumpers and roof antennas that can sustain light deformations and assume their original form. Ventilation grilles are also being researched

that change their shape depending on the air pressure caused by the speed of the vehicle.

Materials with varying viscosity
D30 is a plastic that consists of freely moving molecules that interlock when pressure is applied, causing the material to harden and become shock-absorbent. Motorcycle helmets and other sport articles will soon be equipped with such technology. Re-

Simulation left: thermochromic concrete reacts to heat given off by visitors. Simulation right: wires embedded in a concrete wall warm thermochromic pigments. Afshin Mehin, Tomas Rosen, Christopher Glaister, Royal College of Art, London, 2003

The heat of the light bulb causes the shape memory alloy of the "hanabi" lamp to blossom, nendo, Tokyo, 2006

search is being conducted into appropriate architectural applications.

Materials that change colour or appearance

Over the last decade interest has grown steadily in functional polymers that are able to change their visible properties in response to external stimuli. Chromogenic materials change their colour and transparency depending on temperature, electric voltage, pressure or light, and can be directed by controlling these external stimuli. Depending on the stimulus that controls the material's optical appearance, these chromogenic materials are classified as thermochromic (stimulus: temperature), photochromic (stimulus: light), electrochromic (stimulus: electrical field), piezochromic (stimulus: pressure), ionochromic (stimulus: ion concentration) and biochromic (stimulus: biochemical reaction). Of particular use are thermochromic plastics such as hydrogels, thermoplastic films and duromers, non-deformable plastics and additives that change colour and/or transparency as the temperature changes. A particular application area for these materials is in solar protection to reduce the energy consumption of air conditioning systems in buildings with large amounts of glazing. Electrochromic materials can be made darker actively, while photochromic materials react autonomously to sunlight, an effect used for self-darkening sunglasses. Thermotropic polymers react similarly to rising temperature, changing independently from transparent to strongly diffuse without the need for any external energy supply.

For the manufacture of thermotropic laminated glass, transparent cast-resins are used that contain additives with specially developed pigments. Such laminated glass is highly durable and maintenance-free. Thermochromic products include drinking straws or glasses that change colour depending on the temperature of the fluid or our hands. Thermochromic wall paints can respond to the ambient room temperature or alter the coloration of a facade according to the seasons. These colour pigments can be stimulated using electrical heating wires, enabling architects and designers to turn plain concrete surfaces with embedded pigments and wires into display panels.

Materials that emit light

Certain molecules can temporarily acquire a higher level of energy through an external stimulus. As this energy is given off, part of it will be emitted in the form of visible electrical irradiation. Where this effect occurs almost instantaneously, one speaks of fluorescence (an effect familiar from fluorescent lighting). Where the emitted light follows after a slight delay, one speaks of phosphorescence. Daylight fluorescent paints can be used almost anywhere to make objects light up. Phosphorescent paints and foils are used most commonly for dark or night-time situations as a means of assisting orientation and increasing safety. Electroluminescence is a further principle used most commonly in LED technology. In addition to their use in more dense or more open pixelated patterns, LEDs can also be used in conjunction with light conductors such as

glass fibres, glass panels or transparent plastics to create interesting effects. When illuminated from the side, the entire surface of these conductors lights up. Luminescent surfaces can also be achieved using thick film electroluminescence. An electric current causes pigments in films or cables to shine.

Materials that generate electricity

The performance of silicon solar cells is well-known. Dye-sensitised solar cells are a further development from the field of bionics which utilises organic and inorganic dyes to bring about a kind of photosynthesis similar to that resulting from chlorophyll. This obviates the need for a semiconductor such as silicon. These solar cells are coloured and transparent and can therefore be used as windows. Paint manufacturers are developing coatings for the automotive industry that employ this principle and could be applied as full-surface solar cells to generate electricity.

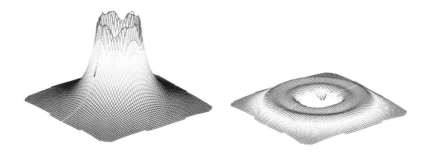

■ 3.3 Smart Structures

The possible reduction of stress concentration at the perimeter of a drill aperture in a biaxially loaded plane using induced strain, Agnes Weilandt

Agnes Weilandt

Transformable structures are increasingly being equipped with ever more functionality. For example, sun control systems are being developed that change their geometry in response to the position of the sun so that the facade is always automatically shaded. These newly developed structures are not just technically impressive; their constantly changing form also lends them a unique aesthetic appearance. With increasing functionality, the structures also become more autonomous, heralding a gradual transition from structures that are merely transformable (for example an adjustable awning) to smart structures and adaptive systems that are able to actively respond to their external environment.

In contrast to transformable structures, adaptive systems exhibit a closed-loop control system consisting of at least three components: sensors, controllers and actuators. The sensors measure the external environmental conditions and pass this information on to controllers that identify and analyse this information to determine the necessary adjustments to the system, passing on this information as instructions. Finally, the actuators put these instructions into effect, changing the system and improving its efficiency. The resulting effect of the actuators on the properties of the system is then measured and monitored by the sensors, closing the control loop.

The variety of different possible adaptive systems is almost endless. Alongside systems that change the physical properties of a building's enclosure, adaptive loadbearing structures also play an important role. Loadbearing structures are designed to accommodate the maximum possible load that may occur during the building's entire life cycle. In most cases, however, the respective peak loads do not occur at the same time so that the individual components of structural system are often over-dimensioned for most typical loads. For example, as a train passes over a bridge, only those parts of the bridge on which the train rests at any given moment are under maximum load while the remainder of the bridge

"Stuttgarter Träger": Institute for Lightweight Structures and Conceptual Design (ILEK), Stuttgart University, 2001

"Stuttgarter Träger", adaptive state

WhoWhatWhenAIR actuated tower, Philippe Block, Axel Kilian, Peter Schmitt, John Snavely:
Built in 2006, the kinetic tower can be actuated by a pneumatic construction (also known as a muscle). The design won a competition for a 12 m high mini skyscraper organised by the Department of Architecture at MIT. The goal was to demonstrate the potential of actuation as a way to build more intelligent structures.

WhoWhatWhenAIR, kinetic tower, computer rendering

Functioning prototype

is less affected. If one were to integrate active elements into the construction that are able to respond to changing external conditions, the need for individual elements to accommodate peak loads can be reduced by redistributing these forces within the structure. When calculating the dimensions of structural members, one would then no longer need to design for peak load situations but for the much lower stresses resulting from load path distribution. This leads to a more economical use of materials. Ultimately, such adaptive systems work by replacing materials or material properties not required for all load situations with induced energy. Pursuing this train of thought further: adaptive systems could in principle be designed to reduce the structural deformation of specific structural elements to zero so that through the application of induced energy an infinitely rigid system can be simulated, something that is never achievable with passive systems.

The model of an adaptive bridge designed at the Institute for Lightweight Structures and Conceptual Design (ILEK) at Stuttgart University in 2001 exemplifies how this potential can be exploited. The activation of the "Stuttgarter Träger" as it is known, is designed so that the deformation of the structure at the point of external loading resulting from a travelling load is always precisely zero. Furthermore the weight of the structure in relation to its bearing capacity can be reduced by up to 50 % compared with a passive system, enabling one to realise an extremely effective depth-to-span ratio of 1:500.

The use of active elements is particularly well-suited for lightweight structures that do not need to cater for a constant invariant load case or where deformation limits are the determining factor for the dimensioning of the structural members. This allows lightweight structures to be made lighter and more efficient and in turn to push forward current limits of what is feasible with regard to construction height and span length. Accordingly, adaptive structures are also a key research area in the field of aviation and space technology, in which weight

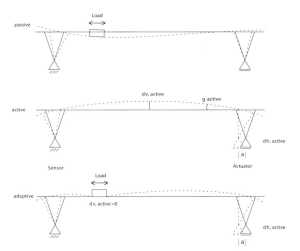

"Stuttgarter Träger": functioning principle

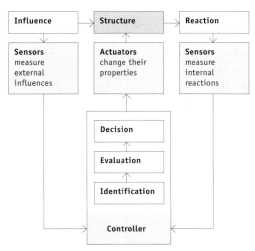

Control system for an adaptive system (after J. T. P. Yao)

plays a crucial role. Here developments have progressed much further than in building construction, and adaptive systems are employed, for example, to reduce the vibration amplitude of helicopter rotor blades. By comparison, active systems in building constructions are characterised by the need to redistribute considerable loads over sometimes long distances but at the same time do not have such high precision requirements. This must be taken into consideration in the choice of actuators.

Adaptive structures are classified as passive, semi-active and active systems: depending on the necessary energy requirements for adapting the actuator properties, one differentiates between systems without external energy input (passive) and those that require external energy input (active or semi-active).

Reactions in passive systems are produced by deformations in the structural framework itself. Such systems include, for example, passive vibration dampers that are used to reduce oscillations resulting from wind, traffic or earthquake loads, or constructions that turn in the wind in order to avoid peak wind loads.

Semi-active adaptive systems function by changing the properties of the system, such as the rigidity or absorption. Electrorheological or magnetorheological fluids are used, for example, as stiffness actuators in vibration dampers. By changing the electrical or magnetic field, these fluids change viscosity and allow a vibration damper to adapt to different oscillation frequencies and sources. Semi-active vibration dampers for use in building constructions were researched and developed in the

1990s. In 2007, the Franjo Tudjman Bridge in Croatia was the first bridge to be equipped with magnetorheological vibration dampers to reduce cable oscillations, a project resulting from work undertaken by Felix Weber at the Swiss Federal Laboratories for Materials Testing and Research (EMPA). Further such systems are planned.

Semi-active systems of this kind can be regarded as stiffness actuators and require less energy than active systems. Active systems, by contrast, adapt to changing loads by producing the exact opposite forces with the help of elongation actuators. Actuators suitable for use with active systems can be divided into unconventional and conventional actuators. Unconventional actuators derive from smart materials but at present do not exhibit sufficient travel distance or actuating force and are therefore

Tristan d'Estrée Sterk – The Office for Robotic Architectural Media & Bureau for Responsive Architecture:
A full-scale prototype of an actuated tensegrity structure for use as part of a responsive building envelope. The structure is designed to use a small number of components to achieve maximal shape change. Two types of aluminium components are used with actuators (pneumatic muscles) and cables.

presently unsuitable for use in adaptive structures. Other actuators such as those that employ electromagnetic (electrical and electromagnetic stepper motors) or fluid-based systems (hydraulic and pneumatic actuators) can provide the necessary travel distances and loadbearing stability for use in building constructions.

In most cases adaptive systems emulate, with technological means, adaptive principles known from nature. Natural adaptive processes are generally categorised according to their speed of reaction in three groups: short-term adaptive processes in near-real-time such as the change in colour of a chameleon; long-term adaptive processes such as the bent growth of a tree on a windy coastline; and evolutionary adaptive processes which take place over several generations. Technical adaptive sys-

tems, such as the aforementioned example of the adaptive bridge, almost always require short-term adaptive systems.

Whether adaptive systems will become commonplace in building construction depends largely on user acceptance. For adaptive building enclosures, for example, the user must decide whether he or she is willing to relinquish own control in favour of an integrated and autonomous overall concept that may objectively provide a higher level of comfort. Adaptive structures will also necessitate a fundamentally different approach to safety concepts. Rather than the conventional approach in which the failure of every individual component is reduced to the very minimum, it may make more sense to prevent the failure of the entire system should an individual component fail or to provide sufficient re-

dundancy to accommodate failure. This so-called "fail-safe" safety concept, which is already widely used in aviation technology and other areas, is now increasingly being discussed and applied in the field of building construction.

■ 3.4 Growth

In biology, growth is defined as the difference between anabolic synthesis and catabolic decomposition. It describes the positive or negative change in the size of an organism over time. At a cellular level this can be caused by a change in the number of cells through cell division or by a change in the size of cells as a result of internal or external pressure. When different areas grow at different rates (differential growth) this can affect not only the size but also the shape and proportions of an organism. Natural growth processes follow different patterns. While the human brain exhibits so-called saturation growth, growing very quickly to begin

with before gradually slowing, the dimensions of the body follow a sigmoidal growth pattern, growing at an ever increasing rate of growth until the age of 13 or 14 before growing more slowly. By comparison, certain organs exhibit a bell-curve-shaped growth pattern: after a phase of (positive) growth, the organs begin to grow smaller as negative growth sets in. In general usage, however, the term growth is often taken to mean exponential growth. This applies, for example, to cell cultures under laboratory conditions: cell divisions occur at regular intervals causing the number of cells to double with each growth phase. Despite the apparent adynamic inter-

val of the individual growth processes, the resulting explosion in size takes place surprisingly quickly and with extreme results.

Growth processes fulfil two major functions: they allow organisms to reproduce as well as to gradually adapt to changing environmental conditions. Applied to architecture, one can identify two distinct, corresponding concepts for the application of growth processes: growth in terms of a change of size that helps a form assume its full size, and growth in terms of continual adaptation, through changes in proportion or properties. Examples that illustrate just how much potential this can offer can

Spider 2, R&Sie(n), Nîmes, 2007

Vertical Farm: Solargreen tower, Soa Architects

be found in both traditional as well as experimental architecture.

From green walls to hanging gardens

The greening of facades with climbers and creepers is a well-known technique that primarily serves decorative purposes, although plants that provide even coverage, such as ivy or vines, can also have a positive effect on insulation properties. In the greening of flat roofs, too, both the aesthetic as well as functional qualities of living organisms (climate modulation, regulation of rainwater accumulation) are utilised in direct conjunction with buildings. In both cases the growth of plants contributes to the design: a wild vine that over the years progressively envelopes an urban villa makes a visual spectacle out of nature's gradual appropriation of the building. Similarly, the seasonal blossoming and colouring of a greened roof renders an abstract temporal cycle visible. The botanist Patrick Blanc has turned this principle into art. His "Vertical Gardens" appear at first glance to be the very expression of uncontrolled plant growth but are actually a carefully orchestrated floral ornamentation. In these gardens, as well as in the preceding examples, the aspect of growth is represented primarily visually. Plants cover the surfaces of architecture, changing them continuously. However, growth processes can also be applied to architecture at other levels.

Vertical farms

In built-up urban areas there is little space for cultivating useful plants and crops. Naturally grown fruit and vegetables have to be transported long distances from outlying regions, incurring high energy costs. The concept of the vertical farm aims to rectify this by employing an intensified means of cultivating useful plants and crops in inner cities.

VertiCrop, High Density Vertical Growth System, Valcent Products

Vertical Algae Technology, Valcent Products

Facade, Musée du Quai Branly, Jean Nouvel/Patrick Blanc, Paris, 2006

The Walkway: Entwicklungsgesellschaft für Baubotanik, Wald-Ruhestetten, Germany, planting and construction March 2005

Plant growth is photoautotrophic: it requires only sunlight as an energy source and easily transportable inorganic substances as nutrients, for example water and salt. By arranging plants in vertical registers behind a protective facade, the yield per square metre floor space can be increased dramatically. Dickson Despommier, a professor at the Environmental Health Science Faculty at Columbia University, who brought this method onto the market in 1999 and continues to conduct intensive research in the field, estimates that yield can be improved by a factor of four to six compared with conventional open field agriculture. Companies are already working on the technical and horticultural realisation of vertical greenhouses. If one were to stack vertical farms above one another to a height of 30 storeys over the area of a residential block in New York, one could, according to Despommier's team, provide enough food for the daily needs of 50,000 people.

Growing environments

The greening of traditionally built masonry walls has long been part of the architectural repertoire. But when the external walls actually consist of living, growing material, fundamentally new conceptual options emerge. On the one hand, a growing building changes perpetually and is never actually finished. On the other, natural vegetation follows its owns natural laws and forms spaces suitable for inhabitation only by chance, if at all. So, which rules should govern how growing spaces evolve and what role can design play in this process?

One of the simplest ways is through a fusion of the disciplines of architecture and landscape architecture. The designer becomes a gardener who plants the materials of the wall and then directs its development by horticultural means (pruning, grafting, twining). This is the method employed for the green catacombs of the Spidernethewood created by the Parisian architects R&Sie(n). Plant growth is used

here to continuously transform the external skin of the building. The protective mesh of leaves and branches grows ever thicker and the extents of the space become gradually more distinct. At the same time the light that penetrates the skin is increasingly obscured and with it the relationship between inside and outside. The space begins to take shape. The above example does not, however, make use of the innate adaptive potential of natural growth processes. Designers such as the Californian architects Tom Wiscombe and Peter Testa have attempted to integrate the self-organising aspects of growing systems in the design stage. Testa uses an experimental software platform to model the growth of areas in space. The designer lays down basic rules for the generation of form, the DNA of the space as it were, and the external boundary conditions. A specific local solution for spatial questions arises as a product of the successive, gradual, program-driven concretisation of space. Here growth is un-

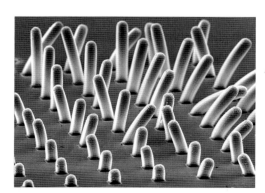

Microscopic enlargement of the growth of carbon nanotubes, John Hart, University of Michigan, 2007

The Walkway: fusion at point of intersection, structural optimisation through biological growth

derstood and utilised as a design method that allows the designer to find the optimal organisation of complex design relationships. Using nature as a model, solutions emerge that are both elegant and efficient.

Growing structures

In contrast to the aforementioned design methodology, natural systems constantly undergo this process of optimisation over their entire lifetime. The founders of the Stuttgart-based Studio Baubotanik have made use of this to develop growing structures. In their Walkway project, living trees are integrated into the structure of a raised walkway in such a way that they gradually fuse at their points of intersection, the latter becoming more and more stable as a product of adaptive growth in response to repeated heavy loading. As a result, the structural performance of the system is constantly improving.

Juan Azulay and David Fletcher also make use of the optimisation potential of growth processes for their design MAK t6 VACANT. The team developed a hybrid system consisting of a non-organic supporting framework and organic 'strangler fig' (ficus petiolaris) plants. Over a period of 30 years, the climbing plants, suspended from a tensile cable construction, will grow towards the ground and thicken to form a plant structure that both strengthens and symbiotically augments the original structure.

Growing materials

Materials research also makes use of innate natural optimisation processes such as material genesis through growth. For example, building materials developed in the laboratory should be trained to adapt to the projected load situation during the growth phase. A research team led by Timo Schmidt is conducting research into building materials that emulate the principle of bone formation using

mechano-sensitive cells that are encouraged to develop their extra-cellular matrix along the principal stress trajectories. A structural element with fixed dimensions could then exhibit differing degrees of stiffness at different points. John Hart at the University of Michigan and his colleague Ryan Wartena have investigated the controlled growth of carbon nanotubes. Together with the architect Elizabeth Marley, the team has developed concepts for applying this in architecture, for example to generate building materials that become more dense according to structural load requirements to create lightweight building envelopes that also function as highly stable loadbearing structures.

Experimental set-ups at the Center for Regenerative Biology and Medicine (ZRM) in Tübingen for the cultivation of mechanically loaded, three-dimensional cell cultures including mechanical simulation unit, media reservoir and sensor system.

 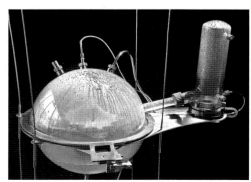

3D bioreactor, cultivation of the ILEK tent on a collagen matrix

3D bioreactor, construction for the 2008 Biennale

B Applications and functions

1

Changing and extending uses and functions

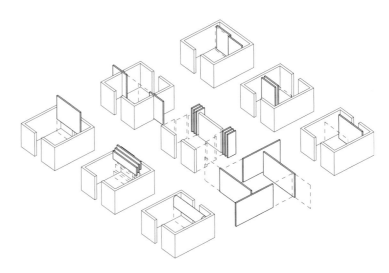

■ 1.1 Variable walls

Positions of dividing elements in space

"Architecture is the art of organising space," according to the French architect Auguste Perret. Movable walls help make spaces more flexible and more functional. More "dynamic" concepts of spaces offer greater potential for using variable walls.

Organising space
The spectrum of spatial concepts ranges from small enclosed spatial units to expansive indoor landscapes: the worker's cubicle on the one hand, the open-plan office on the other, the three-room flat or the factory loft space. Between each of these conceptual extremes, there lies a wide variety of alternative means of differentiating or optimising spaces and functions. The ability of buildings to adapt to changing sociological, psychological and economic situations has become a key factor for prolonging the usable life of a property. The more flexible a building is, the more able it is to react to different patterns of use over several generations of users and the better its overall ecological as well as economic balance.
More visionary approaches go as far as developing buildings whose structures make extensive use of mobile units so that they are fully able to adapt to changing long-term developments. In most cases, however, the cost-benefit ratio of such solutions is excessive and they rarely make it from utopia to reality. Usually, it is more effective to respond to long-term developments by undertaking small-scale conversions, for example by relocating fixed, lightweight partition walls, rather than fitting walls with complicated and expensive movement mechanisms that are only ever rarely used.

Mobile walls are more appropriate for changing spaces for short periods of time. In many cases, spaces need to be adapted to different situations and functions at short notice. Mobile partitions can be used to make a room more spacious, lighter or more peaceful – in other words, they serve more than purely rational and functional needs.

Changing the atmosphere of spaces
Ever changing configurations of separating walls create different spatial impressions. Spaces change their proportions, their illumination, their sound and their degree of intimacy. The ability to bring about these changes oneself and to experience how the spaces change as a result, connects the user directly with the building. Variability can become an experience in itself. Even the aesthetic moment of change can be made into an enriching experience. Theatre staging uses these possibilities to achieve a wide variety of different effects using the same stage set.

Optimising the use of space and variable room sizes
Mobile building elements enable spaces to grow or shrink. The ability to switch between different spatial configurations can create the illusion of more rooms than is actually the case. Carefully conceived and painstakingly executed detailed solutions make it possible to create complex living and working scenarios in very small spaces. The apartment buildings in Fukuoka, Japan, designed by Steven Holl, offer a variety of different spatial solutions in a very

compact space. During the day, variable walls allow the living area to fill the entire space. At night, hinged wall surfaces divide off a section for use as a bedroom. In another apartment, the children's bedroom can be joined to the other living areas when the children leave home.
A further example has been realised by the Austrian architects Franz Sam and Irene Ott-Reinisch. The architects describe their project as follows: "We projected everything one needs to live into a tiny 23.70 m² inner-city apartment. This was only possible by making almost everything mobile and variable. The sliding door of the wardrobe also separates off the kitchen. When the glass shower partition is slid back, it covers the clothes. If one shifts it in the other direction, it partitions off the entrance area. And when both sliding walls are closed, one can enter the living room."

Spaces that serve multiple uses
Buildings and spaces have to be able to adapt to different habitual patterns of use. The ability to change the size of spaces allows them to be used flexibly, to become dual- or multi-purpose. The ability to temporarily divide spaces responds to the way in which the zones are used: the dining area can be associated with the kitchen, the children's room can become a play area, a restaurant can be opened up for large events, parts of a three-court sports hall can be divided off as a fitness gym. It is essential that spaces can be adapted simply and efficiently as this ensures that such possibilities are actually made use of in the first place.

Single leaf   Double leaf   Segmented

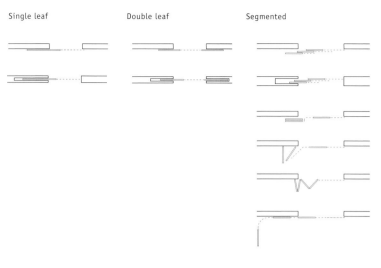

Parking position of dividing elements

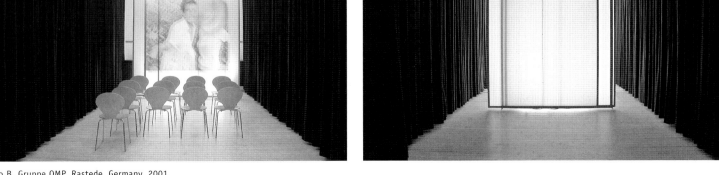

Studio B, Gruppe OMP, Rastede, Germany, 2001

Changing and extending uses and functions

B

1

Hinged Space Housing, Steven Holl, Fukuoka, Japan, 1991

The membrane principle

The variable placement of walls allows one to screen off sounds, smells, views or light. Work and private life are becoming increasingly intertwined. The need to be able to regulate one's work-life balance presents a challenge for architecture: one needs to be able to variably open or close off areas, to ensure privacy in some situations and connection and openness in others. If one views separating walls not as boundaries but as interior panels, curtains or screens, then one can use these to control or direct the amount of light or acoustics of a space. More problematic is the screening of sounds and odours between very different functional areas such as the bedroom and the kitchen.

Mobile walls can be utilised as sound absorbers to reduce sound transmission between different spatial zones. Depending on the requirements, they need to achieve a sound reduction index of between Rw 44 dB (34 kg/m²) and Rw 50 dB (49 kg/m²). The limiting factor is usually the joins between the mobile elements. An Rw value of 39 dB is easily achieved, but higher values are only possible using electrically-operated means of ensuring contact pressure at the seals. Higher noise insulation demands, such as those recommended in DIN 4109 – >47 dB for walls in housing, >52 dB for walls in meeting rooms – cannot be achieved.

The ability to see sounds sources plays an important role in their perception. Footfalls, voices or other sounds behind closed walls and doors typically evoke a sense of unease. Who is it? What are they talking about? What's happening out there? Here,

transparent walls can help: although sounds may be familiar, one feels more comfortable if one can see the source.

Few options are more transparent than mobile walls: when parked to one side they allow a room to be fully open to view. Depending on the choice of material for the wall segment, the use of a graded transition from transparent to translucent can help achieve effective noise reduction when the wall is closed, while still maintaining an optical connection between both spaces.

Light and dark – light redirection

In addition to changing the zoning of spaces and improving acoustics, mobile separating walls can also be used to control the illumination of spaces. Switchable room zones allow a space to receive light from different sides. The orientation of a room can be less relevant if one is able to draw on the qualities of neighbouring spaces. For example, an east-facing bathroom can open out onto a bedroom on the north side of the building, allowing the morning sun to be experienced in a room that would otherwise receive no sunlight.

Walls and regulations: security and fire protection

Architects are also charged with the task of making sure that open-plan and flexible spatial concepts conform to building regulations and norms. Very often regulations cover situations that are temporary or rare, such as night-time security or an outbreak of fire. Fire doors and security grilles can be

used for smaller openings. Larger spaces are divided into fire compartments by using mobile fire walls or shutters. Sliding fire doors make it possible to ensure that large openings can be made reliably fire-resistant.

In normal circumstances, fire doors are held open by electromagnetic fire door holders connected to the fire alarm system. If the fire alarm sounds, the electric current powering the magnets is cut off causing the sliding fire door to close under its own weight. The process of closure is dampened by a hydraulic speed regulator. Full details are given in DIN 18230. To be able to achieve at least 30 or 90 minutes of fire-resistance, special attention must be given to the joins and edges of the door, and the door threshold in particular. Fire safety doors can be single or double-leaf or expand telescopically. They are available in widths of up to 8.50 m and heights of up to 6 m.

The design and construction of separating walls

Compared with fixed, massive separating walls, mobile separating walls offer the advantage of being lightweight, enabling one to react flexibly to changing ambient conditions. They are also able to fulfil the same design and technical requirements as massive walls. With regard to hinges, door fittings and their dimensioning, the choice should be determined by the function, the size and weight of the mobile panel and the frequency with which it is used or opened as well as the individual habits of the users. For the choice of guide rail or track system

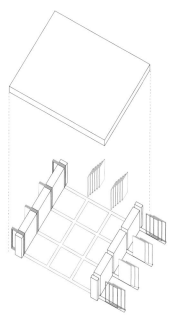

Nine-Square Grid House, Shigeru Ban Architects,
Kanagawa, Japan, 1997

Nine-Square Grid House, Shigeru Ban Architects, Kanagawa, Japan, 1997

there are two principles: standard top-hung systems suspended from tracks for use in interiors can support up to a maximum of 250 kg per wall element or door leaf. Systems such as those used for industrial sheds, with ball-bearing-mounted rollers made of steel, can carry a weight of around 3500 kg. The dimensions of the panels or door leafs vary between 4.00 m and 1.50 m and depend on the weight of the panel and the loadbearing capacity of the runners and tracks or rails.

Bottom-rolling systems run in floor-mounted channels. Rollers transfer the weight of the wall panel or door leaf to the floor. The walls and ceiling are not subject to any tension forces at all. This approach is suitable for heavy wall elements, for example with stone or concrete panels, as well where there is not sufficient structural support for top-hung systems, such as slanting eaves or suspended plasterboard ceilings. The loadbearing capacity is dependent on the rollers. Standard rollers with ball bearings can support a weight of around 400 kg. Special roller gear using components normally intended for cranes and railways can support much greater loads.

The loadbearing capacity of the rollers must be sufficient to support the element and appropriate to the task it fulfils, as rollers are subject to both static and dynamic loads. They should ensure that movement is as quiet as possible. Plastic-coated ball-bearing rollers or plastic rollers with plain bearings in combination with aluminium tracks are generally quietest. Similarly, roller gear must be sufficiently durable for the element they bear and the ease with which they can be replaced; for example,

replacing the rollers on industrial shed doors is not a straightforward task. One should also take care to avoid the bothersome "slip-stick-effect" caused by the surface of the rollers wearing flat in certain sections, an effect that occurs whenever the dimensions and the material are insufficient for the task at hand. For heavy loads upwards of 250 kg, steel systems should be used, although these are generally noisier.

Segmentation

Where mobile wall surfaces are very large but would be too heavy or too large to manoeuvre as a single element, or when the wall has to retract to different positions, the solution is to split a mobile wall into several segments.

Tracks can be arranged in separate parallel planes or in double or multiple track systems. Telescopic systems offer an alternative in which each element pulls the next element out with it, for example by linking them together with a connecting belt. Symmetrical systems allow two elements to be opened simultaneously in a single action. Sufficient space must be available to the left and right of the opening. Folding sliding walls represent a further option. Several elements connected by hinges can be folded together and parked out of the way at a 90° angle to the plane of the track.

Parking position

Whether large openings, room dividers or fire doors, an essential design parameter for movable partitions is the ability to move it to a defined parking

position. In some cases a partition can be shifted around in space until it occupies an alternative position or fulfils another function. Often, however, once retracted the wall should no longer be visible as a wall. A design must make provisions for a parking position: either in front of another wall, in a wall pocket or as a packet of wall sections in a wall niche. A single-track solution is commonly used where a wall consists of a large number of sections that are then pushed together and parked as a packet. These so-called stacking-sliding walls are often automated and are available in linear as well as curved arrangements and can also accommodate changes of direction.

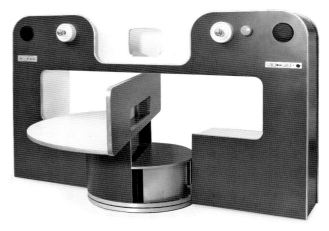

■ 1.2 Variable room elements

Rotoliving, Joe Colombo, 1969

The architectural space that surrounds us is formed by basic elements such as walls, ceilings, floors, columns and stairs. These elements generally delineate the boundaries of spaces within a building and separate them from one another. A combination of several rooms forms the next higher unit. Where the relationship between these architectural elements remains static, space is experienced as a succession of partial impressions. It forms the "sum of successively experienced relationships between places" (Jürgen Joedicke), the appearance of which is determined in practice by three key factors: the articulation of the space; the surface finishes of the space (building material, colour, structure); and natural and artificial illumination. Where rooms are variable, how they change over time becomes a further key factor that determines our relationship to space.

The ways in which a room can be used allow us to develop a functional relationship to it and this can be extended through the introduction of additional fixtures. Depending on needs and function, elements of differing degrees of flexibility can be used. These can be realised traditionally as static elements, fixed units around which we move, or as variable spatial elements which, through their flexibility or mobility, can liberate a space from fixed or constrained patterns of use.

Rather than providing a "frozen" setting for activities, new spatial concepts can be seen as adaptive organisms that make a multiplicity of different uses and atmospheres possible. This understanding of space as process – the design of which incorporates the actions of the user on the one hand and on the other is informed by economic and ecological criteria resulting from the increasing speed of changing needs – requires a set of instruments with which to realise the respective different spatial constellations. Well-conceived mobile room configurations can result in compact environments that take up less space than conventional approaches.

"Schwarzer Laubfrosch" residential conversion, Splitterwerk, Bad Waltersdorf, Austria, 2004

Total Furnishing Unit, Joe Colombo, 1971/72

Variable elements of rooms can be divided into three categories:

1. Space-containing walls
2. Moving platforms (floors, ceilings, stairs)
3. Mobile cells

Space in walls

In contrast to variable partitions that primarily serve to divide or join spaces using two-dimensional surfaces, variable walls also employ the third dimension. On the one hand the depth of such walls can be used to accommodate flexible elements within the wall. Fittings that serve particular pur-poses can be "parked" in the wall and taken out as needed. On the other hand, by making the entire "thick wall" mobile, one can shape various room se-quences. Büro Splitterwerk in Graz, Austria, claims that "just as every computer can run any program, so too must rooms be able to serve any purpose." In a conversion of a house in Bad Waltersdorf, Styria, Splitterwerk realised a new type of apartment that embodies the spirit of this claim. An elongated empty space serves as the living room. The bath-room, kitchen units, bed and table are concealed within the thickness of the walls on each side. The wall opens and the different elements are simply pulled out or put away as needed. There is no suc-cession of rooms, just a central space that can be a bedroom, a dining room, a bathroom or, if necessary, all at the same time.

One of the pioneers of variable living spaces was the designer Joe Colombo. In 1969, based on the as-sumption that living space would become increas-ingly restricted and that, accordingly, all living functions would need to be condensed, he devel-oped multifunctional objects such as Rotoliving or the Cabriolet Bed. Both of these wall-like items of furniture were designed as complementary day and night-time units: with a dining table, television, hi-fi and house bar, Rotoliving contained all the ele-ments of a traditional living room; the Cabriolet Bed

K-Space, 6a Architects, London, 2008

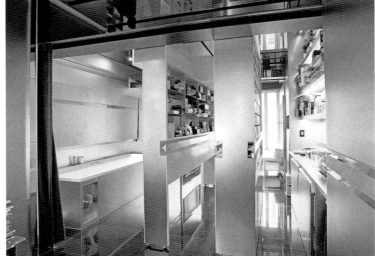

Multifunctional dwelling, Gary Chang, Hong Kong

with its convertible roof and a plethora of electronic aids took the place of the traditional bedroom. Both elements employ pivoting, folding and opening mechanisms to provide a multiplicity of functions. One of Colombo's final designs was for a Total Furnishing Unit, a multi-part compact block that can be placed freely within a room and contains individual wall elements and cells housing the kitchen, bunk and washroom. It forms a living unit containing the most essential functions and is connected to the utilities by pipes hanging from the ceiling.

In Hong Kong, the architect Gary Chang demonstrated how by using variable elements a miniature apartment totalling 32 m² can be converted into a complex residence with sauna, home cinema, office, music and film library, bar, extra-large bath and kitchen fit for a professional. According to the designer, the apartment can be transformed into 24 different spaces. These transformations are made possible by a system of rails on the ceiling to which cupboards, kitchen units and CD shelves are fixed and can be combined in different constellations. One pulls a handle and the entire wall shifts into the centre of the room. A worktop folds out to reveal a minibar. Many further layers of the "wall cube" can be moved to uncover ever more functions and uses. Depending on the owner's respective needs, the apartment can be a large open space or a sequence of different spaces, layers and walls.

Moving platforms

The second category of variable spatial elements concerns horizontal platforms as formed by ceilings and floors as well as inclined surfaces such as ramps and stairs. The ability to transform these elements changes the vertical configuration of a building: the traditional separation of a building into floors is broken down, room heights are not fixed and unusual ways of accessing rooms can result.

In a design for a house in Bordeaux, Rem Koolhaas implanted a hydraulically-operated platform in the

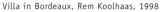
Villa in Bordeaux, Rem Koolhaas, 1998

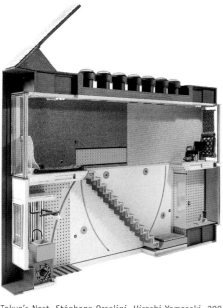

Tokyo's Nest, Stéphane Orsolini, Hiroshi Yamasaki, 2004

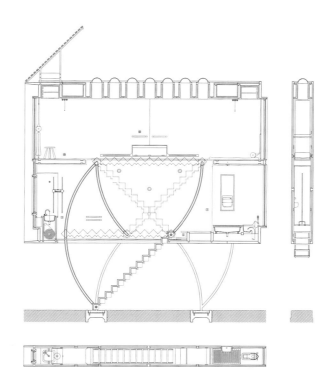

centre of the living area. The motivation for this decision was the disability of the owner: the moving floor provides a means of reaching the upper storey and replaces a lift. But it does much more than that: through its openly visible movement it completely transforms the way the space is experienced. One travels perceptibly through space, each ascent and descent a moment of theatre. Large enough to be furnished, the platform means that particular functions such as working no longer have to be allocated to a certain floor and can be transported to different levels.

An example from Tokyo by the architects Stéphane Orsolini and Hiroshi Yamasaki shows how extremely constrained conditions can be resolved using movable levels. Plots in Tokyo are rare and expensive and every last sliver of space is utilised. The apartment fits a complete functioning two-storey apartment into a 60 cm wide slot between two buildings. The solution lies in a movable staircase that serves both as a connecting and separating element. The folding and swivelling staircase makes it possible to reach the other rooms and connect activities while also separating the otherwise open space into four distinct zones.

The Suitcase House by the Hong Kong EDGE Design Institute, a group of young Asian architects, came about as part of the "Commune of the Great Wall" project near Beijing. In close proximity to the Great Wall of China, an agglomeration of luxury hotels and residences have been built, among them the Suitcase House, a container-like house with a single spacious interior. All the internal walls can be shifted and the room can be divided in a variety of ways. What makes this project different is that the functions of the spaces are contained beneath the floor. In effect they are like suitcases let into the floor: flaps open to reveal underfloor spaces – a kitchen, shower tray or a bed – into which one descends down a few steps.

Suitcase House, Gary Chang, EDGE Design Institute, Hong Kong, 2001

LaboShop, Mathieu Lehanneur, Paris, 2008

Mobile cells

The ability to move entire cells of space around would appear to offer the greatest potential for flexibility. However, on closer inspection the considerable constructional challenges this presents make such effortless transformations of space in practice less attractive.

Moving entire spaces around through three dimensions like containers in a high-rise warehouse – as demonstrated in the WABOT-HOUSE Laboratory research project undertaken at the Waseda University in Japan – has major implications for the geometry of the system of guide rails, the drive mechanism as

well as the rigidity of the cells themselves and the provision of technical services. Where cells are moved around within a contained space, solutions such as those used in warehouses can be employed for the guide-rail system. Energy chain systems such as those used in production facilities or robotics make it possible to provide a flexible electricity supply. Similarly, water supply and drainage can be realised using flexible supply lines, providing there is sufficient space for movement. The installations within the cells therefore represent a limiting factor for the radius of action of mobile cells. The movement of cells that require technical services over

larger distances can also be resolved using docking stations. Again, the flexibility of the system depends on the availability and distribution of docking stations.

A classic example of the use of mobile cells is the Naked House by Shigeru Ban Architects in Japan. Mobile boxes which serve as private spaces or retreats for the individual family members are placed within the open shell of a house. They can be moved around at will on rollers within the volume of the house and can even be rolled outside through a large portal. The spatial constellation created by the repositioned boxes changes constantly. These

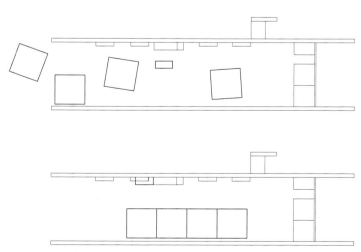

Naked House, Shigeru Ban Architects, Saitama, Japan, 2000

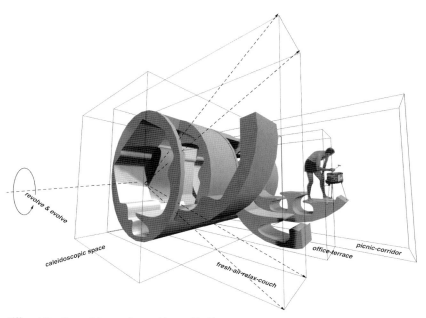

Different TurnOn modules can be used in combination

cells, however, do not contain any special installations such as a kitchen or bathroom, and are not connected to the electricity supply. The lack of a need for complex supply lines and the straightforward manual means of movement on rollers allows the cells to be moved around independently.

The Hanse-Rotorhaus, a multifunctional living concept for compact spaces with a rotating core designed by Luigi Colani, is an example of variable cells that feature technical installations. A circular rotor weighing 800 kg is used to turn a rotating core element with three modules for the kitchen, bedroom and bathroom respectively. These face onto the remaining fixed space. An electric motor gently sets the rotor in motion and brings it to rest in the respective position as needed.

There are numerous further solutions for transformable spaces: "If one wants to create a maximum number of different rooms within a small space, this space must focus on the respective activity" is the concept behind TurnOn, a rotating wheel by the architectural office AllesWirdGut. Every millimetre of the 0.9 m wide and 3.60 m high ring serves the purpose of living. There is no difference between floor, wall and ceiling. Like a hamster wheel, TurnOn rotates around its own axis. When it is time to sleep, the wheel is rotated until the bed is at floor level. The desk is then on the ceiling. Should the area of a single ring be too small, further rings can simply be added. A variety of rings are available: a relax ring, a fitness ring, a kitchen unit and so on. The "wet unit" ring contains a toilet, shower and bath. TurnOn can also travel from place to place on small wheels on land or with the help of inflatable cushions on water.

TurnOn, AllesWirdGut Architekten, 2000

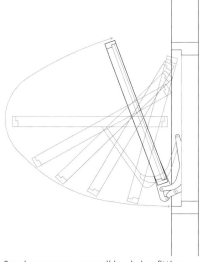

Opening sequence, reversible window fitting
(walchwindow)

■ 1.3 Opening the building envelope

Michael Lange

The expression "opening the building envelope" refers to (building) volumes whose external skin can be opened in one form or other, either in its entirety or partially. Typically the process of opening also conditions that of closing. It does not refer to wrapped enclosures in the sense of Christo and Jeanne-Claude's artistic projects that are opened to reveal what is within in the way a gift is unwrapped. Situations where the entire enclosure can open, such as the Push Button House in New York by the artist and architect Adam Kalkin, are the exception. In most cases larger or smaller sections of the external envelope of a building can be opened, usually part of the side of a building, sometimes the corner. Openable surfaces are not necessarily located solely on the vertical surfaces of a building but can also be found on inclined or horizontal surfaces, such as the roof.

Opening typologies

The first means of differentiating between types of opening methods is by size. The spectrum ranges from small, steel-framed glass-block cellar vents operated by a chain to vast aircraft hangar doors in which the entire frontage of the building opens. A systematic breakdown according to size is not possible, but the way in which surfaces are opened can be categorised. The process of opening and closing parts of buildings is familiar to us from manually opening and closing windows in the home, a comparatively basic mechanism. The first wooden windows were pivot-hung with two hinges on one side around which the window pivots and a handle on the other with the latch mechanism. Later developments added further options such as tilt and turn functionality which made it possible to also tilt the window. Ongoing developments have since resulted in a plethora of different methods of opening which are recorded visually as drawings in the German standards (DIN 18059).

Another means of differentiating between ways of opening is by the type of physical movement involved, i.e. translation and rotation with respect to the Cartesian coordinate system. Other kinds of physical movement such as acceleration, which cer-

"GuglHupf" multifunctional box, Hans Peter Wörndl, Mondsee, Austria, 1993

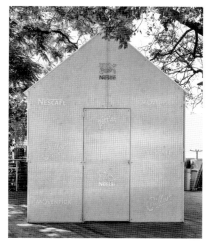

Bar Nestlé, 40th Montreux Jazz Festival, Montreux, Switzerland, 2006

tainly plays a role for electromechanically-operated windows or doors, are not relevant for a typology of opening methods as they primarily concern the drive mechanism. The direction of movement, however, is a further characteristic, and can be "parallel" to the building, whether vertical as is the case with the Nicolas G. Hayek Centre in Tokyo, horizontal as in the Paper Dome in Taiwan (both by Shigeru Ban Architects), or "radial" as exhibited by the Church of the Sacred Heart in Munich by Allmann Sattler Wappner Architekten.

Other possible ways of describing kinds of movement – although closely related to the direction of movement – include the following terms, which sometimes correspond to the name of the respective element: for example, the "sliding door". The simplest and probably also the oldest of these is the aforementioned "pivoting" movement of pivot-hung casement windows. "Flap" (awning) or "tilt" (hopper) constructions employ a similar hinging principle but with the hinges in different places. The location of the hinges is likewise the main difference between "swivel" or "turning" window constructions. Combinations of different types of movements also exist, such as top-hung projecting windows that simultaneously slide down and flap outwards. Parallel opening windows represent a more recent innovation in the field of window design technology and project outwards parallel to the facade. Other means, such as "folding", which

can be seen in the Shelter project in Arlsdorf, Austria, by BEHF Architekten, are rarely used for windows and more commonly found in door and gate installations.

Function and usage

The openable surfaces of a building envelope relate directly through their size, direction, location and manner of opening to the function and usage of the spaces within. The functional quality of the opening element has a direct effect on the quality and usability of the space within.

In particular the manner in which an element opens along with its size can extend or change the ways in which the interior space can be used. The choice

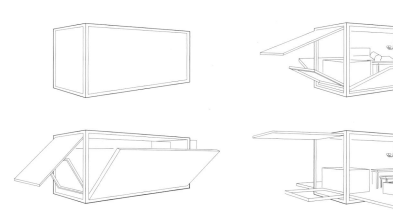

The Push Button House by the New York artist/architect Adam Kalkin, presented at the 2007 Venice Architecture Biennale, is a shipping container that on pushing a button unfolds like a flower, and transforms into a fully furnished apartment.

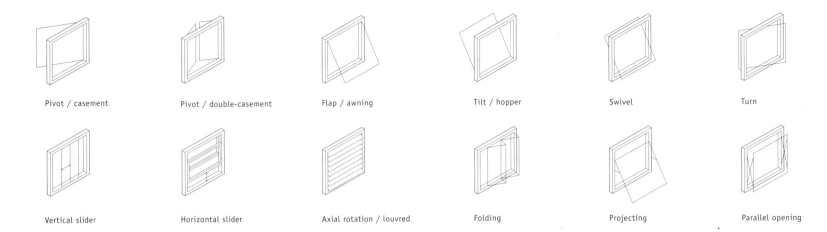

| Pivot / casement | Pivot / double-casement | Flap / awning | Tilt / hopper | Swivel | Turn |

| Vertical slider | Horizontal slider | Axial rotation / louvred | Folding | Projecting | Parallel opening |

Types of opening windows, after DIN 18059

of material and transparency of the openable surface is dictated in part by the indoor room climate and hygiene as well as an appraisal of the illumination, especially where internal or external anti-glare or privacy screens are used. Such elements may also have to fulfil a security function, either to prevent forced access or to protect the inhabitants (for example by being bulletproof). The most commonly used openable building element is most certainly the entrance. However, the quality of opening systems cannot be evaluated solely in terms of the indoor environment. In the case of large, motorised elements, such as those increasingly used to cover spectators in football stadia, the covering material

also plays a central role as it contributes considerably to the self-weight of the construction and in turn to the dimensions of the movable element.
Finally, for residential and office buildings the position of the openable element with respect to the building envelope – whether it lies inside or outside the building or is part of the skin – is important from an energy point of view.

Requirements and solutions

In Central European countries and regions with a similarly temperate climate, an openable element serves as a temporary barrier between different climates inside and outside and must fulfil a series of

requirements such as protection against wind and rain, insulation against noise and heat loss, and safety and security, protecting inhabitants and property.
The technical realisation of openable elements must furthermore take into account the aesthetic impact of construction components such as profiles, channels and guide rails that may be necessary for sizeable movable elements. Thresholds need to be assessed with regard to the degree of seal required and may benefit from additional optical measures such as a channel in the floor. The point at which elements and loadbearing guide rails meet can be simplified by switching to a top-hung arrangement.

Gamma Issa House, Marcio Kogan, São Paulo, 2002

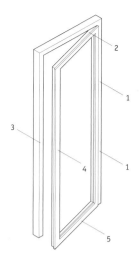

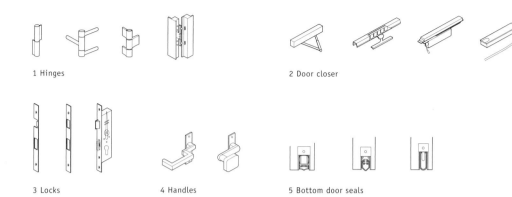

1 Hinges

2 Door closer

3 Locks

4 Handles

5 Bottom door seals

Movable components of a door

Height differences that may result in these critical areas of construction are governed by a variety of technical guidelines and are elaborated in the respective standards (e.g. DIN 18024 "barrier-free design"). Similarly the resting or parking position of facade elements has both a structural as well as a visual dimension.

A good example of an openable building envelope that succeeds in concealing the opening mechanism to create an optically aesthetic result is the Casa Ponte on the Côte d'Azur in France, designed by Marc Barani. The glass frontage can be completely hidden in the floor through a counter-pull device.

The available construction systems can be divided primarily into top-hung or standing systems. Simple examples are the tilt or the flap window: in the first case, the load of the window is transferred through the hinges into the bottom of the frame; in the latter case, the window hangs from the upper part of the frame which impacts structurally on the frame and its anchorage (irrespective of whether the window opens inwards or outwards). In the case of sliding mechanisms, with "standing systems" the weight of the element is borne by rollers or runners that transfer the load to the floor, while "hanging systems", where the rollers and track are located at the top of the element, require a secondary con-

struction to distribute the load. The decision as to which system to use is typically a factor of the architectural appropriateness, the structural requirements and the resulting costs. For example, large sliding door systems, such as those commonly used for industrial works, employ floor-mounted standing systems so that the heavy load of the doors can be distributed directly into the foundation, which is simple to construct. If a hanging construction was used, the entire vertical load above the sliding doors would have to be distributed through the roof and lintel construction to an additional supporting construction that transfers the load to the foundations. Depending on the width and weight of the

The design of the facade of the Glass Shutter House by Shigeru Ban Architects in Tokyo allows the entire frontage to be opened. Like a garage door, the glass elements travel vertically upwards and are parked in the roof space of the house. Full-height curtains then filter the relationship between indoors and outdoors.

Olympic Tennis Centre, Dominique Perrault, Madrid, 2009

Opposite: Cargo Lifter Building, SIAT Architektur + Technik, Brand, Germany, 2000

opening elements, this would necessitate a larger and more solidly dimensioned construction above the opening which, together with the stronger supporting construction to bear the extra load, would be more expensive. Such sliding door arrangements, which can, of course, consist of multiple elements, should be arranged on the internal surface of the building envelope for better protection against the weather.

The aforementioned considerations apply likewise for folding systems. Here too it is possible in principle to distribute the load through the upper or lower edge of the sliding element with the same advantages and disadvantages.

From a cleaning and maintenance point of view, hanging systems can have certain advantages as the lower guide channel is not as large as loadbearing running rails and is less susceptible to dirt accumulation. Floor-mounted rails have to be made of appropriate materials as more moisture is to be expected at floor level: their functionality will depend on their lasting resistance to corrosion. The cost of investment must be weighed up with respect to the expected cleaning and maintenance costs. Stainless steel running rails may appear advantageous in terms of corrosion-resistance but will impact considerably on the initial building costs.

A further key aspect with respect to the reliability of such systems is the drive mechanism. Electric, mechanical, hydraulic or pneumatic drive mechanisms require a control system, particularly with regard to safety aspects as well as the components necessary to trigger or release the safety mechanism.

An essential criterion when choosing a system is the frequency with which the element will be opened or used as this determines the necessary durability of the element and all associated components such as the hinges and drive mechanism, and as a logical consequence also the operating costs for cleaning and maintenance.

Component technology using the example of windows and doors

To fulfil the function and the requirements of the openable element, components must be selected to ensure their long-term functionality.

Here we will consider the generic term "fitting", specifically the hinged side fitting of a window. Fittings and hinges are components whose means of connection and mechanical coupling make it possible to realise the desired function. The relevance and purpose of their individual parts is comprehensible for the layman, for example, a door has several pivoting hinges mounted on one side. One can clearly see that a fitting attached to the door leaf features a sleeve that is slotted onto a second fitting with a pin which is in turn attached to the door frame and forms a swivelling bearing for the hinge. A brass washer between the two minimises the degree of metallic rubbing. By contrast, a tilt and turn window fitting looks more complicated. Depending on the size of the window, window fittings can also include complex latch mechanisms to ensure a reliable seal around the window.

In addition, through the use of different kinds of fittings, a simple window can be made to open in a

variety of different ways. The decision as to which fitting to use depends on whether the hinges should be visible or concealed, whether they are acceptable from a design point of view and on the preferred kind of opening method and/or fitting.

Trends

Window and opening typologies are unlikely to change considerably in the future, however the means of operating them and the materials employed will. With the exception of improved safety and insulation technology, major developments in the housing sector are not to be expected. The need to improve the energy efficiency of buildings and their skin has, however, led to the increasing deployment of electrically-operated openable elements which allow one to control ventilation and air change rates more precisely. In office buildings too, manually-operated openings are becoming less common, again in order to better control the energy balance of the building and ultimately the objective and subjective quality of the office environment. The use of control technology and accompanying mechatronics and actuator and sensor technology is becoming increasingly relevant. In commercial and industrial buildings, where opening elements are usually large and accordingly difficult to operate manually, hand-operated openings will likewise be restricted to smaller elements such as smaller entrance doorways within larger sliding elements.

B

1

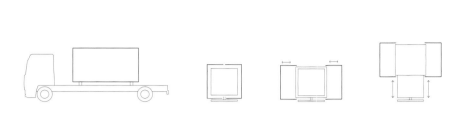

Cocobello, mobile studio, Peter Haimerl,
Vienna, Munich, Rotterdam, 2003

■ 1.4 Mobile and movable building envelopes

Michael Lange

"Mobile and movable building envelopes" takes the concept of "opening the building envelope" a stage further. The Push Button House in New York mentioned previously opens out on all four sides with only the roof remaining in place. Together with the four columns at the corners of the container, the roof plane forms the main stabilising element of the structure. A key criterion is, therefore, the overall stability of the enclosure.

In the same way that the process of opening an element also conditions its subsequent closure, the "movement" of a movable element refers not to a once-only change but to a temporary change of volume that is reversible. More so than with individual movable elements, mobile spatial elements present a greater opportunity to express movement as part of the architectural design.

Different movement typologies

There are no predefined typological norms for the way in which movable or mobile envelopes open or change volume, nor are there other definitions for "movable building envelopes". An examination of the adjective "movable" and the noun "building envelope" does, however, offer a means of typological differentiation.

In the context discussed here, "movement" refers primarily to a change in volume. This change results when the bounding surfaces of a room are shifted from their original position to a new position – which can lie outside the room's own coordinate system – to form a new self-contained space through the new constellation of surfaces to one another.

The term "movement" can also refer to the mobility of an existing space or room whose size, weight and enclosure is designed in such a way that it can be transported easily from one place to the next, allowing it to move largely unhindered as a mobile unit. The means of transport can be manual or aided by machinery.

A further interpretation derived from the term "flexibility" lies in the possibility to change the surfaces

"Fahrt ins Grüne", mobile extension of a timber-frame house typical of the Bergisches Land region, Kalhöfer-Korschildgen, Remscheid, Germany, 2007

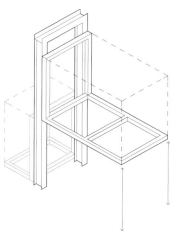

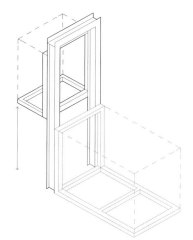

Green Flea pavilion, Büro 213, Potsdamer Platz, Berlin, 1999

and their appearance in response to a change in the room's usage or of its volume.

Finally, one can also differentiate between different ways in which a space changes size: for example a space may spread out, fold open, be held apart, inflate, unscrew, slide open, or add or subtract to name just a few possible alternatives.

Function and usage

A crucial aspect of the design of movable spaces is its structural functionality. The space and its enclosure must be structurally stable in both its "closed" and "open" states to allow it to be used in either case. As a consequence, flexible spatial enclosures are usually small and used only for limited periods of time. Depending on the materials employed, a long-term use can follow, such as is the case with "container villages" which are erected as a temporary measure but serve a long-term use.

The functional flexibility can be expressed through the form of the individual elements as well as the overall system. The construction technology used can be employed in such a way that certain elements in particular areas underline the movement of the building envelope or possibly even elevate it to a central theme of the design.

A "movable envelope" may serve a specific function, for example to improve energy efficiency. Where individual parts of flexible enclosures are equipped with photovoltaic elements that track and follow the position of the sun, they serve additionally as an energy producer. A positive aspect of the construction of such movable envelopes is the ability

to rapidly adapt to the respective environmental conditions, the respective location as well as the opening element itself.

Requirements and solutions

Movable enclosures contain space which we associate with particular qualities. The attainable qualities must make allowances for the factors of transportability and mobility. One of the most important criteria for movable building envelopes is to ensure the lasting functionality of the mobility of the envelope – at least in its closed position. The degree of transportability, which represents a particular kind of flexibility, is highly dependent on the materials used which in turn dictate the weight and size of the individual components.

The durability of such mobile envelopes is dependent primarily on the weather-resistance of the individual components and connection technology. To be able to use the space within, the construction needs to be absolutely rain- and windproof. Further requirements such as soundproofing and thermal insulation will ultimately require additional measures that apply to both the individual moving components as well as how they join together. Typically, such constructions can only be adequately controlled and safely operated using mechanical means. In most cases manual operation is not possible for safety reasons due to the size and mass of the individual elements, as well as possible wind loads that may arise during opening or closing.

Pneumatic or electric systems are ideally suited for machine-operated structures, although both neces-

sitate the provision of an independent energy source within, or at least near to, the movable enclosure. To ensure the lasting reliability of such systems, particularly where machine-driven technology is used, regular maintenance is a factor that must be planned for and implemented. Special requirements such as different classes of protection against forced entry can be integrated but lead to bulkier, heavy-duty connections.

A good example of a mobile and moving enclosure is the Cocobello Container Module by architect Peter Haimerl. Cocobello is a mobile studio for a wide range of different purposes that consists of several collapsible sections that slide apart horizontally and vertically to form a two-storey atelier unit. Once open, the upper floor contains a large atelier, the ground floor the functional areas such as a bathroom, kitchenette and storage. In the closed position the mobile atelier measures just 2.50 x 6.50 x 2.80 m, small enough to be transported without the need for a special transporter. Likewise the 13.5 t weight of the flexible envelope is not a problem to transport. Once connected to a 380 V/16 A three-phase power source, the unit can be extended to its open state – 2.50 x 5.50 x 5.60 x 5.20 m – ready for use.

A further example is the Green Flea pavilion on the Potsdamer Platz in Berlin by the Berlin architectural office Büro 213 – Ute Ziegler, Markus Schell. The pavilion serves as an information point and consists of a flexible three-piece construction whose constellation can be changed to fulfil different requirements. The position of the two volumes can be

The Kitchen Monument, Raumlabor Berlin, Duisburg, 2006

offset against each other using chain hoists mounted on the steel supporting framework between them. Solar cells provide sufficient electricity to cover the energy requirements so that the pavilion is as autonomous as possible.

An example for a membrane construction is the GLOW Lounge by Raumlabor and Plastique Fantastique erected in the Design House Eindhoven for the festival "Forum of Light in Art and Architecture", a temporary structure that served both as a forum and as a light installation. The building is a pneumatically stabilised membrane.

Component technology

Lightweight materials such as aluminium are predestined for use as metallic envelopes, particularly for panel constructions with core insulation for better thermal insulation and noise reduction properties. Steel is likewise particularly invaluable for structural and loadbearing elements, as well as stainless steel where weather-resistance is important. Textile membranes can also provide a structural function when stretched over a framework. Membranes with different degrees of transparency – whether in the form of textiles or single-skin foils – can likewise be used to strengthen framework constructions. Twin-skin or triple-skin foil systems, when inflated in individual sections, can be combined to produce a self-supporting structure. Transparent surfaces can be glazed conventionally or made of more durable, high-grade plastics. To seal the external skin, conventional materials such as EPDM gaskets may be used, typically in several cascading layers that overlap one another, or tubular weatherstrip systems that inflate to create a seal.

Trends

Projects such as those shown here require a certain amount of open space around them – on the one hand to make space for the change in volume, on the other so that they are more easily noticed. In all cases they are of an experimental nature and are very often specifically planned.

Further research into mobile enclosures will without doubt be conducted as they represent a viable alternative to permanent structures, particularly when available in suitable combinations of materials and

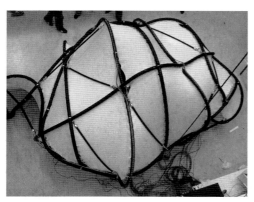

The Muscle Body project interacts with its users who, through their movements in the interior, cause the Muscle Body to continually change shape.

Student project at Delft Technical University, Prof. Kas Oosterhuis, 2005

London Eye, marks barfield architects, 2000

functionally-relevant sizes. In disaster areas too, lightweight, compact and easy-to-transport units will be needed, possibly with self-inflating or self-erecting mechanisms similar to those used for ships' lifeboats. Such units will need to be self-sufficient, not only with respect to the opening mechanism but also the technical facilities for their use. Depending on the requirements in different climatic regions, they may need to be equipped with additional energy-generating or safety-relevant functions. There is certainly sufficient worldwide demand for such small-scale, self-sufficient units, and projects of this kind also have commercial potential. As such, research activities aimed at developing a wide range of cost-effective solutions that are flexible enough to fulfil more general requirements are worthwhile.

Individually-designed mobile enclosures will, according to current estimations, be built only occasionally to fulfil project-specific requirements. As unique constructions they are not made for serial production and therefore not relevant for research platforms. David Fischer's visions for a rotating skyscraper are an example of such a specific solution in which each floor is able to revolve individually about its centre, changing its orientation although not its function.

Rotating Tower, design for a skyscraper with movable floor levels, David Fischer, Dynamic Architecture, Dubai, 2007

B

Applications and functions

2

Conserving
and generating
energy

Moving air, wind turbine, quietrevolution

■ 2.1 Architecture, movement and energy

Brian Cody

Movement is the natural condition of all things. The world consists of atoms that move and collide with one another. If an object in motion is not subject to any external forces, it will continue to move forwards. Photons moving at light speed provide the light needed to read this book, and the reader is surrounded by a fluid whose particles are constantly moving. At a molecular level too, the entire contents of the room are in motion. The higher the temperature of the respective object, the faster the movement of its atoms and the greater their energy content. The field of thermodynamics is concerned primarily with the transmission of thermal energy, but in effect it can be seen as no less than the science of change. According to the second law of thermodynamics every change in our universe leads to an increase in entropy and this in turn is the only constant in the natural sciences that not only takes into account time but also the direction of time. Without movement, however, there is no change. Change is, therefore, necessary and implies movement and as a result also energy.

The relationship between the use of a process and the quantity (and quality) of the energy flow it induces is defined as energy efficiency. There are at least four reasons why we urgently need to vastly improve energy efficiency in society: the foreseeable exhaustion of fossil fuels, the need to drastically reduce the ecological problems resulting from the combustion of fossil fuels, the need to massively counteract climate change and to defuse the ever more apparent geopolitical problems resulting from uncertain energy availability in the future. Global

energy demand can be attributed to three main areas: buildings, transport and industry. The first two categories are responsible for an estimated 75% of the worldwide energy demand and can be directly influenced through architecture and urban design. Alongside making increased use of renewable energy sources, the single greatest means of resolving the aforementioned problems is to maximise energy efficiency. But what does energy efficiency mean in the context of buildings? Although energy efficiency is all the rage, it is also too often fundamentally misunderstood, misused and confused with terms such as "energy demand" and "energy consumption". Maximising energy efficiency is more than minimising energy consumption. Energy efficiency implies performance and is expressed as the relationship between output (use) and input (resources). Current instruments for regulating the energy efficiency of buildings only deal with energy demand and not the actual energy efficiency. At the Institute for Buildings and Energy at Graz University of Technology we have developed the BEEP method with which the actual energy efficiency of a building can be determined so that different design alternatives can be properly compared with one another. The calculated BEEP value is an indicator for the overall *Building Energy and Environmental Performance* (the BEEP) of a building and takes into account the reciprocal relationship between energy demand and room climate. The results from case studies examined using this method show clearly that low energy consumption does not necessarily equate to high energy efficiency.

Irrespective of this fundamental misunderstanding, the issue of energy efficiency in the building sector is generally considered from a very narrow perspective. It is important to realise that considering the energy efficiency of a building involves more than just reducing the heat energy consumption! It concerns the building's overall performance including cooling, lighting and ventilation, and extends beyond the use phase of a building to encompass the energy required to construct as well as to dispose of the building. Similarly, it should also extend beyond the boundaries of the building itself and take into account urban and regional planning. "Whole Systems Thinking" is what is needed if we are to avoid further undesirable and damaging developments.

When one walks around a city such as Hong Kong with open eyes, it is much easier to visualise the flow of energy in the building and transport sectors. While in Europe technical installations are usually concealed behind suspended ceilings or in raised floors, in Hong Kong they are instead plainly visible on the outside of facades and hanging beneath ceilings so that it is easy to imagine the movement of fluids in the pipework that supplies fresh water, removes waste water or keeps the buildings cool. At street level, transformer substations stand next to the pavement converting medium voltage to low voltage, while a level higher ventilation plants buzz behind outside air inlets. On the roofs, technical plants for cooling and ventilating are arranged one behind the other. Similarly, traffic flows on multiple levels simultaneously – cars, trams, underground,

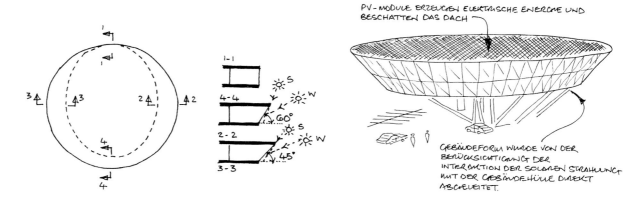

PV-MODULE ERZEUGEN ELEKTRISCHE ENERGIE UND BESCHATTEN DAS DACH

GEBÄUDEFORM WURDE VON DER BERÜCKSICHTIGUNG DER INTERAKTION DER SOLAREN STRAHLUNG MIT DER GEBÄUDEHÜLLE DIREKT ABGELEITET.

Form derived from the sun moving, Sunbelt Management Office Building, Brian Cody with schneider+schumacher architekten, San Diego, California, 2001–2002

buses and people are visible everywhere. So what are the relationships between architecture, movement and energy? Movement has to do with time and in a physical sense describes one's change of position over time.

An awareness of the factor of "time" is also extremely important when planning a building. When one plans a building in a particular place, one also plans, consciously or unconsciously, the not inconsiderable flow of material and energy inputs and outputs that relate to the building over its entire lifetime. As such, time can be seen as the fourth dimension of a building. The relationship between architecture, movement and energy can be examined at four different levels:

On the first level, buildings contain integrated energy supply systems that all have something to do with movement. Probably the most obvious example of these are integral wind turbines. Paradoxically, movement and the accompanying noise emissions and vibrations are probably one of the main reasons why the integration of wind turbine plants in buildings has only rarely been successful.

On the second level are the technical installations that are ultimately responsible for energy consumption in buildings: heating, cooling, ventilation and lighting systems for example. For some of these, movement is more evident than others, and may manifest itself as an unpleasant sensation such as rushing air produced by a ventilation system.

Movements that improve the energy efficiency of a building represent the third level and offer a number of interesting architectural possibilities. One can exploit the movement of the earth around the sun to maximise the energy efficiency of a building. For the design of a low-energy residential building in Berlin-Marzahn, we first undertook a study of the optimal form of the building from the perspective of energy, which in turn influenced the form generated for the building. In a subsequent design for the Sunbelt Management Offices in San Diego, California, the form of the building was derived directly from the interaction of solar radiation with the building envelope. A similar approach was used for the atrium roof of the Infineon Asia Pacific Headquarters in Singapore. If the surface of a building is to be used for energy production, this aspect can also become a part of its overall architectural expression. In a design for the new Opera House in Guangzhou, the interaction of the incident sunlight with the skin of the building was analysed with a view to optimising the transparency of the skin, depending on direction and angle of incidence. The skin consists of photovoltaic modules that are more or less transparent. Depending on the intensity of the annual solar radiation, the density of the photovoltaic cells was optimised so that the transparency of the individual modules appears to differ. As a result, the skin of the building acquires a kind of texture.

Finally, movable parts of a building can also increase its energy efficiency. The climatic concept for the DSD Cyclebowl at the Expo 2000 in Hanover employed easily transportable thermal accumulators in the form of water tanks which were integrated into the ramp of the exhibition. The regen-

eration of their storage capacity by an integral evaporative cooling system not only served as a motor for the design process but also became a central part of the exhibition concept, demonstrating first-hand the company's philosophy and commitment to closed ecological cycles.

A building, and the building envelope in particular, functions as a filter between indoors and outdoors. This can be conceived as a static (non-moving) or dynamic (moving) filter system, the latter offering more potential for energy optimisation. The BRAUN Headquarters in Kronberg, Germany, was the first office building to be conceived with a performance-optimised twin-skin facade so effective that it was possible to do without mechanical services. As such it is one of the few twin-skin buildings that has paid for itself in both economic as well as ecological terms within an acceptably short time span. The automatic opening of the external facade in certain outdoor air conditions transforms the external appearance of the building from a closed, smooth glazed surface to a much more expressive architectural language. Almost ten years later we worked together with the same architects to develop this concept further for the design of a new office and laboratory building in Wels, Austria, which at the time of publishing was under construction. This is made possible by a simple drum element within the facade which can be rotated to effect different ventilation scenarios: for example in winter the external air is pre-warmed in the cavity in the facade while in summer air is allowed to flow directly into the offices without interim pre-heating.

BRAUN Headquarters, schneider+schumacher architekten, Kronberg im Taunus, Germany, 2000

BRAUN Headquarters, movable atrium skylights

The greatest potential for increasing energy efficiency for many building types lies in the areas of mechanical ventilation and lighting, not least because these consume high-grade energy in the form of electricity. Ventilation is also the area with the greatest potential for saving production energy. In the design for the new headquarters of the European Central Bank in Frankfurt am Main, the form of the building is heavily influenced by considerations aimed at maximising energy performance and an optimal natural ventilation of the building. Two optimally oriented towers were placed on the site so that the first tower shades the south facade of the second tower from the sun. A second skin was then wrapped around the two towers forming a central atrium between the two and creating a twin-skin facade around the external faces of the towers. The form and construction of the buildings were then optimised in such a way that both wind as well as solar energy can be employed as direct driving forces for a controlled and effective natural ventilation of the offices. The facades of the atrium are constructed so that they act as "wind catchers" directing the wind into the atrium. The form of the so-called "suction gaps" in the twin-skin external facade of the office towers is conceived so that the gaps suck exhaust air – irrespective of wind direction – out of the offices. Selected functions such as bridges and elevators as well as meeting rooms and rest areas have been relocated from the office floors to the atrium to improve the ratio of gross to net floor areas in the office floors.

In a more recent research project, we have explored this idea further with a view to establishing the technical feasibility of such concepts for tall buildings. There are a number of potential advantages: better operational energy efficiency, a reduction in the consumption of grey energy (ventilation systems, technical plant rooms, ducts), a lower risk of

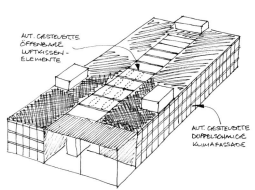

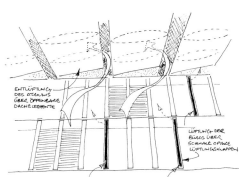

BRAUN Headquarters, conceptual sketches

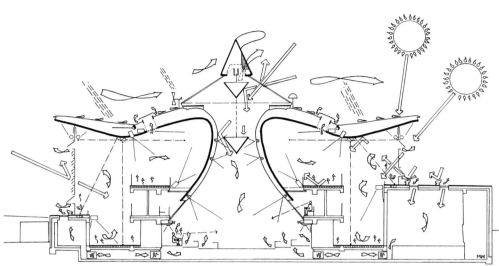

National Assembly for Wales, Rogers Stirk Harbour + Partner with BDSP, Cardiff, 2005

sick building syndrome and cost savings for the operation of a building (energy, maintenance and running costs) as well as for capital investment (systems, technical plant rooms, ducts). These concepts require, as the sketches show, new floor plan configurations and sections.

For a museum project on the island of La Réunion we developed a form based on the traditional courtyard structure but covered with a "big roof" construction. This provides shade for the pavilions beneath and also employs integrated warm water collectors to provide warm water for use with an absorption chiller. The geometry of the construction allows diffuse daylight to penetrate the roof while shielding against direct sunlight. Cooling elements in the roof of the pavilions cool the air which then sinks due to gravity in tubes hung vertically at regular intervals in the exhibition pavilions, flowing into the rooms just above floor level. The warm aim that collects in the upper region of the room is displaced by the cool air flowing into the space from below, setting in motion a process of natural circulation without the need for ventilators.

As part of a research project entitled "Sports Building of the Future" we undertook a study for a three-court sports hall in Puconci, Slovenia, for a subsequent architectural competition. The research project examined the energy concept for a pilot project which through its use of pioneering ideas

was to showcase new possibilities for designing energy-efficient sports buildings. The development employed an analytical process of optimisation conducted using a virtual model. Dynamic thermal simulations, daylight simulations and computational fluid dynamics (CFD) simulations undertaken using the model were used to develop new systems for natural ventilation and lighting that not only improved the energy performance of the building but also highlighted a number of novel design options. Buildings also cause another kind of movement: traffic flows between them. On this meta level more subtle relationships take place between movement and energy on the one hand and architecture and urban design on the other. The configuration and design of urban agglomerations has a considerable effect on the kind and volume of these flows. In ongoing research we are exploring spatial and three-dimensional urban design concepts that employ increased urban density and a mix of functions to reduce or avoid traffic as one of a number of aims. This is not restricted to circulation and movement areas on the ground level only, and public spaces and gardens at different levels contribute to entirely new urban and recreational qualities.

A primary task of future urban design developments is to discover and exploit the possible synergies that result from networking building and traffic systems. In a project on the Adriatic coast we have

developed a comprehensive energy masterplan for a carbon-neutral development on a peninsula with an area of around 100 ha. We propose an integrated network, an energy grid, of buildings and vehicles. The transport system consists of electrically-powered cars running with batteries charged using renewable energy. A combination of central facilities and decentralised systems integrated into the buildings supply the grid with renewable energy. Both the buildings as well as the vehicles can draw or supply energy from or to the grid.

There is vast potential for increasing energy efficiency using concepts for functionally neutral spatial structures which can be adapted to different uses over the lifetime of a building. The development of functionally open architectural concepts and adaptable building concepts will be an important task for the future.

These considerations can be continued beyond the realm of architecture and urban design. In a research project on the relationship between different forms of teleworking and the overall energy efficiency of society, we are examining ways of restructuring the physical and virtual infrastructure of society (buildings, transport and IT systems) with a view to discovering what potential there is to improve the total energy efficiency of society. Instead of modelling the energy structures of buildings or cities, we model those of typical service companies,

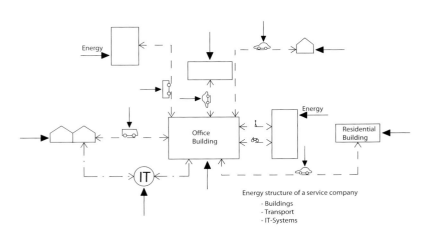

Energy structure of a service company

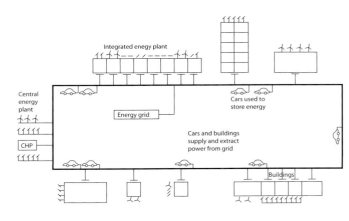

Energy network with buildings and cars

whose infrastructure likewise consists of buildings, transport routes and IT networks. An analysis of the energy structures in our society shows that although architecture and urban design do play a dominant role and therefore offer enormous potential for change, everything that is currently being conceived and realised is not able to make a really meaningful contribution to finding an overall solution to the problems we face. We need to take a completely different approach, to implement fundamental structural changes and rethink and reorganize the physical and virtual structures of society. The energy potential made possible by new means of communication and working must be properly reflected in the physical infrastructure of our society. Structures that appear utopian are conceivable: a city as a three-dimensional grid structure with spaces that one can rent and use on a short-term basis. Meetings and associated transport routes that are coordinated using GPS-like systems. A co-ordination system using digital control technology makes it possible to ensure that all buildings are exploited to their full potential. Buildings then become highly adaptive structures that are able to adjust to changing requirements in real time. One lives for a particular period of time at a particular location before moving on to the next. One owns the minimum necessary but can also use as much as one wants. The days of mankind as a gatherer

(though not as a hunter) have finally come to an end. Here too, such deliberations are the result of the interrelationships between architecture, movement and energy.

All research projects mentioned in the text have been undertaken by the author and his team at the Institute for Buildings and Energy at Graz University of Technology in Austria. The energy concepts for the projects described in the text were developed by the author and his team at Arup in association with the following architects: Coop Himmelblau (Guangzhou, La Réunion, Giza, Frankfurt am Main, Shenzen), schneider+schumacher architekten (Kronberg, San Diego, Wels), Ortner & Ortner (Duisburg, Montenegro), Carsten Roth (Vienna), Assmann Salomon und Scheidt (Berlin), Atelier Brückner (Hanover), TEC PMC (Singapore).

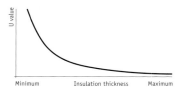

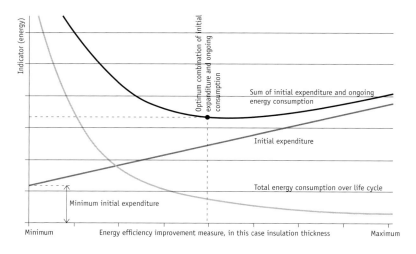

■ 2.2 The principle of efficiency

York Ostermeyer

To be able to make a reliable assessment of any system, the choice of a suitable frame of reference and system boundaries is a decisive factor. All findings regarding a measure to be undertaken within the system should always be seen against the background of the defined system boundaries, outside of which they have limited or no validity. Energy efficiency is a good example of this problem that is of practical relevance for architects. The values currently calculated using established models for assessing the energy efficiency of a building examine in essence the operational consumption. For the example of an opaque wall, efforts are concentrated on achieving a certain U-value which can be influenced by the thickness of the insulation material (see diagram above left).

If one were instead to consider the efficiency of an opaque wall in terms of the ongoing losses resulting from heat loss, the optimal situation would be represented by an infinitely thick wall. However, such a construction is not energy-efficient as efficiency expresses the relationship between the effort expended and the resulting effect. A heavily-insulated opaque wall may be very effective in minimising heat loss, but it is not efficient in this respect. It is obvious that such considerations can only tell us so much about the overall system of a building or even about the system of a wall. A central aspect of the development of the Energy Savings Act (EnEV) in Germany was, therefore, to expand the frame of reference. Correspondingly, the system boundaries were extended to include the introduction of a heating energy performance coefficient and primary energy factors that go as far as taking into account the extraction cost of the energy carrier.

One would be forgiven for expecting that this more holistic view would now result in environmentally-friendly and energy-efficient building constructions. However, despite the greater importance now accorded to domestic heating systems and the energy carrier, in the case of the aforementioned opaque wall, the variant with infinitely thick insulation would still be the optimal solution. The reason why opaque walls are realised with only a limited thickness of insulation is simple: very thick layers of insulation are expensive. This initial expenditure for the construction is lacking from our consideration. So, here too the revised system boundaries are unsuitable and do not produce meaningful results. Only the inclusion of factors such as necessary economic expenditure, space limitations and structural reasons can exclude such extreme results. However, only by including the effort necessary to create the opaque wall and the resulting insulation thickness/effect can we derive a calculated optimum value.

In real constructions this interplay between effort and effect is evaluated almost exclusively in economic terms. But an optimal wall construction in monetary terms is not necessarily an energy-efficient wall. To be precise, it is a cost-optimised wall for a chosen period of time (which usually corresponds to the credit or amortisation period) whose parameters may be modified depending on economic boundary conditions such as subsidies, price changes and credit terms. At best, the energy balance/ecological balance may be approximated by the economic balance. That is, however, only rarely the case. Nevertheless, the ecological aspect is often emphasised – although possibly valid with re-

spect to conventional existing buildings – even when it was not central to the decision-making process.

Alongside the choice of an appropriate frame of reference, the second key parameter is therefore the choice of an appropriate balancing or evaluation criterion. Current debate highlights a number of problems in this respect: much is made of saving energy when what is meant is reducing emissions; similarly, a client asks the architect to design an energy-saving house, but in actual fact he is worried about rising energy costs and wants a cost-saving house.

The consequence of this problem becomes clear when one considers that energy costs are set to rise in future while at the same time energy production will be more environmentally friendly. If we incorporate these relationships in our deliberations, the operational costs need to be weighted with respect to the initial cost. A cost-oriented balance will then tend towards more initial cost while an energy-based balance will tend towards more operational costs. The precise description of the balancing criteria is therefore of key importance for the correct result.

In the context of the current climate debate, greater efficiency has been accorded more importance in all areas. In many cases, ways are being sought to maintain current standards as efficiently as possible. Here it is necessary to find an appropriate balancing criteria. This represents a chance for adaptable and mobile architectural elements that are able to achieve more with less expenditure of resources.

This demand is not new and was discussed in the 1980s in conjunction with the assessment of per-

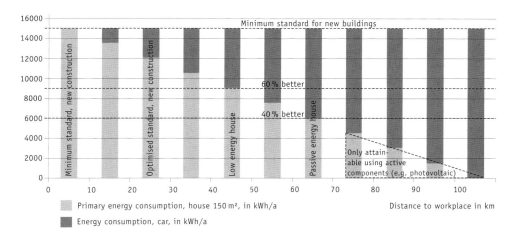

A maximum emissions balance considers not only the energy efficiency of a house but also its location (which may be outside the city) by factoring in emissions caused by commuting. Houses located further away need to exhibit exceptionally high energy efficiency standards to be able to compete with a house in the city.

Relation of distance to workplace to housing standard

Conserving and generating energy

sonal emissions. At the time, however, insufficient reliable data was available concerning the energy required and ecological impact of the production of many products. In recent years the situation has improved considerably with the help of computer-aided modelling. Today, the relationship between effort and effect – the efficiency – can be determined according to criteria that have a much more meaningful relation to environmental impact than money. These include, for example, the cumulative energy demand (grey energy) that supplements operating consumption or the environmental impact points (UBP) model. These can serve as a basis for adjusting subsidies so that an economic assessment more closely resembles the desirable ecological assessment.

An extended frame of reference of this kind could help clarify the flawed basis for a number of current but problematic approaches.

Passive energy houses (with around 50 kWh/m²a less primary energy consumption than the EnEV minimum standard) are being subsidised on the periphery of cities despite the fact that relocating to the outskirts may make it necessary to purchase a second family car, raising the petrol consumption by around 500 litres (some 5000 kWh) per year. The diagram above shows the consumption of different building standards in relation to their distance from the workplace, assuming that the resulting journey is undertaken 300 times per year with a small private car (5 litres per 100 km). For the chart, a 150 m² apartment fulfilling the EnEV minimum standard has been taken as the minimum criterion. Here the home is located directly adjacent to the workplace so that no car is required. Where the distance from the

workplace results in a total journey distance of 18,000 km per year with the low-consumption car, the building will need to fulfil passive house standards to compete favourably in terms of energy consumption with the first house adjacent to the workplace. After one adds to this the additional cost of achieving the passive energy house standard (approx. 10,000 kWh) and the cost of manufacturing the second car (approx. 50,000 kWh every 5 to 10 years for a VW Golf), relocating to the outskirts can no longer be justified in terms of energy balance.

The insulation of buildings is often undertaken using rigid foamed polystyrene panels although the building in question may already have a low energy demand. Such foams are much cheaper than sustainably won insulation materials, although the latter have a much better eco-balance. Nevertheless, the end result is presented as an environmentally-friendly building due to its low energy consumption.

Because ecological products typically represent only a small market segment, they are often more expensive than established products although the necessary cost of their manufacture is comparable. By assessing the respective product performance over a wider frame of reference, it would be possible to clarify differences in performance over the lifetime of a product in order to improve their competitiveness with the help of state subsidies.

In addition to these controversial cases, there are other concepts which are generally held to be worthwhile but fail on more detailed examination. The eco-balance of many decentralised rainwater utilisation systems, for example, is heavily dented by the considerable effort required to lay the necessary

pipes. The subsidisation of electricity generated by photovoltaic systems skews the balance in favour of energy generation with the result that cell types are recommended that in terms of strict energy balance are only sensible for more southerly regions. A direct assessment in terms of energy balance, however, favours in some cases cell types containing highly toxic substances. For this reason assessments should always be undertaken with as many different and relevant criteria as possible.

What makes the aforementioned approaches problematic is the use of inappropriate reference criteria (money), the compounding of different criteria (money and energy together) or the use of too restrictive system boundaries (e. g. an assessment according to operational consumption only). In this respect, it would be desirable for architects to take on the role of an agent and adviser to the client, to promote these aspects in the planning process and in public awareness. No other participant in the planning process has such a good overview of the consequences associated with particular decisions. From this standpoint architects would have the ability to develop functional and sensible overall concepts and with it to reaffirm their relevance for building planning and promote new models in the field of planning. Ways in which architects can employ movement for such concepts to not only optimise but also create synergies between aesthetics and function will be examined in the following sections. The basis is always to ascertain the best possible holistic view through the choice of a suitable frame of reference and a reliable basis for calculation.

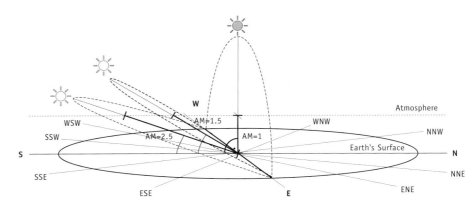

Dependency of the angle of the sun and air mass

■ 2.3 Solar gain in context

York Ostermeyer

The changing climate over the course of the day and the year is something we are all intuitively aware of. A whole variety of habits have their origins in the time of day or year – seasonal attire, summer holidays, springtime lethargy to name just a few – and many aspects of everyday life are arranged around the respective climatic conditions. In our collective understanding, however, we only rarely accord the same to houses.

Many contemporary architectural concepts are increasingly placing greater emphasis on consciously utilising available solar irradiation. Most commonly the energy of the sun is exploited as solar gain to reduce the heat demand of buildings. Numerous publications detail how the intensity of solar radiation varies with the path of the sun. The three central parameters that affect the intensity of solar radiation are the angle of the receiving surface with the respect to the sun, the degree of cloud cover and the atmosphere between the sun and the receiving surface.

Little consideration is given, however, to the outdoor temperature, which in combination with the desired indoor temperature allows one to derive the temperature difference. On first examination, this is proportional to the transmission and ventilation heat losses which together result in the overall heat energy demand of a building. The lack of consideration given to this ambient condition can be attributed to our inability to influence it. While the amount of solar radiation differs for each side of the building, the outdoor temperature remains more or less the same. For a static building it is possible to

regulate the effect of the sun (and with it the degree of solar gain) through the well-judged placement of windows and the positioning of shading elements with respect to the sun. For the opaque parts of the building, the construction is treated uniformly, as the requirements on all sides of the building resulting from the temperature difference are more or less identical. Exceptions arise where the surfaces warm up as a result of solar radiation. But as the majority of heat losses occur overnight and solar gain through opaque elements is almost negligible as a result of current levels of insulation, the above argumentation is valid, at least for a first examination.

For architectural concepts in temperate and cold climatic zones, this direct correspondence between solar irradiation and outdoor temperature represents a problem. Although the air and building surfaces warm up (with a slight lag) as the sun shines on them, the problem is that when the need for solar gain to cover a building's heat demand is greatest, the level of solar irradiation is typically at its lowest. An ocean climate or certain wind currents may improve this relationship, but this applies only to isolated circumstances.

Given the fact that people are so readily able to adapt their habits and activities to the prevailing climate, it seems surprising how static and inflexible buildings are by comparison. Adaptation is commonly limited to the addition of glare-reducing or shading elements. The advent of modern materials and systems, however, has opened up many more progressive possibilities.

Possible gains

Energy gains received through a building's external envelope arise primarily through utilising solar energy. Although it is possible to utilise thermodynamic potential to extract warmth out of outdoor air, this requires mechanical means in the form of a heat pump. In theory this approach can be regarded as a moving solution, but in reality the movement is not perceivable by either the users or onlookers. As such, the aspect of movement as a functional or aesthetic component of architecture is lacking. The following discussion applies, therefore, to passive uses made possible by building envelopes.

In general one can express heat gain as follows:

Heat gain = Solar irradiation x g-value

The energy transmittance (g-value) is an important property of glazing. For our more general purposes, we shall assume here that the g-value also encompasses further factors that affect transmission alongside the properties of glazing, for example dirt accumulation, glazing frame proportion and shading. The g-value therefore represents the total energy transmittance of a particular building component with respect to the solar spectrum of our sun.

Losses

Energy losses from a building can be divided into ventilation heat losses and transmission heat losses. In the following discussion we will take a simplified approach and consider only transmission heat losses: on the one hand, modern well-sealed construc-

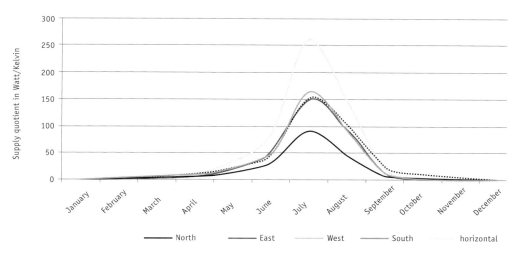

Supply quotient for standard German climate

tion methods have today almost totally eradicated the occurrence of unintentional ventilation heat losses, and on the other, the use of controlled ventilation and heat recovery makes it possible in almost all cases to cover the remaining ventilation heating demand using internal heat sources (which in turn have not been listed under the gains in our discussion). Transmission heat losses can be expressed in a simplified form as follows:

Transmission heat loss = U-value × Temperature difference

The promise of flexible facades
Where the amount of transmission heat losses and solar gain are equivalent:

Solar irradiation x g-value = U-value × Temperature difference

In such circumstances, the thermal energy gains and losses for a particular building component balance each other out. The same equation can, therefore, be rewritten with the material-specific values on one side and the climatic characteristics on the other:

$$\text{Solar irradiation / Temperature difference} = \frac{\text{U-value}}{\text{g-value}}$$

This makes it possible to describe the material characteristics needed to achieve a thermal balance for a specific set of climatic conditions. For the sake of simplicity, the climate-specific quotient is termed here as the supply quotient and the material-specific quotient as the utilisation quotient. By way of example, the chart above shows the typical supply quotient for a standard German climate for each of the four directions of the compass at a desired indoor temperature of 20°C.

It is clear that the aforementioned need for flexibility will need to take account of the orientation. For this reason, one can observe a specialisation among solar gain concepts for smaller buildings: solar gains are generated by the south-facing facade to compensate for losses occurring through the north facade. This presumes, however, that the necessary balance within the building actually works. The larger a building is, the more difficult it becomes to ensure that this happens. The use of flexible facades is, therefore, of particular interest for larger buildings or those that are divided into zones.

Opportunities for the resident to positively influence the supply quotient consist primarily of

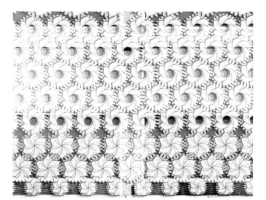

Concepts for movable facades, student projects for "MOVE" seminar, Leibniz University Hanover

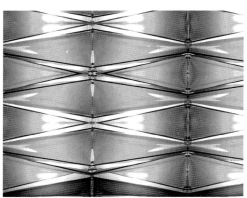

Blossom Hotel, schneider+schumacher architekten, Kish Island, Iran, 2004

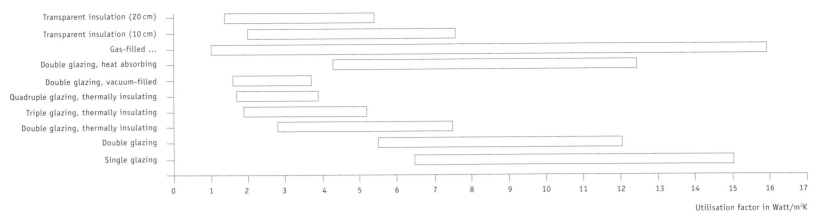

Transparent insulation (20 cm)	
Transparent insulation (10 cm)	
Gas-filled ...	
Double glazing, heat absorbing	
Double glazing, vacuum-filled	
Quadruple glazing, thermally insulating	
Triple glazing, thermally insulating	
Double glazing, thermally insulating	
Double glazing	
Single glazing	

0 1 2 3 4 5 6 7 8 9 10 11 12 13 14 15 16 17

Utilisation factor in Watt/m²K

Utilisation quotient for different materials

adjusting the indoor temperature to more closely match the outdoor climate. This results in a reduced temperature difference which in turn positively affects the supply quotient. If, for example, the residents can tolerate a mean indoor temperature of 18°C in winter and 22°C in summer, the temperature difference decreases in winter and rises in summer, leading to a more evenly distributed supply quotient (chart above right).

The aim of this elaboration is not to adapt the interior conditions to outdoor conditions (in which case the summertime adjustment would not apply) but to smoothen the course of the supply quotient

so that a building element with little means of adjustment can deliver a thermally-balanced performance for a maximum number of hours.

In principle almost all building materials offer a positive solar utilisation quotient, but for most the level is negligibly small.

Here we shall look more closely at building materials that combine a high level of energy transmittance (g-value > 0) with respect to the solar spectrum with a useful U-value (possible thermal gains by transmission from materials with a high thermal mass are disregarded here):

– Glazing
– Transparent insulation materials
– Transparent plastics
  (for example in the form of gas-filled cushions)

As with all static building elements, the places where these building materials can be used are limited when they are unable to move. Where no adaptation is possible, there is a precise supply quotient for each static material in which it fulfils the aforementioned requirements. Given the strongly fluctuating level of the supply quotient, the time span in which thermally-balanced conditions actually pre-

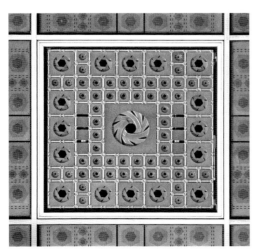

Institut du Monde Arabe, Jean Nouvel, Paris, 1987

Torre Agbar, Jean Nouvel, Barcelona, 2005

Social housing, Edouard François, Louviers, France, 2006

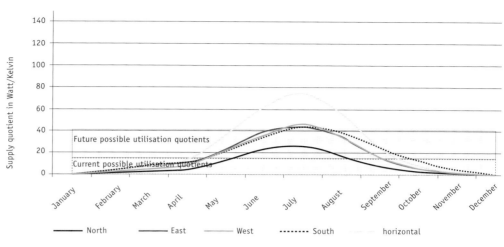

Diagram showing a more evenly distributed supply quotient and an extended utilisation quotient

vail is severely limited (typically amounting to only a few hours over the course of a year). By contrast, flexible constructions and switchable material properties are able to provide a variable utilisation quotient (shown in the table above left as regions) that makes it possible to greatly extend the period in which their thermal performance is balanced.

A variety of technical possibilities are commercially available. The use of solar shading systems makes it possible to reduce the g-value considerably when there is a very high supply quotient. The current norms allow a reduction factor of 0.2 (80 % reduction) using flexible externally-mounted shading sys-

tems. Flexible systems allow one to limit solar gain while still maintaining sufficient daylight levels.

Variochrome glazing alters its g-value when a current is applied, changed or removed. However, the resulting electricity consumption required for large parts of the year is an aspect that should be viewed critically.

Other elements are able to adapt their U-value, for example gas-filled elements in which the amount and kind of the fill-gas used determines the U-value and g-value.

All these building components have enormous development potential. The electricity consumption of

variochrome glazing will continue to sink and the ability to regulate gas-filled elements is improving continually. The transparency of these elements will also increase with improvements in plastics technology. Flexible shading systems are able to filter more precisely and to deflect necessary levels of daylight into rooms without them overheating. In combination with a smoothened supply quotient resulting from adjusted user requirements, buildings with flexible facades will in future be able to do without any heating or cooling for large parts of the year.

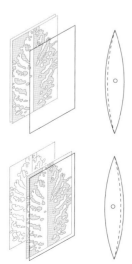

Pneumatic sun protection, Cyclebowl, Atelier Brückner, Expo 2000, Hanover

Facade closed

Facade open

Metha membrane heliostat, Schlaich Bergermann und Partner, Almeria, Spain, 1990

■ 2.4 Factor 1.4 – The potential of movement for solar gain

York Ostermeyer

On the forefront of architecture, a variety of concepts have emerged that are able to react flexibly to maximise the respective available solar irradiation. Here we shall examine the example of solar cells that turn to follow the position of the sun according to the criteria discussed in the previous two chapters. To obtain a precise and reliable representation, it is necessary, as described in the chapter on "Architecture, movement and energy" above, to assess the balance according to as many different relevant indicators and assessment criteria as possible. For space reasons, we will examine only the energy balance. Photovoltaic elements generate electricity, the highest order energy carrier. For their manufacture, however, high temperatures are required that are achieved using combustion processes. As such, the results from the following examinations with varying indicators, tend towards higher initial expenditure.

Cell properties

The manufacture of photovoltaic cells is costly. To use the terminology introduced above, photovoltaic systems require a high initial expenditure. The elec-

Photovoltaic cell types	Efficiency, in practice per cell (module)	Efficiency, theoretical per cell (module)	Grey energy in kWh/m²	Power coefficient per degree Celsius over 25° C	Assumed efficiency (direct/diffuse)
Crystalline cells					
Single-crystalline silicon	18 % (15 %)	24.7 %	1850 – 2550	-0.38 % bis -0.51 % (-0.41)	(20 % / 11 %)
Polycrystalline silicon	15 % (13 %)	19.8 %	1410 – 1530	-0.38 % bis -0.5 % (-0.41)	(16 % / 10 %)
Polycrystalline silicon band cells	14 % (13 %)	19.7 %	–	–	(16 % / 10 %)
Thin film cells					
Amorphous silicon	10 % (7,5 %)	13 %	480 – 500	-0.12 % bis -0.23 % (-0.18)	(5.5 % / 10 %)
Copper indium diselenide cells (CIS)	14 % (10 %)	18.8 %	950 – 1000	ca. -0.36	(10 % / 11 %)
Cadmium telluride cells (CdTe)	10 % (9 %)	16.4 %	500 – 600	-0.2 % bis -0.6 % (-0.3)	(9 % / 17 %)
Chromatophores	7 % (5 %)	12 %	–	–	(3 % / 11 %)

PV cell types

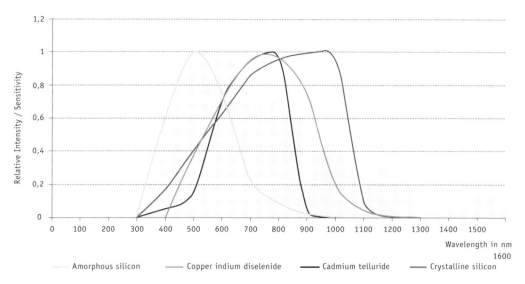

Solar spectrum and spectral sensitivity of different cell types

Amorphous silicon ——— Copper indium diselenide ——— Cadmium telluride ——— Crystalline silicon

tricity they produce over their lifetime comes from two sources – direct and diffuse solar radiation – which have very different degrees of efficiency.

Our sun radiates with a spectrum that corresponds to a black body with a temperature of around 6000 °C. On its way to the earth's surface certain parts of the spectrum are filtered more strongly than others by the earth's atmosphere, which with an air mass of 1.5 results in the grey area in the diagram above. The materials within the photovoltaic cells are able to convert the different wavelengths of radiation to differing extents, resulting in varying degrees of efficiency.

In particular, the silicon-based cells widely used in Central Europe are optimised for utilising direct sunlight, where they are at their most effective and perform better than all other currently available cell types.

Because the manufacture of the cells requires such a high initial expenditure, it makes sense to max-

imise their utilisation of solar radiation. As the largest proportion of electricity is generated by frontal exposure to sunlight, in particular where silicon-based cells are concerned, the ability to turn the cells to follow the course of the sun through the sky makes it possible to maximise the electricity generated. Cell types with other constituents that are less or not at all dependent on direct sunlight benefit little from such systems. As such, all further considerations here will only consider silicon-based cell types.

Analysing climate

Installations for generating electricity from the sun are only rarely isolated concepts for own use, and as such the aim is typically to maximise the total annual profits rather than fulfil personal demand. For this reason, it is usually possible to calculate an optimum orientation for every individual location. In the northern hemisphere, photovoltaic plants face

south (often turned slightly westwards to minimise the effects of morning mists). The inclination of the surfaces depends on their location on the globe. At the equator, the angle is 0°, locations in the northern hemisphere need a steeper angle. The table below lists the solar irradiation levels for five different locations. For each of these, values are also given for an optimally-oriented static setup, an optimally-oriented tracking system, for static installations on the south and west walls and a tracking system mounted on the west wall.

A comparison of these values clearly shows the additional margin resulting from using flexible systems. Optimally-oriented tracking systems can receive between 1.3 and 1.5 times more solar radiation than an optimally-oriented static system. The benefit of a tracking system over a static system mounted on the west wall is much less pronounced as these elements are in shadow for half of the day and receive only diffuse solar radiation.

Location	Horizontal in kWh/m²a	Optimal static in kWh/m²a	Optimal tracking in kWh/m²a	Static South wall in kWh/m²a	Static West wall in kWh/m²a	Tracking West wall in kWh/m²a
Helsinki	965	1189	1687	918	710	943
London	940	1075	1381	759	594	780
Berlin	1017	1183	1568	855	654	905
Rome	1559	1821	2432	1227	1227	1251
Cairo	2000	2201	2950	1258	1258	1486

Annual solar radiation on different surface types

Substructure of a solar tracking mirror

As the values shown do not differentiate between direct and diffuse solar radiation, the table is not valid for all kinds of solar cells. Cell types that are more effective at converting diffuse solar radiation into electricity perform considerably better when mounted on west-facing walls than cell types optimised for direct sunlight.

Depending on the cell type used and its predicted lifetime, it is simple to determine whether the degree of effort necessary to install a tracking system at a particular location is feasible. The table on page 139 shows the results for single-crystalline (assumed efficiency: 15%) and polycrystalline (assumed efficiency: 13%) silicon-based cells for an assumed lifetime of 20 years.

The 20-year balance for single-crystalline cells is not necessarily positive. If one were to extend the balance assessment over the entire lifetime, it becomes clear how important the choice of an appropriate cell type and adaptive tracking is.

The use of movable components to help the solar cells track the sun brings more yield in all locations. This plus may, however, not be significant compared to the additional expenditure required to install and operate the tracking system. One will need to offset the energy consumption required for the motors as well as the impact of the additional raw materials to be used.

Given the many aspects an architect has to consider, an analysis purely in terms of the energy balance

may be extended to include other factors. These can range, for example, from a communicative benefit that results from the conscious use of solar cells, or a multifunctional approach where solar cells also double as shading elements or as a screening element. Both aspects represent other kinds of added value and may justify deviating from the most optimal solution in energy terms. One way or the other, the choice of an appropriate cell type remains relevant as either of the silicon-based cell types are equally able to fulfil the aforementioned aspects.

Shading
Silicon-based cells are particularly susceptible to shading as not only the conductivity of the shaded

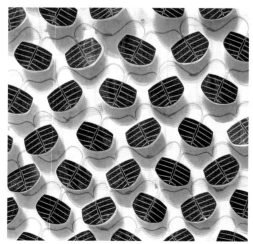
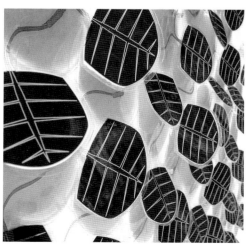

Solar ivy combining solar and wind energy use, Grow, SMIT/Samuel Cabot Cochran, 2005

Cell type	Manufacture in kWh/m²	Yield after 20 years (static) in kWh/m²	Balance after 20 years in kWh/m²	Yield after 20 years (tracking) in kWh/m²	Additional yield from tracking system in kWh/m²
Helsinki					
single-crystalline	2200	3567	1367	5061	1494
polycrystalline	1470	3091	1621	4386	1295
London					
single-crystalline	2200	3225	1025	4143	918
polycrystalline	1470	2795	1325	3591	796
Berlin					
single-crystalline	2200	3549	1349	4704	1155
polycrystalline	1470	3075	1606	4077	1001
Rome					
single-crystalline	2200	5463	3263	7296	1833
polycrystalline	1470	4735	3265	6323	1589
Cairo					
single-crystalline	2200	6603	4403	8850	2247
polycrystalline	1470	5723	4253	7670	1947

Expenditure-yield assessment for photovoltaic systems in different locations

area of the cell suffers but also the entire cell along with all the parallel modules in the respective block. When using photovoltaic cells as movable elements, the need to prevent the individual elements from shading each other quickly becomes a dominating aspect of the design of an overall concept. Two possible approaches are common:
– Reduce the number of tracking elements and calculate the distance they need to stand apart from the known course of the sun.
 Advantage: where there is sufficient space, the yield can be optimised using fewer elements.
 Disadvantage: the yield of the units that can be installed is not much above the value that could be reached with a larger static area.

– The use of a single large element that as a consequence cannot overshadow itself.
 Advantage: maximum yield.
 Disadvantage: complex structural constructions are necessary as the large surface is more susceptible to wind loads; in design terms, the photovoltaic elements will be the dominant visual element.

Where photovoltaic cells are integrated into facades, the use of opaque cells is typically restricted to smaller confined areas. Other limitations may arise where tracking solar cells conflict with other functions of the facade, such as the ability to see out or to open surfaces, or because they are mounted in

difficult-to-reach parts of facades where it is difficult to perform maintenance. As a result photovoltaic tracking installations are only rarely used on building facades although the concept of tracking harbours interesting design possibilities and is also advantageous from an energy balance perspective.

Cherry blossom: static

Sunflower: tracks the sun in the course of the day

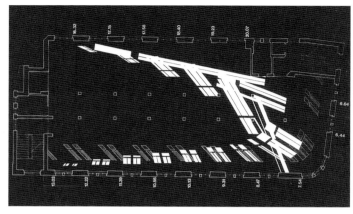

Sun Spots Project, schneider+schumacher architekten, 2004

■ 2.5 Daylight direction using moving deflectors

Roman Jakobiak, Andreas Schulz

The vitalising effect of daylight can be attributed to a large degree to its seasonal and locally specific dynamics. The further one travels from the equator, the more pronounced the seasons become. While direct sunlight exhibits an intensity of illumination exceeding 100,000 lx and an irradiance of more than 1000 W, the intensity and irradiance under cloudy skies or in the shade may be a mere fraction of that. The position of the sun, the level of cloud cover and turbidity of the atmosphere are together responsible for the amount and brightness distribution of daylight during the day.

The enormous breadth of the dynamics of light during the day contrasts markedly with the strongly regulated quality criteria for the illumination of interiors – here the breadth of what is deemed acceptable is much narrower. It is the task of an intelligently designed daylight plan to filter the abundance of daylight available outdoors to create a friendly, lively and comfortable indoor environment, taking into account biological, ecological and economic criteria. The intensity of the almost parallel radiation of the sun presents both great challenges and particular opportunities: on the one hand the need to shield against glare and overheating, on the other to provide interiors with essential daylight. In architecture, the characteristic seasonal and daily rhythm of the sun's path across the sky has given rise to different strategies for dealing with the dynamic element of the sun.

Fixed solar-geometric systems

Illumination with sunlight
Overhanging eaves are a traditional means of screening out the sun that derives from vernacular architecture. The principle is simple: when the sun is high in the sky in summer, the walls and windows are shaded to prevent the building from overheating. By contrast, the low sun in winter is able to shine onto the windows and walls contributing through solar gain to heating the building. A strict

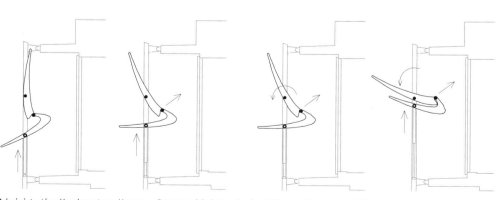

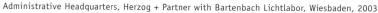

Administrative Headquarters, Herzog + Partner with Bartenbach Lichtlabor, Wiesbaden, 2003

Sun Spots Project, schneider+schumacher architekten, 2004

seasonal difference in the angle of the sun's altitude is only pronounced enough on the south face of buildings (or the north face in the southern hemisphere). Accordingly, this is where fixed horizontal shading elements are most effective.

While an overhanging roof may offer seasonally specific protection against the sun, it also limits the available sunlight when the sky is cloudy irrespective of season. A progression of the principle of overhanging eaves is the light shelf, which is most suitable for use in non-residential buildings. It shades only the lower part of a window while allowing daylight to enter above it, simultaneously affording illumination as well as protecting against direct sunlight. A properly functioning light shelf will shade the lower part of the window entirely during the summer months and reflect a portion of the direct sunlight into the depth of the room. Because the shading element reduces the level of illumination near the window, the contrast between the level of illumination next to the window and deeper inside the room is reduced. A fixed overhang of this kind is most effective at geographic latitudes of between 30° and 45°. Above a latitude of 45°, however, the horizontal fixed element has to be so deep that it can exceed the height of the window. Due to these increasingly disadvantageous proportions, light shelves in higher latitudes are inclined or adjustable. The inclined arrangement, however, has the disadvantage that it obstructs the view outdoors as well as the winter sun. The ability to adjust the element, on the other hand, means that it has

to be operated to be useful and is no longer maintenance-free.

For light shelves to be effective as a light-deflecting system, the upper surface must be highly reflective. As outdoor facades rapidly accumulate dirt, the light-directing function quickly deteriorates without regular maintenance. To reduce the degree of soiling, light shelves are sometimes also mounted internally. However, this more or less sacrifices their solar protection function and the light deflection is also less effective. Nancy Ruck's study *Daylight in Buildings* provides a detailed analysis of daylight systems and their quantitative assessment.

Many daylight systems can also be miniaturised and integrated within the cavity of multi-pane glazing. This is the case with mirrored lamellae which replicate the functionality of a light shelf: they protect against steep incident sunlight while directing lower sunlight deep into the room. However, as fixed elements within the glass pane they obstruct the view outside. Such systems can therefore only be used in glazed areas where a view outside is not important.

Illumination from the sky

The solar selectivity of overhanging eaves and light shelves aims to protect against overheating in summer while making use of the sun's warmth in winter. Given the current standard of thermal insulation of the external envelope and the high internal heat loads inside buildings resulting from the building's use, it is more important for the overall energy ef-

ficiency to prevent overheating in summer than to exploit solar gain in winter. From this point of view, orienting a building to face north represents an ideal approach to fixed daylight regulation: diffuse light from the sky provides sufficient daylight illumination while direct sunlight almost never reaches the interior, and when it does, only to a small degree. This same principle is employed by north-facing windows as well as the classic north-facing shed-roofed skylight.

Movable solar-geometric systems

Fixed solar-geometric systems are most suitable for surfaces oriented due south or due north. In other orientations they may have a contributory effect but on their own are unable to afford illumination while simultaneously protecting against the sun and glare.

Illumination from the sky

A functional principle of movable solar-geometric systems is the ability to shield against parallel direct sunshine while transmitting diffuse light from the sky that comes from other directions. For this the solar protection system has to adjust according to the position of the sun. In most cases horizontally-arranged swivelling lamellae are used. By using mirrored lamellae or prisms, direct sunlight can be reflected back towards its source. This principle is known as retroreflection. Another principle involves projecting the direct sunlight onto sections of opaque surfaces, for example using cylindrical lenses.

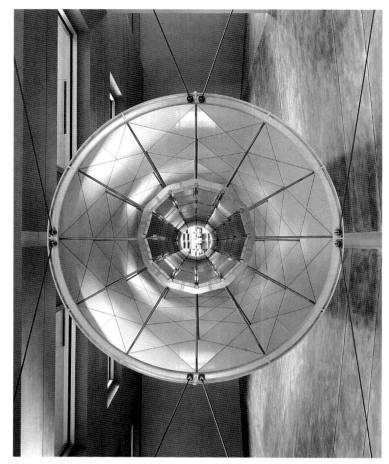

Solar Light Pipe, Carpenter Norris Consulting, Washington, DC, 2001

When these surfaces are covered with photovoltaic elements or thermal solar collectors, the concentrated solar energy can be used to generate electricity or warmth. Such "energy facades" can then serve as a power source. A vertical arrangement of the lamellae is likewise possible but less common.

Irrespective of the orientation of the facade, the systems discussed here will provide a stable level of indoor illumination under changeable skies.

Dual-axis solar tracking systems are rarely used for solar protection due to the high cost.

Illumination with deflected sunlight

A screen or a simple adjustable sliding louvre transmits only a small portion of daylight and deflects the direct daylight component. While most louvres simply scatter the light, adjustable sliding louvres are able to deflect light according to the angle of

the blades: they protect against glare and distribute deflected light across the ceiling, illuminating the room with reflected daylight. Due to the very high intensity of direct sunlight illumination and the comparatively low levels of illumination in interiors, small changes in the daylight control system can have a significant effect on the indoor illumination. Accordingly, solar protection systems that transmit a portion of the direct sunlight into the interior create a much more dynamic indoor illumination than the selective systems discussed above.

Non-selective systems can be optimised by controlling the degree of light transmittance and distribution. A simple system is the block-out operation used by adjustable louvre systems in which the blades of the louvre adjust according to the position of the sun, swivelling just enough to prevent direct sunlight from shining through. While the

block-out operation optimises only the shading function, light-deflecting systems are also able to actively contribute to light provision. Through the use of mirrored lamellae in the upper section of louvred blinds above the eye-level of a standing person, a portion of the direct light can be deflected onto the ceiling to illuminate the depth of the room without dazzling the inhabitant. Lamellae with a special profile allow different degrees of light transmission depending on the blade angle. With this arrangement a single system can fulfil multiple functions: anti-glare, daylight provision and, depending on where it is installed and the quality of glass, solar protection. Highly-polished systems need to be precisely controllable to avoid certain blade angles causing glare.

An alternative to such a highly complex solution is to employ a combination of different daylight con-

T-Home Headquarters, Van den Valentyn Architektur with Licht Kunst Licht, Bonn, 2008

trol systems each with a clear functional purpose. A degree of control can also be achieved using fixed systems: electrically-switchable glazing, for example electrochromic glass, allows the g-value to be modified by darkening or lightening the pane of glass.

Illumination with channelled sunlight
Using heliostats, the direct radiation of the sun can be directed to other fixed mirrors or directly onto the object to be illuminated. Due to the high intensity of solar radiation, even relatively small mirrors are able to transport a considerable amount of light. Heliostats are used where an impression of direct sunlight needs to be created. Other systems go a step further, directing light not just through the air but channelling it through pipes or flexible light-conducting elements. The indoor illumination produced using these systems is static and cannot be differentiated from artificial light. Such light-channelling systems do not afford a view outside.

As mentioned at the outset, the task of daylight planning involves designing the building and daylight control systems in such a way that they filter the widely varying dynamics of daylight out in the open so that it can be used to effectively illuminate interiors in accordance with the relevant criteria. Movable daylight control systems are able to effectively respond to changing lighting conditions and distribute the required amount of illumination in the interior while simultaneously protecting against overheating by blocking unnecessary sunlight. Indoor lighting should nevertheless retain its vitality. A levelling-out of daylight fluctuations is not the intention. Ultimately, the aim is to create lively and attractively illuminated interiors using as simple means as possible.

B   Applications and functions

3 Interaction: Recognizing, controlling and representing movement

Tarantula Amusement Park, Madrid

■ 3.1 Elevators and conveyors

During industrialisation, two main means of conveyance were developed that were to have a formative impact on architecture: the elevator and the escalator. Today, both the elevator and the escalator have developed into highly complex and technically advanced product lines offering a high degree of safety and comfort. Both play an important role in the conveyance of people. For this, a wide range of different technical devices for lifting, moving and processing loads are available. The spectrum of kinetic apparatuses ranges from hydraulic lifting platforms to cranes and hoists to complex conveyor systems used in plant manufacturing. The following section examines transport systems that are especially relevant for architectural applications.

Elevator technology

In the last century a series of technical solutions have been developed for raising and lowering an elevator car. The simplest of these is a cable winch around which the cable winds to raise the car. In ancient Greece, Archimedes had already developed a hoist that used a pulley block and winch to raise and lower a load. This combination of roller and cable was used repeatedly in the centuries that followed to create simple vertical hoists or horizontal cableways.

During the period of industrialisation in the 18th century, the first elevators were powered by machines, for example to transport people and goods in and out of mines. In 1853 Elisha Otis famously demonstrated his "safety brake" for elevators at New York's Crystal Palace: should the cable fail, an automatic brake was activated that prevented the car from falling. A few years later in 1880, Werner von Siemens demonstrated the first electric elevator in Mannheim. Around the same time high-performance steel cables came onto the market based on an invention by the German mining administrator Julius Albert in 1834 in Clausthal which opened up new possibilities for conveyor technology.

The effort required when using a cable winch is considerable and equates to the entire load. Cable winches that employ a counterweight require less effort. The counterweight is connected to the car via a pulley and is dimensioned so that the system is in balance when the car is half-full. The drive mechanism uses a traction sheave which uses friction to drive the cable. The maximum load that the motor has to move is half of the maximum car load.

Hydraulic elevators developed parallel to cable-driven elevators and are used primarily for smaller passenger elevators and lifts for heavy loads as the maximum possible length of a hydraulic piston is limited to around 25 m. Direct-acting hydraulic elevators employ a piston directly beneath the car so that, as with the simple cable winch, the effort required to move the load corresponds to the total load of the car and contents. The space requirements are dictated by the height of the piston assembly when fully retracted. A telescopic arrangement of several pistons one inside the other makes it possible to further minimise this distance. Indirect-acting hydraulic elevators are more economical with space. Here the car is attached to the piston via a cable and roller. With this arrangement, the travel distance of the piston is halved but the effort required is doubled.

A further drive concept involves motorising the car directly. The car becomes in effect a vehicle with its own motor and climbs up and down a rail or track. In its simplest form, this system is used for transportable construction lifts. Climbing elevators are also used for specific purposes in industrial buildings and can also be used for people. The comfort of the rides is, however, somewhat limited.

Machine room

A machine room is in most cases necessary for both cable-driven and hydraulic elevators. For cable-driven systems this is best located at the top of the elevator shaft, although by additionally passing the cable over a pulley the machine room can alternatively be located at the base. This increases the length of the cable and requires more components that are subject to wear. For hydraulic elevators, the machine room can be positioned more flexibly as the pressure lines can be located up to 10 m away from the piston.

In the last ten years, so-called machine-room-less (MRL) elevators have become increasingly popular. These are mainly cable-driven elevators which employ a compact traction sheave assembly that can be mounted within the driveshaft itself, utilising the space that is needed in any case for the overtravel.

Application areas

A differentiation is drawn between whether passengers, passengers and freight, or just freight are to

	Standing car with internal drive mechanism	Standing car with external drive mechanism	Suspended car with external drive mechanism	Continuous conveyor
Horizontal				
Diagonal				
Vertical				

be transported. Stricter safety requirements apply for the transport of passengers. This includes emergency facilities and an intercom system in the car and pinch-guards for all movable parts that people may come into contact with. The number of permissible passengers is calculated based on the size of the car using tables for different types of buildings and number of users. Cars suitable for use by the disabled must fulfil minimum dimensions as given in DIN EN 81-70.

For the transport of heavy goods, the lift must also be able to accommodate a secondary means of transport used to move the primary load, depending on its size and weight. A variety of different standard elevator types are available on the market that serve the most common application areas: small goods lifts, passenger elevators, passenger and freight elevators, service elevators, bed elevators, car elevators and freight lifts. Specific solutions are also available for special application areas.

Control technology

In the simplest cases, the individual journeys are fulfilled one after the other. This single journey control system makes most sense for freight lifts as a fully laden elevator cannot take on additional loads mid-journey.

Cabins ("Bubbles") of the Grenoble-Bastille cable car, Denis Creisseis, France, 1976

Examples of different elevator
drive concepts.
Traction sheave drives and
hydraulically-powered
elevators with a side-mounted
hydraulic cylinder represent
the state of the art.

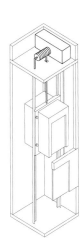

Cable winch

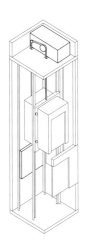

Traction sheave
with counterweight

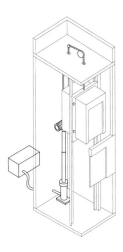

Hydraulic piston

Climbing elevator

Passenger elevator Mercedes-Benz Museum, UN Studio,
Stuttgart, 2006

For passenger elevators this form of control system is now regarded as outdated due to the long waiting times that ensue. Instead, collective automatic control systems are used that stop additionally mid-journey to allow other passengers to get in. This can happen irrespective of direction or, through the prior selection of the desired direction (up or down), only when the elevator is travelling in the same direction. Through the use of additional induction loops or ceiling or weight sensors, the system can detect whether the elevator is already full and temporarily override intermediate stops.

To further increase the capacity of the overall system, destination control panels can be implemented at the main entry points which allow users to indicate their intended destination. The control system then determines the shortest overall journey time based on the currently active journey requests. While the overall capacity increases, the time an individual may have to wait, and therefore the perceived time for the entire journey, may be longer.

Performance

The performance of passenger elevators is optimised so that the desired number of people reach their destinations as quickly as possible. The dimensions of passenger elevators are calculated according to the parameters of transport capacity, waiting time and round trip time. Basic information regarding minimum number and size of the necessary elevators are generally given in the respective building regulations. A more powerful control system can improve the overall capacity significantly. This is of particular importance for high buildings and long travel distances. In large buildings, elevators may be organised as an internal traffic system with different elevators for long-distance journeys and local journeys. This can optimise the overall journey time.

Lastly, elevators are continually being developed in terms of energy efficiency. Regenerative drive systems will in future allow the reconversion of potential energy in electricity as a fully laden car travels downwards.

Escalators

In the development of the escalator, the implementation of safety aspects was necessary before the first public escalator could be put into service at the World Expo in Paris in 1900. Today a series of technical safety mechanisms have become standard practice and are anchored in the European standard DIN EN 115: in particular the entry and exit points at each floor must be carefully adjusted to the er-

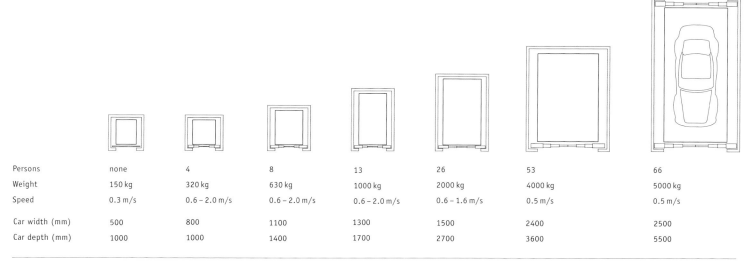

Persons	none	4	8	13	26	53	66
Weight	150 kg	320 kg	630 kg	1000 kg	2000 kg	4000 kg	5000 kg
Speed	0.3 m/s	0.6 – 2.0 m/s	0.6 – 2.0 m/s	0.6 – 2.0 m/s	0.6 – 1.6 m/s	0.5 m/s	0.5 m/s
Car width (mm)	500	800	1100	1300	1500	2400	2500
Car depth (mm)	1000	1000	1400	1700	2700	3600	5500

A comparison of standard elevator types

Interaction: Recognizing, controlling and representing movement

Car production line for the VW "Touran", Wolfsburg, Germany

Facing page:
Lift Inclino, St. Moritz, Switzerland

Right:
Functional principle of an escalator

gonomic needs of the users. The steps initially move horizontally before moving diagonally upwards or downwards. A moving handrail also provides support and tactile orientation 40 cm before the feet reach the first step. The serrated surfaces of the moving metal treads pass beneath a notched comb plate to prevent clothing from becoming trapped in the mechanism. In addition, emergency stop buttons allow the escalator to be deactivated quickly, and in Europe stop buttons are compulsory for all escalators at an interval of less than 30 m.

Construction
Escalators are delivered either as a complete unit and craned into place from above or in individual segments which are assembled on site, an altogether more laborious construction process. In both cases the body of the escalator unit is slung unsupported between the floors. The span length and the low permissible bending tolerance – one thousandth of the span length – often necessitate sizeable substructures at the bearing points at the edges of the floor slabs to support the high loads. An escalator spanning a floor height of 4 m with an ascent angle of 30° can weigh up to 7000 kg. The construction of horizontal moving walkways is simpler as in many cases these do not need to span unsupported.

Energy consumption
Escalators in commercial environments usually have to cope with twelve hours usage per day for six days in a week. Public escalators may be used for up to 20 hours a day, every day of the week. A typical escalator (1 m wide, 30° angle, 5 m floor height, 0.5 m/s speed) running idly without load will consume between 50 kWh (commercial) and 105 kWh (public) per week. With an estimated mean load of 25 kg per step, an escalator in a commercial environment such as a shopping centre may consume 300 kWh per week. For a public escalators with an estimated mean load of 35 kg per step, this can be as much as 780 kWh per week. It is clear that considerable energy savings can be achieved by using weight sensor plates to activate the mechanism only when needed.

Design options
Due to the large number of such functional and construction-related parameters, the design options for escalators are restricted to certain aspects. The choice of materials for visible surfaces such as steps, floor panels and handrails is usually limited to a few alternative choices. The side panels of the balustrades can be glass or opaque. The supporting framework of the escalator mechanism is usually encased but can be clad with transparent panels.

Performance
In addition to their technical construction, the dimensions of escalators are also largely regulated by standards. Escalators with a tread width of 600 mm, 800 mm and 1000 mm are permissible with an angle of ascent of 35° for travel heights of up to 6 m and 30° for greater height differences. Travelling walkways typically have an angle of inclination of between 0 to 6° or 10° to 12°. Speeds of between 0.45 m/s and 0.5 m/s are usual; for long distances across large heights, speeds of up to 0.75 m/s are possible. From this one can calculate the capacity which typically ranges between 4500 to 8000 persons per hour. By comparison a 1 m wide stair in unobstructed use may serve between 200 to 400 persons per hour in one direction.

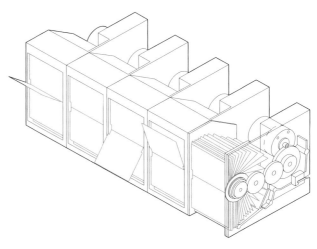

■ 3.2 Recognizing and representing movement

Mechanical Pixel: Split-Flap Board, after Ralf Tornow and Frank Mössner

Interaction

Interaction describes the reciprocal interplay between two or more participants. It is a communicative act in which the actions of all participants react to the respective actions of their counterparts. Each participant has a given scope for action that encompasses several alternatives and operates within this scope as an independent individual. Today, technical systems are able to imitate interactive processes. While their reaction to human presence follows predefined rules, these have become so extensive and offer such complexity that they create the impression of an individual response to our actions. This impression is heightened when the computer's calculated response is relayed not by an individual kinetic component but by an additive array of connected elements. The sum of individual reactive elements creates a larger form that responds with almost lifelike vitality.

The concept of interactive technology (or reactive technology to be more precise) has been explored artistically in numerous media installations. Often the viewer takes on the role of an active user whose physical signals, for example in the form of movement or sounds, bring about a reaction in the respective object or installation. This is mirrored back to the viewer encouraging them to respond. A playful interaction between man and object results. The potential offered by such intuitive means of interaction for concrete applications such as equipment interfaces is enormous.

Movement as a trigger

In the simplest cases, the object simply reacts to the presence of people achieved using a sensor. The use of such closed loops to adjust the indoor room climate or lighting is common practice. An extension of this concept would result in buildings that

are able to adapt room for room to the respective pattern of use. A sound follows the inhabitant through the room, energy is used only where it is needed. But personal movement also encompasses much more complex means of expressions such as gestures and body language which, like the spoken word, are an essential means of communication. Three different strategies are possible for representing this movement or even responding to it through interactive processes:

- A centralised means of capturing movement using a camera with subsequent inductive computer analysis of the image and the centralised calculation of a corresponding reaction.
- The decentralised capture of movement using a large number of very simple sensors with subsequent deductive analysis and the

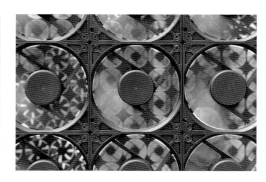

Installation Flow 5.0, Studio Roosegaarde, Rotterdam, 2007 – 2009

HypoSurface

centralised calculation of a corresponding reaction.

– An entirely decentralised means of capturing movement and a direct, local reaction to the respective movement through a large number of small elements.

An example of the last type is an installation by Studio Roosegaarde entitled Flow 5.0. This interactive object consists of a freestanding wall whose entire 8 m long structure is equipped with 640 small fans. Each individual fan is linked to an infrared sensor that sets the fan in motion as a warm body approaches. These individual reactions are connected to one another via a central controller and can therefore be adjusted. The sum of the individual fans creates a wind with the contours of the body of the viewer. This wind follows each and every movement and stimulates one's perception precisely at the point where the viewer stands and

can sense it and nowhere else. Because the fans increase or decrease the apparent transparency of the wall locally depending on their speed of rotation, this interactive process can also be experienced visually.

The capture or sensing of patterns of movement caused by a large number of people over extensive terrain is more complex. For this the architect Carlo Ratti, Director of SENSEable city lab at the Massachusetts Institute of Technology (MIT), has exploited the now widespread use of mobile telephones. For the project Real Time Copenhagen, the density of mobile telephone signals during the Kopenhagen Kulturnatten 2008 (Copenhagen Night of Culture) was superimposed onto a map of the evening's events in real time. The interactive presentation visualizes the stream of visitors, in turn influencing them by displaying the most interesting routes through the site of the event at that point in time.

A more extensive targeted analysis of patterns of human movement in space requires a carefully methodical approach utilising computer-aided modelling techniques. The British consulting firm Space Syntax is a specialist in the field and uses self-developed simulation programmes to capture and extrapolate human patterns of movement in spaces ranging from office floors to entire urban quarters in order to ascertain a better idea of how these spaces function. This approach is not only valuable for individual planning decisions. By feeding this data back into regulatory systems, for example for the allocation of empty office space or for directing traffic flow, this could in future serve as a basis for a working mechanism for interactively influencing spatial structures.

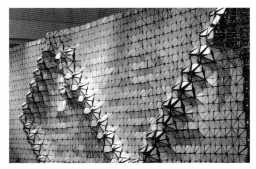

HypoSurface, Mark Goulthorpe, Massachusetts Institute of Technology

Facing page:
ICE Interactive Communication Experience,
Klein Dytham architecture, Tokyo, 2002

LED display embedded in a glazed facade as information wall,
Powerglass by Glas Platz

Movement as a representation of movement

Interactive processes between man and machine usually employ visual perception as the central means of communication. The actions of the user create a visible reaction on a display or input device: moving pictures that allow rapid and direct feedback. The interactive media wall "ICE", created by Klein Dytham architecture together with the installation artist Toshio Iwai for the news and financial data service Bloomberg, registers the movement of the viewer using numerous infra-red sensors behind a 5 x 3.50 m wall of translucent glass. Depending on the selected mode, of which four are available, different patterns of movement are projected onto the screen, animating the viewer to respond anew.

It is no surprise that the visual power of a display can be further heightened through the use of three dimensions. For large-format projections, however, special 3D-glasses would be required that allow the viewer to assemble a spatially convincing scene out of two slightly different perspectives for the left and right eyes. The HypoSurface, developed by Mark Goulthorpe, a professor at MIT, is all the more impressive: it is a display consisting of thousands of motorised metal plates that move in a wave-like form at a maximum speed of 100 km/h and project up to 60 cm out of a flat surface. In conjunction with cameras, microphones and a sophisticated control software, the system responds to the user's input with abstract three-dimensional representations of fluid movements.

By comparison, traditional media facades are relatively simple, relying exclusively on fleeting mo-

mentary impressions of continually changing images to dissolve the surfaces of built objects in a flow of dynamic images. Urban intersections such as those in Times Square in New York or the Shibuya Station in Tokyo are particularly impressive examples of such environments. The repertoire ranges from running tickers displaying stock exchange data to alternating stills to moving film sequences and advertising spots. Motion is used here to attract attention: the brasher the better so that they are noticed among their neighbours. The spatial presence of the individual buildings is of secondary importance.

The Elbe Bitwall 1 installation by Christian Moeller shows that this effect can be used more subtly for artistic abstraction. Here the principle is not used to achieve maximum reach but to realise an artistic response to a characteristic landscape. The slow flow of the River Elbe is translated into a continually moving black and white cloud of pixels and displayed on a vertical column-like, mechanical bitmap display. While the original image of the passing river bank can still be experienced in an abstract form, the central motif is the continual movement of water.

Moving pixels

The term display usually denotes a device for displaying changing images on objects the size of a mobile telephone or computer. Currently TFT displays have dimensions of around 100 x 60 cm with a typical pixel size of between 0.1 and 0.3 mm. But if this principle is applied at a larger scale, for example for a surface the size of a wall or even an

entire facade, fundamentally different technical requirements apply.

In such cases, the distance at which an image is perceived ranges from a few metres to several kilometres in the case of an animated skyscraper facade. The pixels are then correspondingly larger and spaced farther apart in order to ensure that images remain legible. Glass surfaces with embedded, individually controllable light-emitting diodes at a pixel interval of 60 mm already produce a legible image at distance of around 10 m. At very large distances, individually lit windows of an office facade can even function as pixels for displaying simple images.

The shift in scale from conventional display technology makes it possible to realise changing picture cells using mechanical means. The pixel becomes a technical device which by shifting or turning individual components can be made to present a different colour. An additive combination of this single small-scale movement can then be used to create dynamically changing surfaces that in turn can set entire facades in motion.

C

Buildings
and building
elements

Swivel
Rotate
Flap
Slide

Fold
Expand and contract
Gather and roll up
Pneumatic

Church of the Sacred Heart

Munich, D, 2000
Allmann Sattler Wappner Architekten

The Church of the Sacred Heart in the Neuhausen district of Munich is the product of a competition held in 1996. The glazed external envelope of the building lends it an object-like quality and at first glance is not immediately identifiable as a church. The 48 m long, 21 m wide and 16 m high rectangular volume only reveals its ecclesiastical character when the two giant, 14.20 m high and 9.30 m wide doors at the gable end of the building are opened onto the forecourt. The inner facade of the church is then revealed, a slatted wooden casing made of maple lamella which encloses the actual interior of the church. The external envelope of the building is a post-and-beam construction clad with insulating glass units, which creates a transparent veil while allowing the altar area to be concealed behind translucent and opaque glass elements.

The hydraulically-powered portal (Wörsching Ingenieure) lends the church a variety of attractive features, combining them with a grand visual gesture. The resulting space it defines in front of the church allows the congregation to hold church services outdoors on special occasions. Each door weighs 22 tonnes and turns around an axis located a third of the way along the door leaf. The hydraulic drive for the door leaves is located in a plant room below ground. The electrical impulse for the opening mechanism is controlled by a hand-operated switch regulated by a combination of a dead man's control and wind sensor for safety. Rectangular metal stiffeners maintain the structural integrity of the construction to ensure it can withstand wind loads.

The 436 blue-coloured translucent and transparent glass squares embedded in the church doors create an intense play of colours in the entrance area. Designed by Alexander Beleschenko, the structural glazing elements depict motifs from the Gospel of John in specifically arranged patterns of nails. When both of "God's gates" are closed, visitors enter the church through small doors in the middle of the large opening portals.

Building-height doors open the church to the forecourt

0:00   6:00   12:00   min:sec

....

Dimensions W x H 9.30 x 14.20 m per door leaf (2 leaves)   **Weight** 22 t per door   **Drive** 2 x hydraulic cylinders

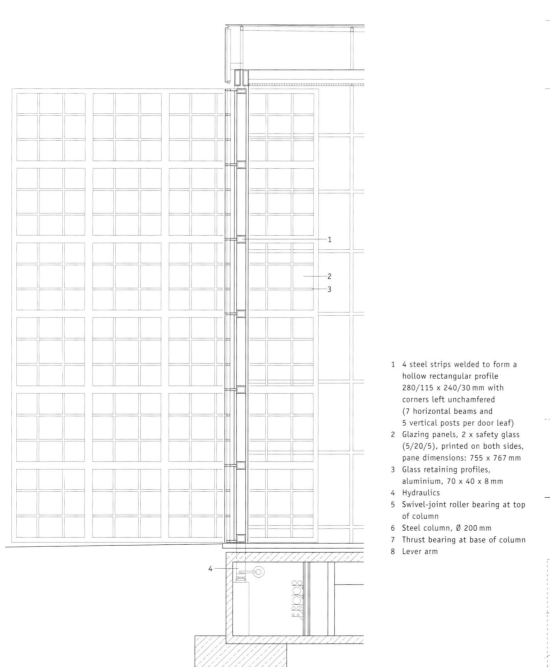

1 4 steel strips welded to form a
   hollow rectangular profile
   280/115 x 240/30 mm with
   corners left unchamfered
   (7 horizontal beams and
   5 vertical posts per door leaf)
2 Glazing panels, 2 x safety glass
   (5/20/5), printed on both sides,
   pane dimensions: 755 x 767 mm
3 Glass retaining profiles,
   aluminium, 70 x 40 x 8 mm
4 Hydraulics
5 Swivel-joint roller bearing at top
   of column
6 Steel column, Ø 200 mm
7 Thrust bearing at base of column
8 Lever arm

Swivel

Longitudinal section, 1:115   Detail, door leaf bearing, 1:15

BMW Training Academy

Unterschleißheim near Munich, D, 2004
Ackermann und Partner

The building contains seminar, lecture and training rooms arranged on two storeys around a central atrium. The entrance elevation features swivelling vertical sunscreens that resemble sails arranged at regular intervals along the full width of the frontage, allowing the glazed facade behind to be almost fully shaded throughout the day. The sail-like sunscreens underline the technical appearance of the training academy and symbolise the dynamic mobility of the BMW Group.

Each set of parallel sunscreens, six on one side, seven on the other, are connected by a coupler drive-en on the other, are connected by a coupler drive-

shaft in a channel in the floor and can be swivelled using an electric motor. The angle of the sunscreens automatically adjusts with respect to the position of the sun but can also be manually operated to position them in a particular arrangement, for example to allow vehicles to pass behind them. Each of the sails rotates around a full-height, vertical aluminium shaft that is positioned off-centre. To minimise the eccentric forces, the screens have a lightweight construction and profile reminiscent of aircraft wings, with a supporting construction made of aluminium profiles clad with riveted aluminium sheeting.

In normal automatic operation, the screens rotate continuously and very slowly. In manual operation, a dead man's control is used to prevent injury or damage to the system. Depressing and holding the safety switch causes the sunscreens to turn at a rate of 90° per minute. When the switch is released, movement is halted automatically.

Each group of six or seven sunscreen sails can be rotated together

0:00

0:30

1:00

min:sec

....

Dimensions W x H x D 2.50 x 6.67 x 0.25 m per sunscreen   **Number** 43   **Weight** 1000 kg per element   **Drive** Electric motor with coupler driveshafts for 6 – 7 elements

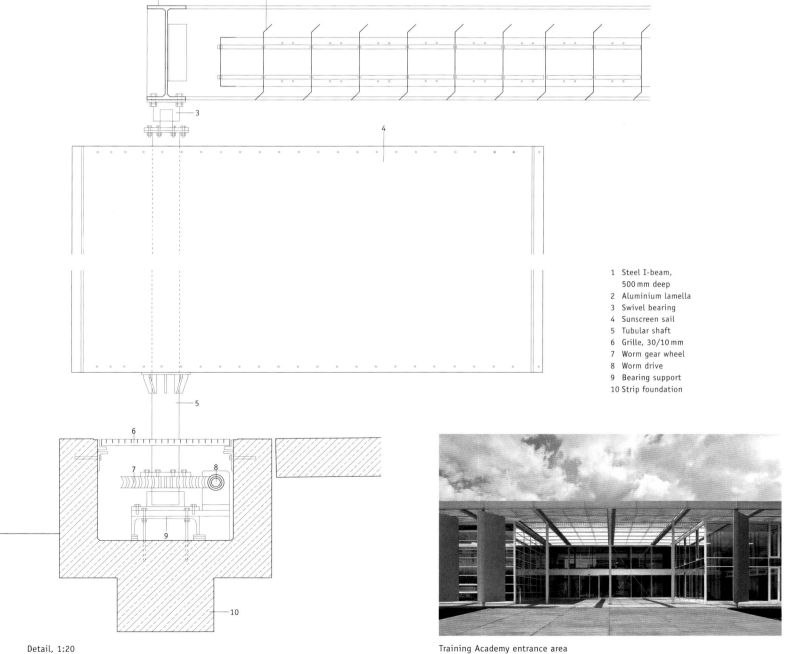

Swivel

1 Steel I-beam,
   500 mm deep
2 Aluminium lamella
3 Swivel bearing
4 Sunscreen sail
5 Tubular shaft
6 Grille, 30/10 mm
7 Worm gear wheel
8 Worm drive
9 Bearing support
10 Strip foundation

Detail, 1:20

Training Academy entrance area

Ernsting's Family Distribution Depot

Coesfeld-Lette, D, 1999
Schilling Architekten

The design of the industrial premises for a textile and clothing company is dictated by the primary processes of the delivery and distribution of goods. The deliveries building, with an entrance portal designed by the Spanish architect Santiago Calatrava, and a works hall for processing the goods was extended by adding a warehouse and a new distribution depot. As with the earlier buildings on the site by the architects Reichlin, Reinhard and Calatrava, the distribution depot, designed by Schilling Architekten, was the product of an architectural competition in 1996.

The form of the ensemble, consisting of two building volumes, closely follows the internal functional arrangement. The shallow roof of the warehouse slopes downwards following the incline of the surrounding landscape. The final section of the slanted roof consists of three parallel segments that when open reveal loading bays for up to twelve lorries. These individually movable segments can be opened in the mornings and closed in the evenings. In the closed position, the large rising gates, each with a surface area of 320 m², lie in the same plane as the roof and seamlessly continue the line of the roof down to the ground.

The mobile gate sections rest at their centre of mass on four inverted V-shaped steel supports, minimising the force required to pivot them around the horizontal axis through their centre of mass. Electric hoists on the inner side of the supports set the roof in motion: each segment has a pair of contracting electric spindle motors that cause the leading edge of the gates to rise. The transition between the gate and floor levels has been carefully detailed. Three raised grilles for drainage and ventilation are lowered using a system of cables as the gates open so that they lie flush with the floor and provide a seamless transition from outside into the loading bays. The grilles prevent access to the narrowed gap beneath the partially closed roof and lend the process of opening and closing a special grace.

Three hinged rising gates close off the loading bays

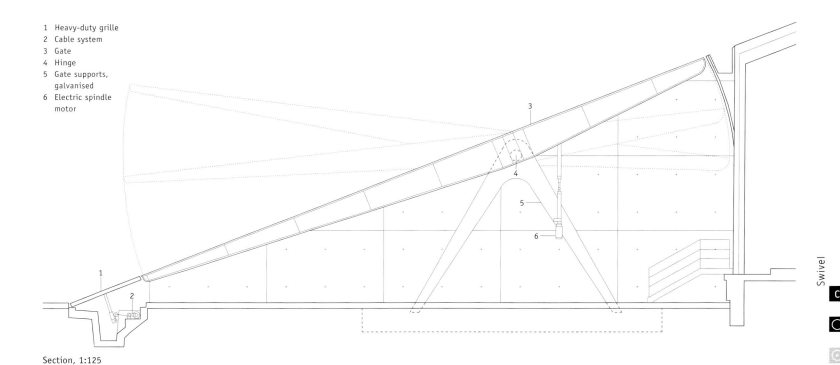

0:00   0:07   0:15   0:22   0:30   min:sec

Dimensions L x W 20 x 16 m per gate **Number** 3 gates **Drive** 2 electric spindle motors per gate

1 Heavy-duty grille
2 Cable system
3 Gate
4 Hinge
5 Gate supports,
   galvanised
6 Electric spindle
   motor

Section, 1:125

Swivel

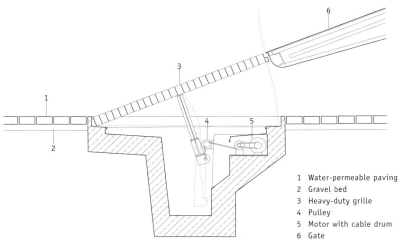

1 Water-permeable paving
2 Gravel bed
3 Heavy-duty grille
4 Pulley
5 Motor with cable drum
6 Gate

Detail, floor grille, 1:50

Inverted V-shaped supports for the fulcrum

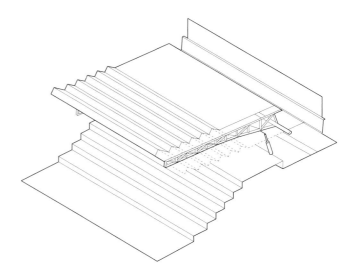

○ Lakeside Stage

Lunz am See, A, 2004
Werkraum Wien with Hans Kupelwieser

To provide an attractive venue for the annual Summer Festival hosted in Lunz, Lower Austria, since 1997, a competition was announced in 2003 for a new stage on the banks of the lakeside resort. The winning entry was a multifunctional artwork by the artist Hans Kupelwieser, who teamed up with the Vienna-based engineering office Werkraum Wien to realise the project. The resulting construction is an ingenious lakeside stage complex consisting of a floating stage, a forestage and an open spectator stand, which can be converted to a covered stand as required. The structure therefore serves the dual functions of a bathing island and a venue for performances.

The stand construction rests on two bearing blocks. The roof is guided and fixed in position by hydraulic extending props. Using a system of pumps, water from the lake is fed into a trough higher than the pivot point at the rear of the roof. By releasing the hydraulic valve, the weight of the water causes the 13 x 13 m timber and steel roof, which rests on top of the stepped concrete seating, to rise silently upwards. When open, the roof acts as an acoustic shell as well as protection against the rain. To lower the roof, a vent is opened to allow the water to drain off along a concrete channel – used otherwise as a diving platform – back into the lake. The hydraulic lines are opened and the props allowed to sink back to the closed position.

When closed, the lower booms of the roof trusses slot snugly into a parallel arrangement of channels in the concrete stand beneath. The stepped roof covers the concrete seating exactly, its upper surface providing a lakeside sun deck to sit and sunbathe.

The floating pontoon on the lake was developed by a German shipyard. The 8 x 5 m aluminium construction is connected by demountable walkways to the shore. In the winter months, the pontoon is sunk by filling it with water and spends the winter at a depth of 3 m beneath the frozen lake. In summer it is filled with air and raised to the surface again.

Sun deck and spectator stand

The roof opening

Covered spectator stand

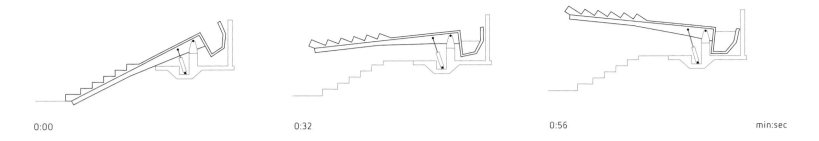

0:00   0:32   0:56   min:sec

Dimensions L x W 12.50 x 12.60 m roof   Drive water, volume 14 m³

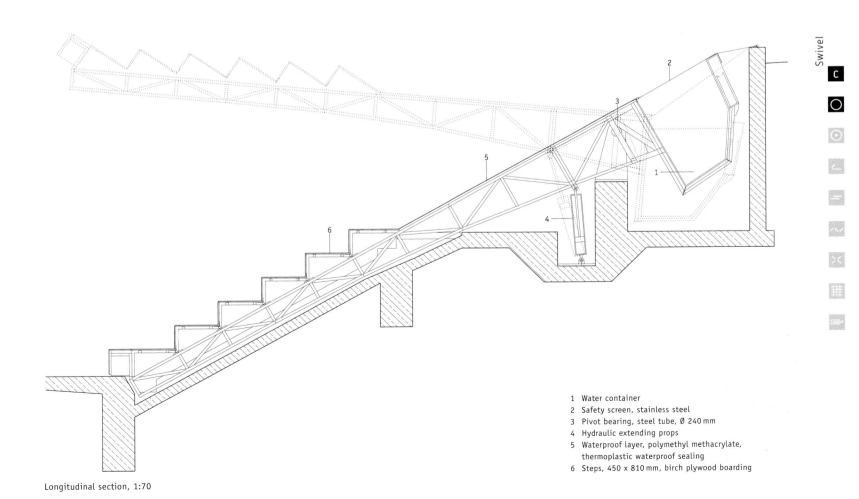

Longitudinal section, 1:70

1 Water container
2 Safety screen, stainless steel
3 Pivot bearing, steel tube, Ø 240 mm
4 Hydraulic extending props
5 Waterproof layer, polymethyl methacrylate,
   thermoplastic waterproof sealing
6 Steps, 450 x 810 mm, birch plywood boarding

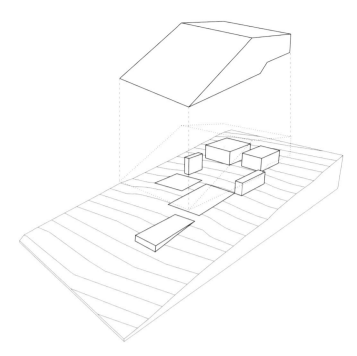

F House

Kronberg im Taunus, D, 2009
Meixner Schlüter Wendt Architekten

The form of this 325 m² floor area single family house is a response to the local authority's planning policy, which stipulates that houses must have pitched roofs. Building on this, the architects extended the typical roof pitch, increasing its length dramatically to create a house with a distinctive silhouette. The concrete, steel and timber construction rests on columns and beams and appears to hover over the surrounding orchard. Its facade cladding made of sheet-aluminium composite panels picks up the colouring of the slate typical for the region. In response to the sloping site, the house is divided into three levels: cellar, garden and upper storey. The garden-level floor is reached from the higher ground to the north and is the main living area, fully-glazed and seamlessly embedded into the slope.

A particularly interesting aspect of the design is the articulation of the southern tip of the wedge-shaped roof, which extends some 4 m over the terrace. Two wing-like sections of the roof can be raised upwards by 60° to allow more light into the living room on the garden-level below. The two flaps are mounted on shafts at their centre of gravity and are raised using electrically-powered motor-driven telescopic rams. Grooved ball bearings take up the axial loads of the kinetic construction and stops in the fixed sections of the roof wedge prevent the flaps from rotating freely. The folding sections and the materiality of the roof create the impression of a military flying object that has come to rest on the idyllic slopes of Kronberg's orchards.

Aluminium wings regulate the entry of direct sunlight

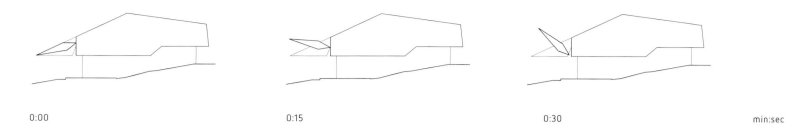

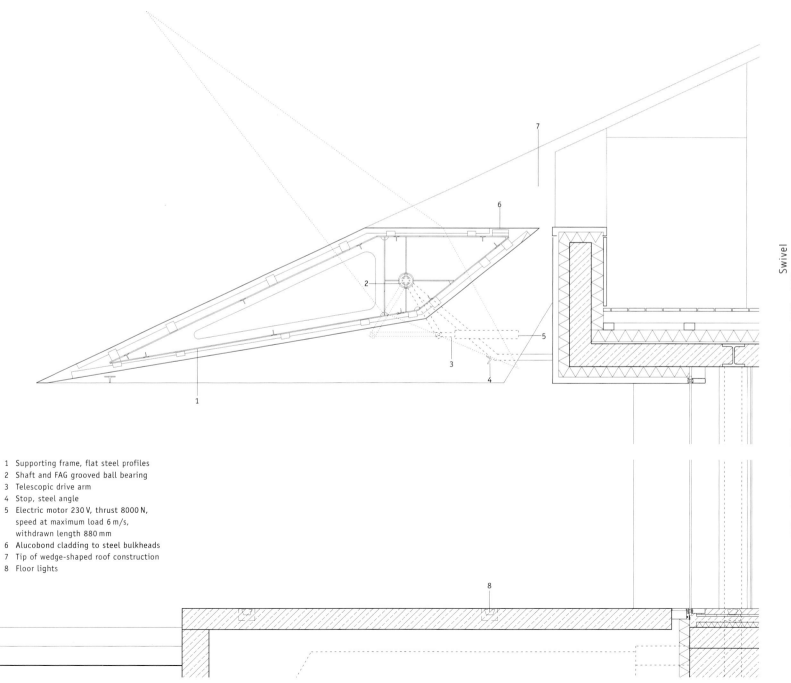

0:00   0:15   0:30   min:sec

Dimensions W x H x D 340/380 x 130 x 400 cm, rotation angle 60°   **Number** 2 wings   **Drive** electric motor with telescopic rams

Swivel

1 Supporting frame, flat steel profiles
2 Shaft and FAG grooved ball bearing
3 Telescopic drive arm
4 Stop, steel angle
5 Electric motor 230 V, thrust 8000 N,
   speed at maximum load 6 m/s,
   withdrawn length 880 mm
6 Alucobond cladding to steel bulkheads
7 Tip of wedge-shaped roof construction
8 Floor lights

Section, 1:33

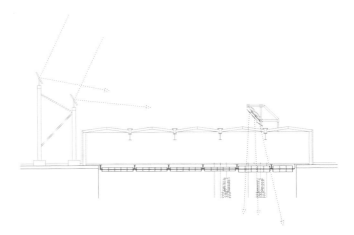

Genzyme Headquarters

Cambridge, Massachusetts, USA, 2004
Behnisch, Behnisch und Partner

The headquarters of the Genzyme Corporation, a biotechnology company, unites sustainable plant technology and intelligent daylight redirection with a communicative and comfortable working atmosphere. The building is organised around a central, full-height atrium that opens onto twelve differently shaped storeys. At each of the 920 flexible workplaces, the employees can manually override the fully automated blinds, air supply and conditioning. Light-deflecting louvres and the light-flooded atrium reduce the need for artificial light. On the roof, seven heliostats are mounted on steel masts and can be turned on two axes to follow the sun. They direct sunlight via a bank of fixed mirrors

– also consisting of seven units each with 63 individually adjustable mirrors – through a thermally-glazed skylight into the interior below. Inside the 13-storey atrium, hundreds of prismatic acrylic glass plates reflect and scatter the sunlight, creating lively, dynamic patterns of light. Connected by ball-joints to its stainless steel supporting rod, each panel can be adjusted freely. Like a set of giant mobiles, they react to air movements creating a random component to the otherwise carefully articulated building. A fountain and reflective "light wall" enhance the effect of light reflection. In the construction of the skylight, 1130 prismatic lamellae mounted on 21 shafts regulate the intensity and

quality of the incident light. This "prismatic ceiling" is divided into two sections, each separately controlled by a linear drive motor. The lamellae in the smaller section are arranged vertically during the day to allow light reflected downwards from the mirrors to pass. The remainder are arranged perpendicular to the angle of the sun, so that they reflect direct light and allow only deflected diffuse light to reach the interior.

Modern environmental technology and minimal energy expenditure by American standards led to the awarding of a LEED platinum rating in 2005.

Heliostats that follow the position of the sun

Prismatic lamellae arranged at 90° and 70°

The sparkling chandelier made of prismatic acrylic panels

0:00   2:30   5:00   7:30   10:00   h:min

Dimensions 340 x 68 cm per prismatic module   **Number** 21 shafts, 1130 prismatic lamellae   **Drive** electric linear motor   **Angle of rotation** max. 140° and 90°

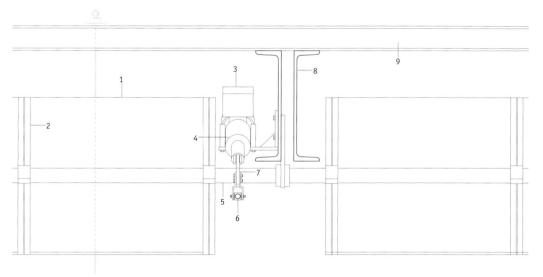

1 Prismatic lamella, acrylic glass, energy
  transmission g = 0.15,
  light transmission LT = 0.7
2 Two-part connecting web
3 Linear drive motor, electric, 110 V/0.12 kW
4 Hydraulic elevating ram, travel = 400 mm
5 Prismatic drive shaft, Ø 60 mm, l = 3840 mm
6 Transfer rod, transfers movement to parallel
  shafts
7 Lever, per section
8 Supporting structure, twin channel sections,
  d = 450 mm
9 2 x channel sections, 100 mm

Swivel

Detail, longitudinal section of control mechanism 70° angle, 1:15

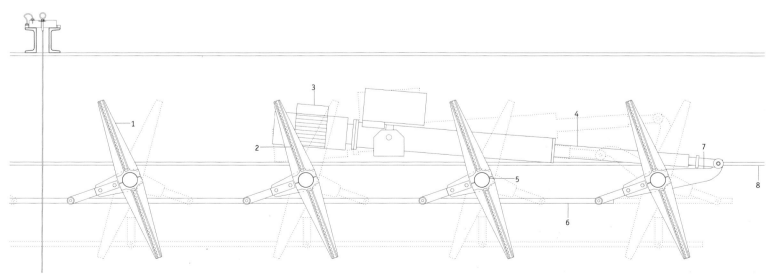

Detail, cross section of control mechanism 70° angle, 1:15

Wind Silos

International Trade Center, Charlotte, North Carolina, USA, 2006
Ned Kahn Studios

For many years the Bank of America had been looking for an artistic means by which to improve the nondescript east elevation of the International Trade Center car park. Ned Kahn's design conceals the parked cars behind a steel construction mounted on columns whose form is inspired by grain silos. The curved forms and the light that plays over them captivated his enthusiasm for the interplay of science and art. Inspired by principles from atmospheric physics, geology, astronomy and kinetics, the design expresses environmental phenomena without representing them figuratively. Instead, by observing this work of art natural processes are made visible.

The 150 m long and 23 m high facade is divided into 15 curved steel-frame segments, each clad with perforated corrugated stainless steel sheeting. 40 % surface perforations allow a certain amount of light and wind to pass through the facade. The furrows in the front face of the corrugations each hold a fixing rail for an almost 5 m high reflective veil that extends along the entire length of the facade. The rails hold 30 000 polished stainless steel discs, each 120 mm in diameter, which are suspended freely from the ends of 115 mm long projecting spacer rods. Together they form a veil that follows the undulations of the silos. Each fixing rail is anchored to the underlying structure and holds 30

such dangling discs which reflect the light, the clouds, the colour of the sky and the entire surroundings.

The overall appearance is in a state of constant flux as the lightweight discs respond to changing lighting conditions and the play of the wind. The boundary between the conspicuous sculpture and its environment blurs. The facade is dematerialised, allowing the observer to experience the phenomenon of the wind in a new way. To a certain extent, the movement is still visible when there is no wind as the discs have no fixed resting position. Only the wind regulates the movement and with it the appearance of the wind silos.

Metal discs moved by the wind

View from behind the facade

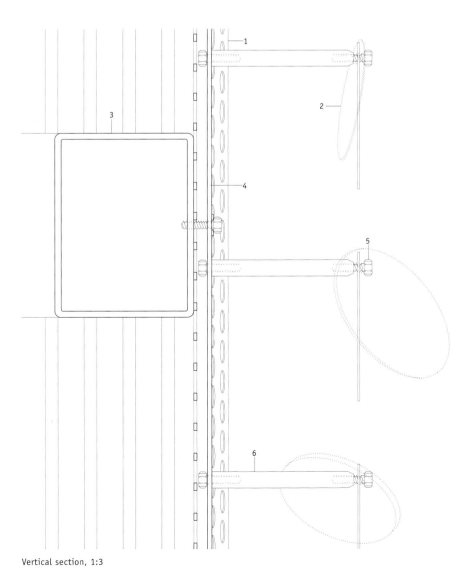

Dimensions veil strip L x H 140 x 4.90 m, Ø 120 mm stainless steel discs, spaced 183 mm apart, radius of movement 360°   **Number** 30 000 stainless steel discs

1 Corrugated stainless steel sheeting, 40 % perforated
2 Stainless steel discs, Ø 120 mm
3 Curved hollow profile, steel, 160 x 120 mm
4 Fixing rail, aluminium U-section, 50 x 13 mm
5 Hexagon screw, stainless steel, Ø 6 mm
6 Spacer rod, stainless steel, l = 115 mm, Ø 13 mm

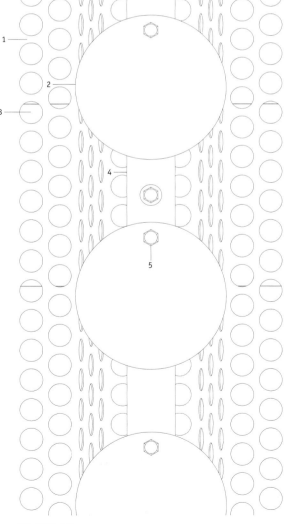

Vertical section, 1:3

Elevation, 1:3

Swivel

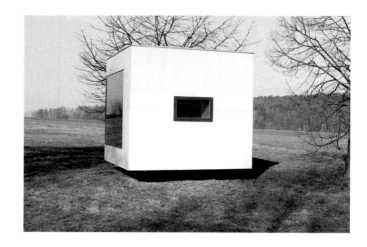

◉ Rotatable Housing Cube

Dipperz, D, 1996
Sturm und Wartzeck Architekten

The rotatable housing cube represents the first stage of a housing project in which the individual living functions are to be housed in several such cubes. The idea is that a number of separate cubes are positioned near to one another and that the resident leaves one cube to enter the next. Accordingly, the natural surroundings are used as circulation space and become an active part of the living environment.

A further key aspect of the concept is the ability to rotate each cube manually as desired according to the position of the sun. This is made possible by mounting the 3 x 3 m cubes on turntables set into the concrete foundation. Steel I-beams are welded to the top surface of the 1 m diameter turntables – a prefabricated element made for articulated lorries – which bear the floor slab of the housing cube. The remainder of the cube is a timber-frame construction.

The triple low-energy glazing ensures maximum solar gain in winter and the 6 m² of photovoltaic panels on the roof supply each cube with electrical power. Although virtually self-sufficient, a supplementary mains electricity connection in the centre of the concrete foundation covers any additional energy required.

The interior of the prototype is designed so that concealed folding elements can be pulled out as required. Wall flaps and floor panels can be folded down or pulled out for use as a table, or slid to one side to reveal a bed.

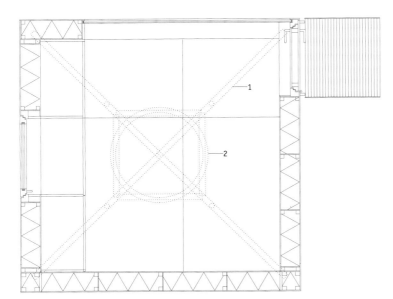

Dimensions 2980 mm edge length of cube, Ø 1050 mm turntable **Drive** manual

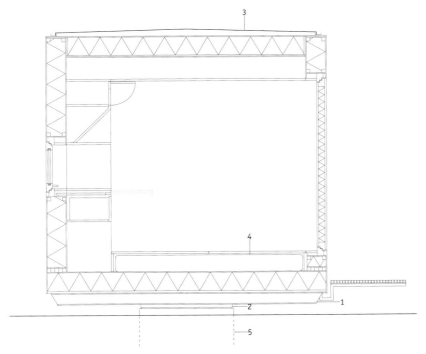

Section, 1:40

1 Steel I-beam, Ø 120 mm
2 Precision turntable, ball-bearing-mounted,
   external Ø 1050 mm
3 Photovoltaic panels, 6 m²
4 Bed beneath folding panel
5 Concrete foundation, annular formwork,
   external Ø 1151 mm
6 Steel flange ring, 8 mm (height 42 mm)
7 Lubricating nipple for ball bearings
8 Steel roller bearings, Ø 13 mm

Rotate

Floor plan, 1:40

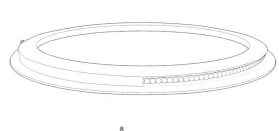

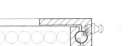

Section through precision turntable with ball bearings, 1:4

Council House 2

Melbourne, AUS, 2006
DesignInc

The City of Melbourne aims to achieve zero CO_2 emissions for the municipality by 2020. A major contribution to this strategy is the reduction of CO_2 emissions by commercial buildings by 50 %.

Council House 2 was planned as a low-energy residential scheme with a view to providing a working example for the local development market. In addition to maximising the use of passive energy, utilising solar and photovoltaic panels, and an energy-efficient construction, particular attention was paid to using building materials that conserve resources.

All concrete and timber elements, for example, are recycled materials.

The air handling system cools fresh air using so-called "shower towers". Water is used to cool the building materials which in turn chill the air used to condition the building. Exhaust air is extracted through large exhaust-air chimneys with turbines on the roof.

Six wind turbines on the north edge of the roof generate electricity during the day using the chimney effect. Warm air rises up the chimneys causing

the large turbine blades to turn. This creates negative pressure in the ventilation system causing fresh air to be drawn in through air intakes on the south side of the roof.

The Savonius wind turbines are connected by a rotating shaft to a generator made out of a Fisher & Paykel washing machine motor that generates energy at around 100 revolutions per minute. The large turbine buckets are additionally driven by the wind. At night they contribute to ensuring a continuous supply of fresh air in the building.

North elevation

Wind turbines for night-time air exchange; during the day they generate electricity

Dimensions H 4 m, Ø 3 m   **Number** 6 turbines   **Drive** wind, air rising out of building

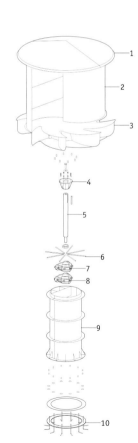

1 Conical cover
2 Turbine vanes
3 Turbine buckets
4 Connecting piece
5 Rotating shaft, Ø 140 mm
6 Stiffening elements
7 Main rotary bearing
8 Auxiliary rotary bearing
9 Cylindrical sleeve, Ø 950
10 Base anchor bolts

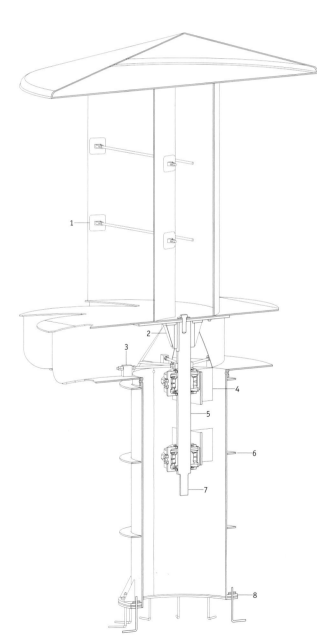

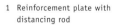

1 Reinforcement plate with
  distancing rod
2 Connecting piece
3 Stiffening elements
4 Positioning fins for rotary
  bearing
5 Rotating shaft, Ø 140 mm
6 Reinforcement ring
7 Connector piece for
  generator
8 Base anchor bolts

Rotate

Exploded isometric (not to scale)

Sectional perspective (not to scale)

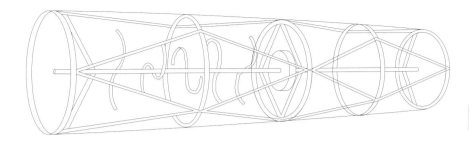

◎ Lakefront Supportive Housing

Chicago, Illinois, USA, 2004
Murphy/Jahn Architects

Lakefront Housing was built for Mercy Housing, an institution which develops, promotes and finances projects that support families and the elderly, disabled, ill or homeless. A particular requirement of this project was to employ environmentally-friendly building materials and implement a new energy concept developed together with Transsolar ClimateEngineering. The top four floors of Lakefront Housing contain 96 residential units ranging from 25 to 28 m² in size, each with its own kitchen and bathroom.

The communal areas are located on the ground floor. Recycled and recyclable building materials were used for sustainability. The energy concept includes 48 hot water collectors, rain water utilisation and grey water reuse. On the roof, eight horizontal wind turbines, developed by Aerotecture International Inc., provide enough electricity for the entire building. The orientation of the building, whose long side faces southwest, the primary wind direction, and whose short side faces northeast, the secondary

wind direction, offers optimal conditions for utilising wind turbine energy. The 2 m high turbines, each mounted in a housing with a diameter of 1.50 m, are all the same size and arranged end-to-end along the building's axis. The rotors, with a diameter of 1.40 m and a wind area of 4 m², generate approximately 1500 watts at a wind speed of 65 km/h. A three-phase rotary generator transforms the alternating current from a pair of turbines into direct current.

The complex structure of the wind turbines with numerous bracing struts

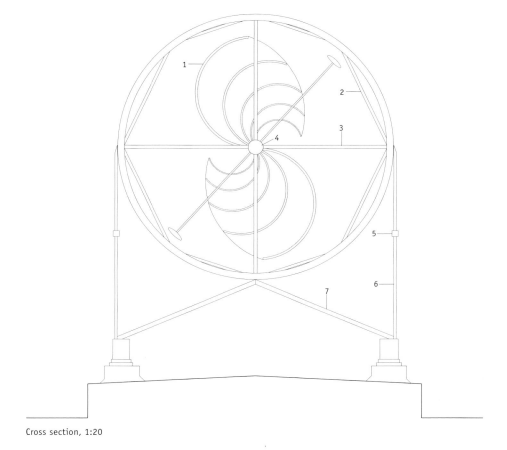

Dimensions Ø 1.50 m housing   **Number** 8 pairs of turbines   **Weight** 39 kg per rotor   **Wind surface area** 4 m² per turbine

Cross section, 1:20

The rotors are covered with polycarbonate panels

1   Rotor, polycarbonate panel covering
2   Space frame members, Ø 20 mm
3   Mounting for fixing rotating shaft to the frame
4   Turbine shaft, Ø 75 mm
5   Horizontal connecting rods between the columns
6   Frame assembly for rooftop installation
7   Support leg bracing

Rotate

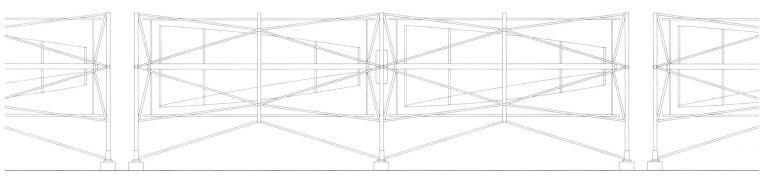

Longitudinal section, 1:50

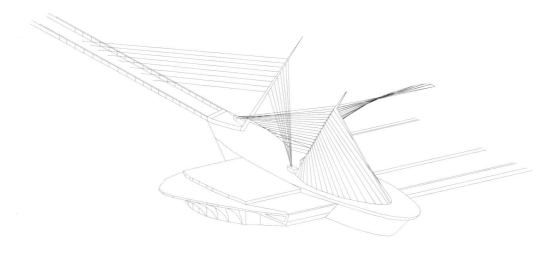

Quadracci Pavilion

Milwaukee, Wisconsin, USA, 2001
Santiago Calatrava

Commissioned to conceive a new attraction for visitors to the Milwaukee Art Museum, the Spanish architect Santiago Calatrava designed a sail construction situated on the banks of Lake Michigan. Calatrava's Quadracci Pavilion, which resembles a flying bird, came out as the winning entry in a competition organised by the trustees of the Art Museum which attracted designs from 77 architects.

The 27 m high steel and reinforced concrete construction contains the new entrance hall for the museum. Depending on the requirements for the exhibition area, the "brise soleils wings" weighing 115 tonnes are opened or closed. If wind speeds should exceed 37 km/h, a computer-controlled system intervenes and the wings are closed automatically. The 36 steel elements vary in length between 8 and 32 m and take 3½ minutes to open and close. With a wingspan of 66 m, the imposing sail-like construction is wider than a Boeing 747.

Seventeen steel frames, varying in length between 8 and 30 m, are arranged parallel to one another around an oval ring beam, the space between them spanned by 236 different-sized panes of glass. The framework meets at the top along the central axis where the steel columns intersect at an angle of 48.36°. Arranged symmetrically on either side of this axis are rotating tubular steel elements to which the wings are fixed. Each rotating steel out-rigger is linked to its neighbour by a distancing piece so that a fluid motion results. The overall impression, however, is that each wing opens independently of the other. The wings are raised by 22 hydraulic pistons arranged in slightly different starting positions so that the elements turn 90°. This spectacular construction allows light to spill into the foyer during the day. At night, lights integrated beneath the ring beam illuminate the foyer and cause the entire construction, when seen from outside, to light up like an oversized "shining lantern".

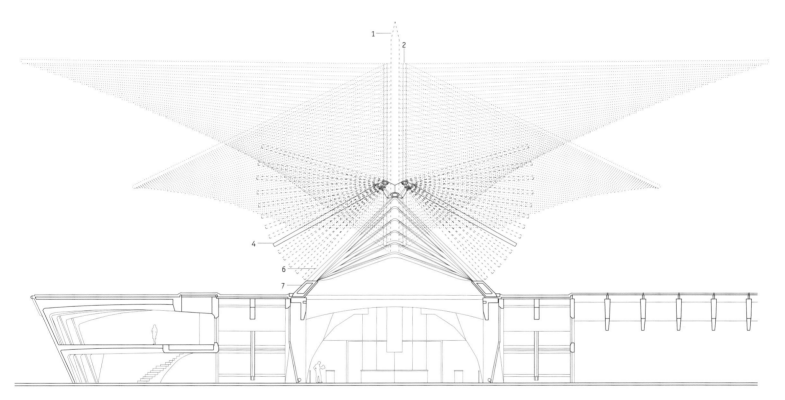

0:00   1:45   3:30   min:sec

Dimensions 66 m wingspan, 8 to 32 m steel lamella length   **Number** 2 wings, 36 lamellae each   **Weight** 115 t wing construction   **Drive** 2 x 11 hydraulic pistons

Section, 1:333

1 Steel pylon, Ø 635 mm, 13 mm thick
2 Rotating tubular steel element
3 Hydraulic piston
4 4 steel flats welded to a hollow section, reinforced internally, 330 mm

5 Connecting rod, steel
6 Steel frame of the glass facade
7 Ring beam, reinforced concrete
8 Steel disc welded to rotating steel tube

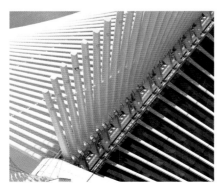

Hydraulic cylinders connected in series

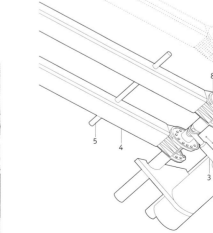

Detail of wing connection and hydraulic piston

Flap

Leaf Chapel

Kobuchizawa, J, 2004
Klein Dytham architecture

The Risonare Hotel Resort lies at the southern foot of the Japanese Alps in Kobuchizawa in the prefecture of Yamanashi, with a view of Mount Fuji and the Yatsugatuke peaks. The hotel is arranged like an Italian village. The Klein Dytham architecture practice was commissioned to build a wedding chapel. The design idea revolves around two leaves which have seemingly fluttered to the ground. One of the leaves is made of steel and glass and leans against an inclined slope to the rear which contains subterranean ancillary rooms and a separate access to the

chapel. The pattern of the structural members reminds one of the veins of a leaf.
The metaphoric associations continue in the second, movable, 15 m wide leaf. The twin-skin steel construction with convex steel profiles concealed between the two, is perforated with 4700 holes. Each hole holds an acrylic lens, scattering a decorative pattern of spots of light across the floor and facade that is reminiscent of a lace veil.
The ceremony begins within the enclosed chapel. At the moment when the groom lifts the bride's veil,

the "steel veil" of the chapel rises, revealing a view of the garden. After the guests leave the chapel and head into the garden, the chapel closes in readiness for the next wedding party.
The steel veil weighs eleven tonnes and is raised by a lever mechanism powered by two hydraulic rams arranged beneath the vertex of the chapel. The roof can be raised in 38 seconds and lowered in 45 seconds. Two infrared sensors and safety switches must be operated by four people simultaneously to raise the roof through an angle of 45°.

The chapel opens during the wedding ceremony

0:00   0:13   0:25   0:38   min:sec

Dimensions Ø 15 m **Weight** 11 t movable parts **Drive** Lever mechanism with 2 hydraulic rams **Movement radius** 45°

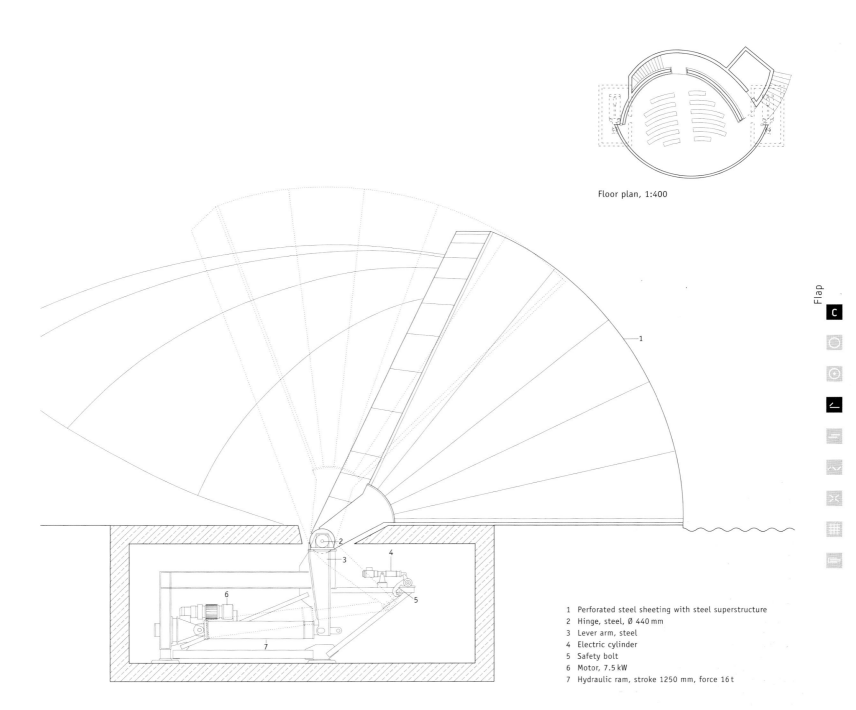

Floor plan, 1:400

Flap

C

1 Perforated steel sheeting with steel superstructure
2 Hinge, steel, Ø 440 mm
3 Lever arm, steel
4 Electric cylinder
5 Safety bolt
6 Motor, 7.5 kW
7 Hydraulic ram, stroke 1250 mm, force 16 t

Dome drive mechanism, 1:75

Palatinate Cellar

St. Gallen, CH, 1999
Santiago Calatrava

For the redesign of the vaulted cellars under the former monastery, the city and canton of St. Gallen selected the architect Santiago Calatrava. The Pfalz (the palace) had originally been a monastery before becoming the seat of local government for the canton. The vast cellar lies beneath the central part of the east wing of the historic building. After the redesign and conversion, the cellar now houses the city's conference centre with space for up to 300 people to attend events of all kinds. Its resemblance to a conch lends the subterranean room its

unusual character and simultaneously underlines Calatrava's architectural language.
The cellar is reached from the public square in front of the Pfalz. What makes the entrance special is the fact that when closed it drops to the floor of the square and is barely visible. When the arched opening of the entrance rises, a ramp becomes visible that leads underground covered by an elongated metal vault. As the ramp descends to the cellar, the width of the passage narrows from 3.10 m at the top to 2.00 m at the entrance to the cellar and has a

maximum headroom of 3.15 m along its inclined length. The metal construction consists of 24 parallel steel hollow-section profiles that are fixed with a hinged joint to the entrance archway. As soon as the arch tilts back and rises, the individual lamellae fan out to form the roof. The steel lamellae converge to a single axis at the far end. This simple idea of a fanning construction lends the Pfalzkeller its particular charm and leads the visitors into the subterranean chambers of the original monastery building.

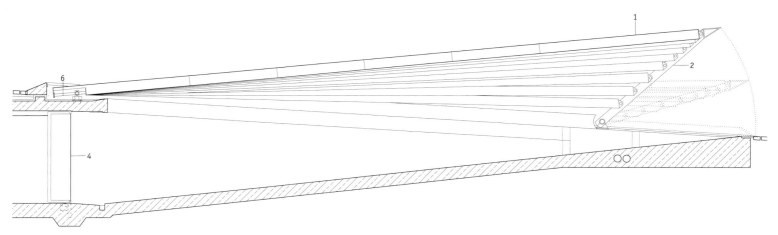

Longitudinal section, 1:133

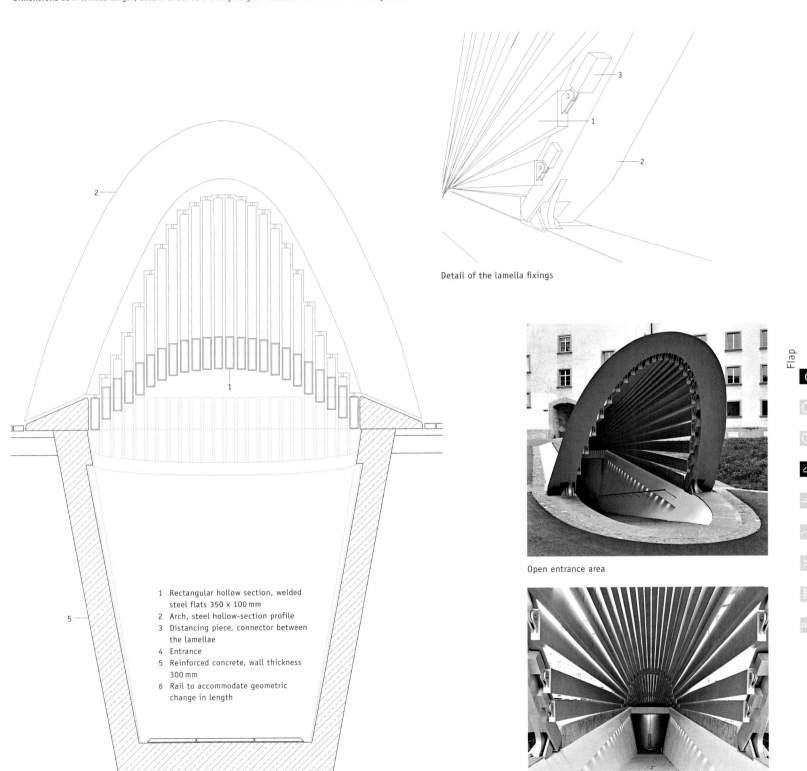

0:00   0:45   1:30   min:sec

Dimensions 22 m lamella length, 3.15 m entrance archway height   **Number** 24 lamellae   **Drive** hydraulic

Detail of the lamella fixings

1 Rectangular hollow section, welded
   steel flats 350 x 100 mm
2 Arch, steel hollow-section profile
3 Distancing piece, connector between
   the lamellae
4 Entrance
5 Reinforced concrete, wall thickness
   300 mm
6 Rail to accommodate geometric
   change in length

Cross section, 1:40

Open entrance area

Arch formed by steel lamellae

Flap

C

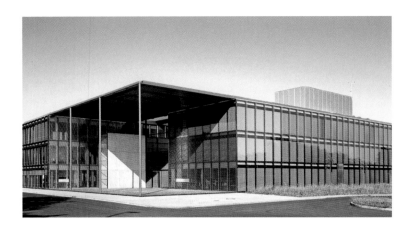

BRAUN Headquarters

Kronberg im Taunus, D, 1999
schneider+schumacher architekten

The design of the building reflects the high quality of products and excellence in industrial design for which the client is known.

The rooms inside the elongated rectangular volume of the three-storey U-shaped building are wrapped around a central covered atrium. Underlining the openness and transparency of the building, this central space can be used for exhibitions and events and also serves as a thermal buffer zone between indoors and outdoors, regulated by motor-driven, air-filled membrane cushions in the roof.

With the exception of the entrance area, the external face of the building consists of a dual-skin facade that is able to react to different weather conditions. The storey-high elements function in a similar way to historical box-windows, preventing solar gain in summer and heat loss in winter as well as reducing traffic noise from the busy road outside. The outer layer is centrally controlled, each pane opened by two motor-driven chain actuators – three at the corners where the wind loads are higher – concealed in the underlying frame. The panels of toughened safety glass are held at only four points creating an even surface to the facade that, as the windows gently open, changes its appearance dynamically, varying according to the changing angle of the individual panes.

The inner windows are double-glazed insulating units that can be opened for cleaning. A narrow opaque room-high window vent alongside each window allows the otherwise airtight window unit to ventilate the room. When a user opens the insulated vent in winter, the respective outer pane opens automatically, closing again after a few minutes. Thermostats in the cavity between the panes regulate the opening and closing mechanism in such cases. For safety reasons, and to reduce noise, the windows open at the relatively slow speed of 9 mm/s.

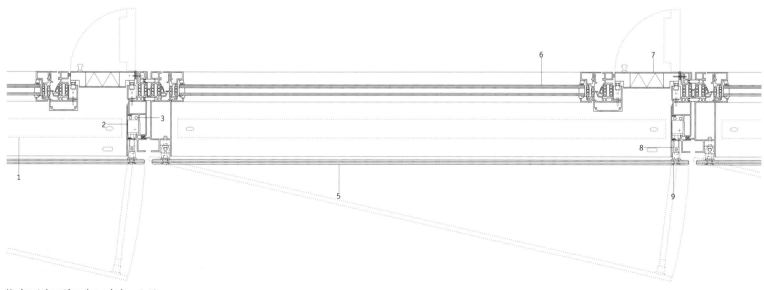

Horizontal section, box window, 1:10

0:00   0:20   0:40   min:sec

Dimensions W x H 1450 x 3440 mm box window, opening angle 13.3°, opening width 300 mm   **Speed** 9 mm/s   **Drive** 2 or 3 24 V motor-driven chain actuators per element

1 External blinds, controlled individually and centrally
2 Motor-driven chain actuator, tandem, W x H x D 518 x 28 x 42 mm, operating voltage 24 V, compressive force 150 N, tensile force 225 N, tensile holding capacity 3000 N
3 Control mechanism, concealed in frame
4 Thermostat
5 Fully-glazed sash, toughened glass 12 mm, point supported, W x H 440 x 3440 mm
6 Cleaning sash, laminated safety glass, insulating glazing
7 Ventilation flap, insulated, magnetic closing mechanism
8 Chain head with stainless steel, chain length between motor housing and cotter pin hole max. 339 mm
9 Cotter pin hole, bolt M10

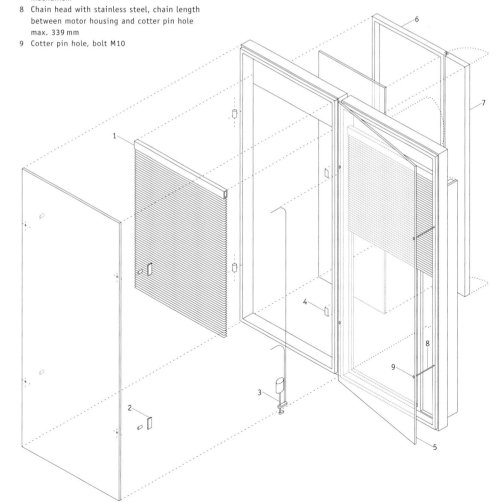

Exploded axonometric, box window element

Closed uniform glass facade

Feathered appearance of facade with deployed sashes

Flap

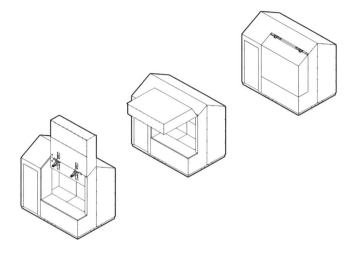

←

m.poli Kiosk

Madrid, E, 2006
Brut Deluxe

At first sight, these miniature houses seem rather unspectacular, but on closer inspection one discovers just how ingenious these "monopoly houses" really are.

The idea of the m.poli kiosk is, indeed, inspired by the well-known board game. As with the game itself, maximum effect is best achieved in reality by placing not just one but a collection of several kiosks in the right location. In combination, a group of individual miniature houses creates a small townscape – a micro-city.

In December 2006, one hundred such kiosks were installed around Madrid to showcase the handicrafts of local craftsmen and women. What makes both the concept as well as the construction special is the hydraulically-operated flap that can be opened outwards by up to 180°, revealing, or closing to conceal, the contents within.

The steel flap measures 1.96 x 1.75 x 0.50 m and is powered by four hydraulic cylinders activated by a push-button inside the kiosk. For safety reasons, the element moves only when the button is pressed

and held down. An acoustic warning also sounds to indicate that the flap is in the process of opening or closing.

The flap can be locked in three different positions, allowing the appearance of the kiosk to be varied. When closed, one sees only the clear contours of a house with pitched roof; at an angle of 90°, one sees a typical kiosk; and at an angle of 180° the house acquires an oversized chimney. The flap also serves as a sign advertising the contents, and is backlit at night.

Kiosks in different locations

0:00   0:30   1:00   min:sec

Dimensions W x H x D 1.96 x 1.75 x 0.50 m movable element   **Weight** 380 kg per flap   **Drive** 4 hydraulic cylinders

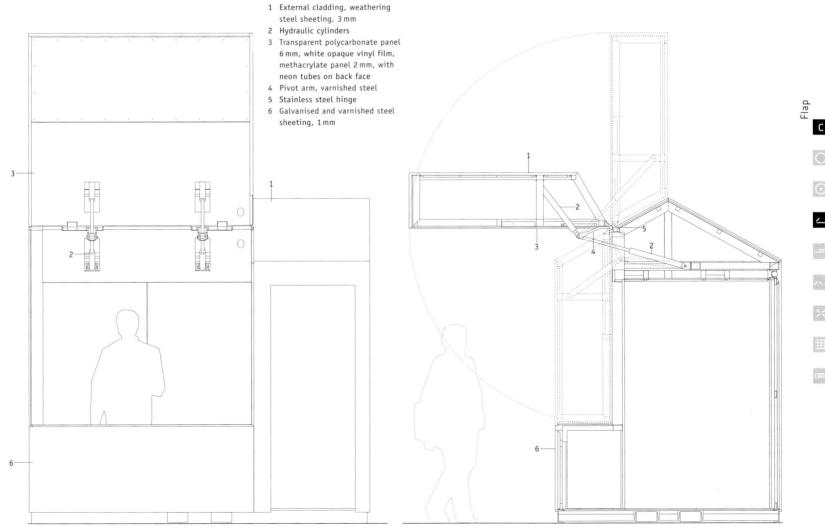

1 External cladding, weathering
   steel sheeting, 3 mm
2 Hydraulic cylinders
3 Transparent polycarbonate panel
   6 mm, white opaque vinyl film,
   methacrylate panel 2 mm, with
   neon tubes on back face
4 Pivot arm, varnished steel
5 Stainless steel hinge
6 Galvanised and varnished steel
   sheeting, 1 mm

Front elevation, 1:33

Cross section, 1:33

Flap

Shop Entrance

Bamberg, D, 2007
Nickel und Wachter Architekten

As part of the redesign of a well-known traditional shop in a historic listed building in Bamberg, the entrance situation needed to be improved in a way that harmonised with the existing building. In a first step, a pillar directly adjoining the building was removed that cramped the entrance to the shop. While the wrought-iron lattice gate to the courtyard could be retained, the fencing near the entrance next to the pavement was removed and relocated further back from the street so that it separates the entrance from the private courtyard to the rear. In front of the entrance, a raised sandstone plinth, a detail typical of the region, was created to provide a transitional space between the building and public street.

To facilitate entrance to the building itself, a metal portal encasement for the entrance was designed. A mobile construction element makes it possible to fold out the entrance stairs and a small canopy every morning, and to retract these again in the evening when the shop closes. In a closed position, this protects against vandalism and break-ins while also affording greater space to access the courtyard and rearward buildings. In summer the steps can be fitted with wooden treads, in winter with non-slip metal grating.

The moving parts of the entrance casing are driven by a hand-operated crank handle that turns a ball-bearing-mounted steel crankshaft. A chain drive mechanism provides sufficient force to lower the stairs. Operating the crank handle causes the steps and canopy to open outwards simultaneously. They are stabilised by a gas-pressurised shock absorber. The winding mechanism is entirely concealed within the sheet steel side casing. To secure the construction in the open position, the canopy is locked with a retaining bolt.

Canopy and stairs are retracted

Dimensions W x H x D 1.25 x 2.50 x 0.30 m **Weight** 350 kg **Drive** chain with hand-operated crank handle

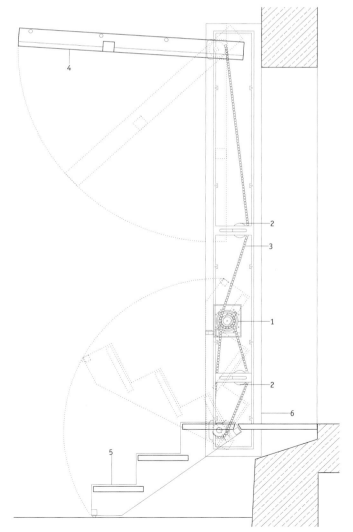

Detail, drive mechanism, 1:20

1 Sprocket wheel on ball-bearing-mounted crankshaft
2 Tensioning roller
3 Drive chain
4 Canopy, hinged; frame and upper surface: sheet steel; lower surface: timber battens
5 Stairs, hinged, natural wood treads
6 Sheet steel encasement

Flap

House No 19

Utrecht, NL, 2003
Korteknie Stuhlmacher Architecten with
Bik Van der Pol

House No 19 is an initiative by the City of Utrecht's art organisation "Beyond" that offers a place for international artists to live and work in Utrecht. The intention is that the "artists in residence" observe and respond to the transformations resulting from the rapid growth of the new urban area Leidsche Rijn, which will add 30 000 new dwellings to the city. The artist's atelier "House No 19" is one of several projects that examine the effect of the new urban development. It serves as a temporary residence and atelier for artists and from time to time as a base for cultural interventions and events. The 18 x 4 x 3.20 m building was developed in collabora-tion with the artists Bik Van der Pol and is positioned between the Dutch landscape of canals and meadows and the encroaching city. The elongated interior heightens this contrast by providing strongly directional views onto the surroundings.

This practical and inexpensive working and living space can be divided into several internal and external areas. A roof terrace can be accessed by a stepladder.

The sturdy construction of thick laminated timber boards stiffened with two steel frames allows the box to be transported in one piece to a new location. The introverted character of the house can be changed entirely by opening the six window shutters and three folding flaps so that its interior becomes an exhibition area for the city and its residents.

The timber panel flaps are connected by a system of ceiling-mounted pulleys and steel cables to a hand crank. It takes about two minutes to lower the flaps, after which the steel cable can be released and reeled in completely with the hand crank. The mechanism and construction of the moving parts are made of commercially available steel elements and not concealed in any way.

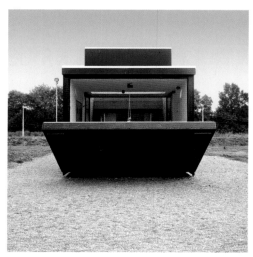

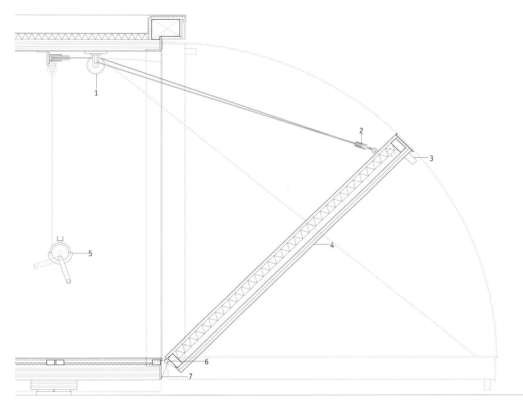

0:00   0:40   1:20   2:00   min:sec

Dimensions W x H 4 x 3.50 m per door flap   **Number** 4 door flaps   **Drive** manually-operated hand crank   **Angle of rotation** 90° (max. 110°)

Vertical section, 1:33

1 Fixed ceiling-mounted pulley, steel,
   Ø 160 mm, two or three per flap
2 Detachable pulley with crane hook,
   detachable from the flap
3 Flap end stand, two mounted on the
   outside top edge of each flap
4 Fold-down flap, 26 mm three-ply solid
   timber panel with steel stiffening frame
   60 x 120 mm
5 Crank with mechanical brake mechanism,
   hand-operated
6 Hinge, two per door flap, steel, welded
   to the base of the steel frame
7 L-section steel frame as stiffening frame
   for transit

Flap

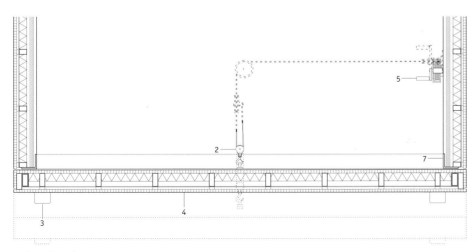

Horizontal section, 1:33

The cable routing is visible in the interior

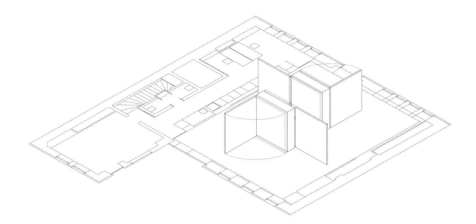

BDA Wechselraum Gallery

Stuttgart, D, 2005
Bottega + Ehrhardt Architekten

To offer its members a new central venue, the Baden Württemberg section of the Association of German Architects (BDA) redeveloped part of the Zeppelin Careé shopping and hotel complex near to Stuttgart Central Station. The ground floor of the building was originally a wine bar but had been used as a bank archive prior to the conversion. After removing the archive, the architects were faced with the disparate spaces of a wine bar. The former bar area was cramped by two massive sections of wall that supported the floors above. The stipulations of the conservation authorities and budget constraints gave rise to the idea of a continuous band around the perimeter of the space. This band serves as a kind of wallpaper behind which everything not related to the gallery can be concealed. A clearly perceptible notch at the top and bottom of the wall reinforces the formal expression of the band. The band is not interrupted by windows or openings. These are instead concealed behind flush-mounted folding or sliding sections which, when opened, allow a view outside or passage into an adjacent space. Two equal-sized timber partitions, one pivoting, one sliding, have been attached to each of the two wall sections in the centre of the space. These partitions can be folded or slid out to divide the room into different sections, lending the exhibition space its name – the *Wechselraum* (changing space). The office, kitchenette and toilet are located in an adjoining space hidden behind a sliding element and can be separated off and hired out as required.

Wall panels divide the *Wechselraum*, sliding and pivoting elements temporarily change its appearance

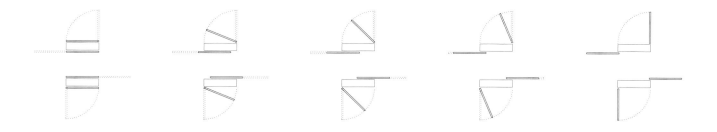

Dimensions W x H x D 2.61 x 2.33 x 0.10 m each pivoting/sliding door   **Number** 2 pivoting and 2 sliding doors   **Drive** manual

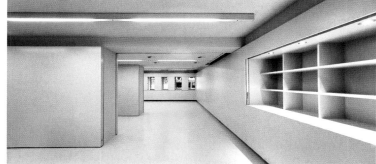

Openings and niches in a band along the wall

1 Suspended ceiling
2 Track, 60 x 60 mm
3 Roller assembly
4 Steel angle section,
   150 x 88 x 8 mm, l = 45 mm
5 Ball bearing
6 Pivoting door, MDF,
   261 x 233 x 10 cm
7 Sliding door, MDF,
   261 x 233 x 10 cm
8 Steel plate with pin,
   30 x 100 x 8 mm, l = 150 mm
9 Flush retaining bolt,
   45 x 125 x 3 mm
10 Washer, Ø 40 mm
11 Floor guide

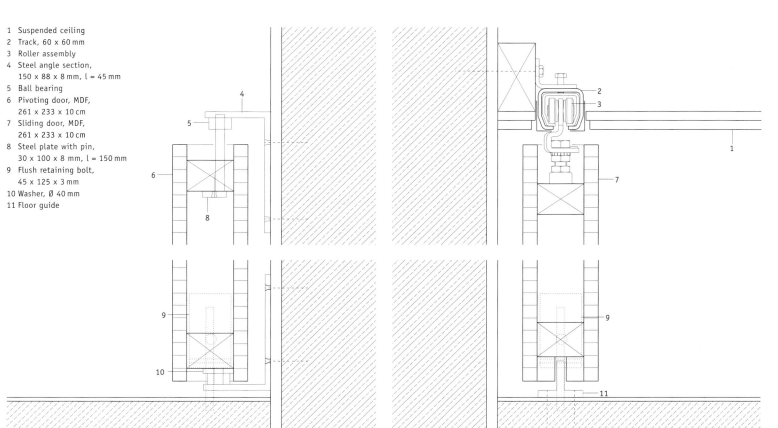

Pivoting door, 1:5

Sliding door, 1:5

Flap

C

EWE Arena

Oldenburg, D, 2005
asp Architekten Stuttgart, Arat – Siegel – Schust

The EWE Arena is part of the Weser-Ems-Halle trade fair and events complex in Oldenburg in North Germany. It is a landmark building in the urban landscape, visible from far and wide, and can be seen on arrival at the railway station. Its serves primarily as the home ground for Oldenburg's national league basketball and handball teams and is also used as a concert hall and as spillover floor space for trade fairs. Visitors are led through a circular hall directly to the foyer at the main entrance. From here two staircases lead to the fully-glazed spectator area that runs around the perimeter of the building. A large mobile sunscreen is mounted externally in front of the glazed facade. Measuring 36 x 7.60 m, the screen moves around the building, following the position of the sun. The construction travels along a stainless steel track mounted on the upper ring of the facade. Each segment has one powered roller and one freewheeling roller. Side-mounted pinch rollers ensure that the segments stay in the track.

The upper ring of the facade supports the entire weight of the construction while the lower ring resists lateral wind loads. A second retaining track on the lower ring holds the segments in place.

The sunscreen can travel 200° around the perimeter of the building and consists of 200 m² of photovoltaic cells which generate 27 200 kWh of energy per year.

The sunscreen travels along a cantilevering precast concrete ring

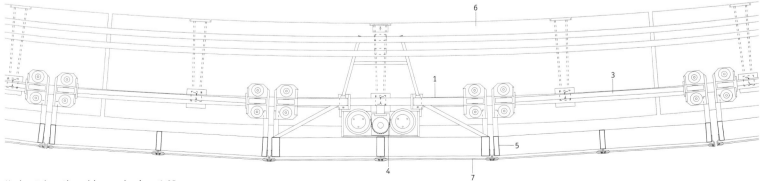

0:00   2:30   5:00   7:30   10:00   h:min

Dimensions W x H 36 x 7.60 m   **Number** 18 segments, 72 photovoltaic modules   **Weight** 28 t   **Drive** electric motor

Four photovoltaic modules per segment

1 Track, 180 x 100 x 5 mm
2 Post and rail facade
3 Track, 120 x 60 x 5 mm
4 Belt drive
5 Frame segment, aluminium
   hollow-section profile,
   200 x 50 x 4 mm
6 Precast concrete element,
   5.50 x 1.10 x 0.14 m
7 Photovoltaic modules

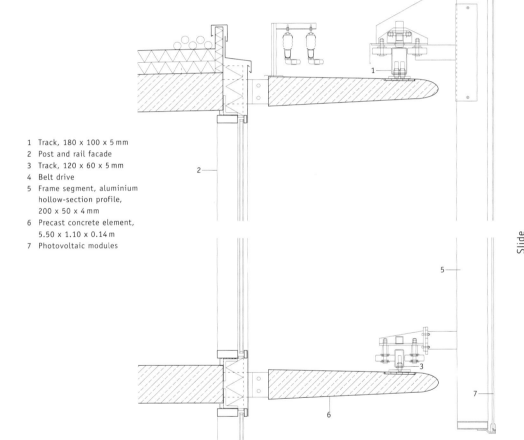

Vertical section, 1:25

Slide

C

Horizontal section, drive mechanism, 1:25

Meridian Buildings, Astrophysical Institute

Potsdam, D, 2004
Joachim Kleine Allekotte Architekten

A grant from the EU Regional Development Fund provided the funding for renovating the Meridian Buildings at the Astrophysical Institute in Potsdam, which were originally designed and realised by the then Chief Architect G. Thür under direction of the City Architect W. Eggert and are now part of the "Prussian Arcadia" World Heritage Site. With the restoration and conversion of the three listed buildings, the renovation of the AIP campus is almost complete.

These special buildings with their characteristic, 4.50 m high half-tunnel vaults date back to 1913 and were erected to house the three meridian circles. Their form is determined entirely by their func-

tion. Two of the meridian housings are connected by a central building that today serves as the institute's media and communications centre. The third freestanding building to the northeast is now used as a museum.

Given the state of disrepair of the buildings prior to renovation, surprisingly only a sixth of the steel and 30 % of the timber needed replacing. As part of the conversion, spaces that were previously unheated were insulated and the previously open observation slits in each of the two connected buildings were glazed. Only the external surfaces of the six sliding half-rounded roof sections needed restoring. Each observation slit can be covered by a pair

of roof sections. Today they serve as sun-shading elements.

The sliding roofs can only be opened by hand. A hemp rope is used to turn a series of rods and pulleys mounted on the long side of the room, which in turn drive an external rack and pinion arrangement that moves the sliding section of the roof. The sliding roof sections travel along rails and can be moved independently of one another. A pedal next to the drive rope releases the brake. Depending on the level of exertion, the roof can be opened or closed in two to three minutes.

Renovated historical drive mechanism

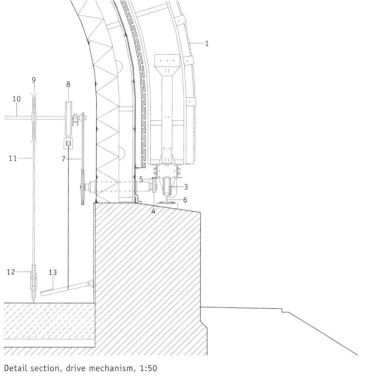

| 0:00 | 1:15 | 2:30 | 3:45 | 5:00 | min:sec |

Dimensions W 2.25 m, radius half-tower 4.50 m   **Number** 2 sliding roof sections per building, 6 altogether   **Drive** manual

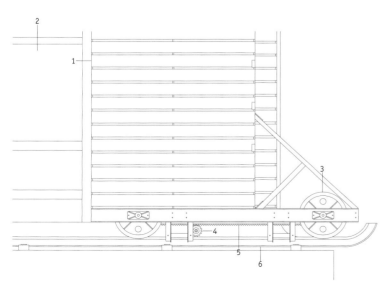

Detail section, drive mechanism, 1:50

1 Larch boarding
2 Glazing over the observation slit
3 Railway wheel, Ø 640 mm
4 Drive pinion, Ø 160 mm
5 Rack
6 Rolled steel vignoles rail
7 Positive clutch drive chain
8 Strap brake with counterweight
9 Traction sheave, Ø 675 mm
10 Driveshaft
11 Hemp rope
12 Pulley block, Ø 280 mm
13 Brake pedal

Elevation, drive mechanism, 1:50

Hand-operated mechanical drive system with hemp rope

Slide

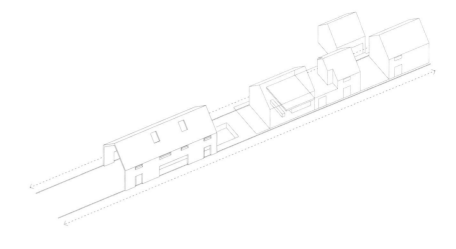

Sliding House

Suffolk, East Anglia, GB, 2009
dRMM Architects

The Sliding House in a village east of Cambridge lies on a slight rise surrounded by open landscape. The volume of the building with an overall length of 28 m consists of three parts – the main building (16 m), a garage (5 m) slightly offset and an annexe (7 m).

The southwest end of the building is a glass and aluminium construction; the remaining sections are timber-frame with larch timber boarding. What makes the building exceptional is a second, sliding sleeve that envelopes the whole ensemble.

Depending on the position of this mobile roof/wall enclosure, the degree of openness or enclosure can be altered. Being also 16 m long, the mobile sleeve covers the pitched roof of the main house, lining up exactly with the gables. When parked in one of the many other positions, a whole range of different spatial situations can be created. The courtyard in front of the garage can become an extra covered parking space. In summer, the sliding roof shades against the sun. In winter, its function is reversed: during the day it is retracted to allow passive solar gain in the glazed section, and returned at night to shield against heat loss.

The 20-tonne travelling second skin consists of a steel frame construction with an insulated and moisture-proofed timber infill. Like the main house, it is also clad with larch timber boarding. The main house and the sleeve share a common 1 x 1 m structural grid so that elements in the facade, such as doors, windows and skylights, line up with the openings in the mobile sleeve when it is parked in different positions.

The mobile sleeve slides along 33 m long railway tracks, resting on 14 steel wheels powered by four 24 V electric motors. The motors can be powered by mains electricity or two 12 V car batteries each, which in future will be charged by photovoltaic solar cells.

The maximum speed of travel is 0.322 km/h (0.2 mph). The roof takes 6 minutes to travel the entire distance.

0:00   3:00   6:00   min:sec

Dimensions L x W x H 16.0 x 5.80 x 7.20 m **Weight** 20 t **Drive** 4 electric motors, 24 V

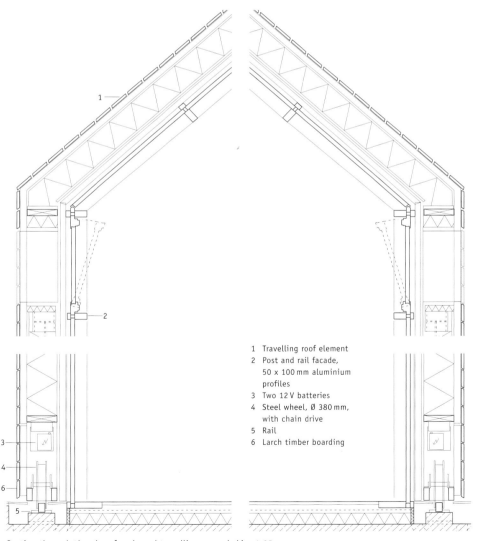

1 Travelling roof element
2 Post and rail facade,
   50 x 100 mm aluminium
   profiles
3 Two 12 V batteries
4 Steel wheel, Ø 380 mm,
   with chain drive
5 Rail
6 Larch timber boarding

Section through the glass facade and travelling second skin, 1:25

Slide

Weekend House

Keremma, Tréflez, F, 2005
Lacaton & Vassal Architectes

The weekend house on the coast of Brittany consists of three buildings, all of the same size and shape, each with a floor area of around 100 m². When the house is occupied, large sections of the facade, up to 7.10 m in length, are slid to one side to enclose a three-sided courtyard. Together they create a screen that shields the outdoor space against the onshore wind from the north and forms a sheltered, south-facing sandy courtyard extending right into parts of the glazed buildings. The sliding sections of the facade and the division of the house into three parts means that it can react to changing usage patterns. In winter, only the space that is actually occupied needs to be heated, but if necessary there is also room to sleep 20 people. The open

structure affords each building a direct connection to the surrounding landscape. The position of the sliding panels determines the relationship between inside and outside.

The panels are slid to one side by hand, either connecting the buildings to one another, or sliding out of the way in front of other fixed sections of the facade. Several sets of rollers on the upper edge of the sliding sections allow the panels to travel along the entire length of a track. The bottom edge of the panels consists of a U-section steel profile that moves over floor-mounted roller bearings fixed at intervals to the foundation with steel angles. Between the buildings, the sliding panels run on a steel frame consisting of a hollow steel rail resting

on HE-A section steel columns, an arrangement which serves as a steel pergola when the panels are not open.

The panels themselves are made of aluminium to minimise their weight. This makes them easier to open and close and reduces the risk of accident, as there is no in-built safety mechanism. This aspect was important for the elderly clients, as the complex is also used by their children and grandchildren.

The buildings themselves have a steel skeleton construction and the supporting steel HE-B beams are left exposed in the interior. Eternit panels form the external cladding to the structural frame and the opaque roof.

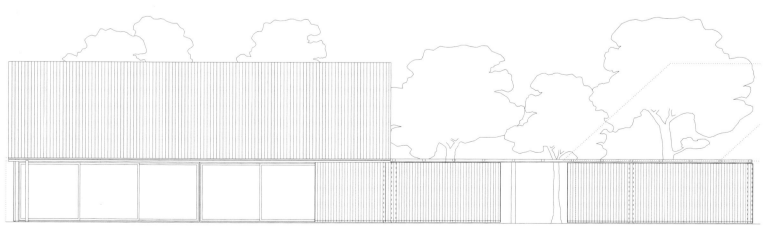

Elevation of the central building, 1:133

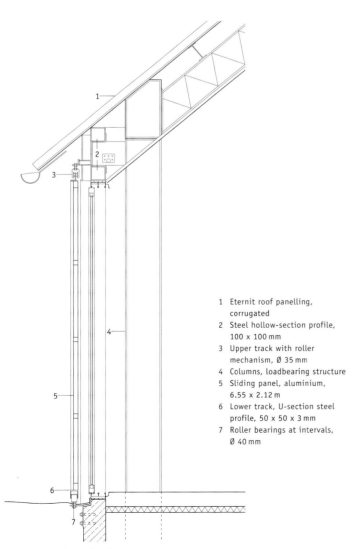

Dimensions L x H 3 – 7.10 m x 2.12 m per element   **Number** 14 sliding facade sections   **Drive** manual

1 Eternit roof panelling, corrugated
2 Steel hollow-section profile, 100 x 100 mm
3 Upper track with roller mechanism, Ø 35 mm
4 Columns, loadbearing structure
5 Sliding panel, aluminium, 6.55 x 2.12 m
6 Lower track, U-section steel profile, 50 x 50 x 3 mm
7 Roller bearings at intervals, Ø 40 mm

Section through the facade, 1:25

The loadbearing structural steel framework

Sliding panels regulate the degree of privacy

Slide

Metro Station Saint-Lazare

Paris, F, 2003
Arte Charpentier Architectes

In front of one of the main railway stations in Paris, the RATP, the public transport agency, wanted a building that signalled above ground their investment below ground. Three existing underground lines intersect with a new fully-automatic metro line. A new street level entrance to the metro station was planned by the Parisian architects Arte Charpentier and Abbès Tahir.

The lenticular shape of the entrance is a product of the combination of a torus and a sphere. Beneath the glass and stainless steel construction, a lift, two escalators and stairs provide access to the ultra-modern station 20 m below street level.

The 108 different-shaped, bidirectionally-curved glass panes rest in a grid of nine transverse and eleven longitudinal ribs which have been welded to an elliptical arch. The slender triangular profiles all lie in the same plane, maximising the amount of incident light in the interior.

At night, two similarly curved stainless steel gates slide together to close the 7.10 m wide entrance, thereby completing the arc of the building's form. The different radii of the upper and lower guide rails allow the 3.50 m high and 5.50 m wide elements to tilt back slightly to fit the bidirectional curvature of the facade. The supporting framework of the gates consists of planar-curved steel tubes with a diameter of 140 mm. Between these span 5 mm wide and 40 mm deep ribs which hold a series of horizontal stainless steel lamellae. Barrel roller bearings at the foot of each element accommodate the 12° change in tilt. Two further roller assemblies and a motorised drive unit are permanently fixed to the foot of the frame. Mounted on plastic-coated steel wheels with ball bearings, they support the vertical load as well as facilitate movement along the rail. Here too, barrel roller bearings accommodate the changing angle of the gate. The gates move at a speed of 4 m/min.

A dead man's switch and safety contact strips on the edges of the gates ensure that the gate stops in a space of 10 mm if obstructed. Electrical as well as mechanical stoppers ensure that the gates do not travel beyond the end of the rails.

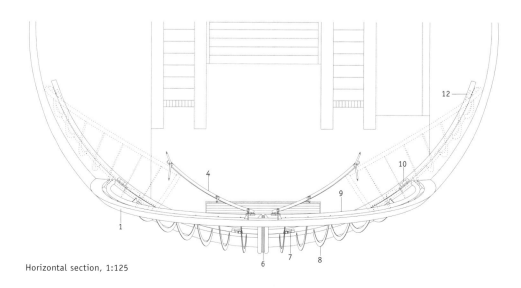

Horizontal section, 1:125

0:20

0:32

0:50

1:06   min:sec

Dimensions W x H 5.50 x 3.50 m per gate   **Weight** 1600 kg per gate   **Horizontal rotation radius** 29°   **Drive** 0.25 kW per motor

1 Arched entrance opening with drainage channels, 7.10 m wide
2 Laminated safety glass with bidirectional curvature
3 Contact roller, barrel bearer
4 Upper guide rail
5 Horizontal stainless steel lamella, matt, 40 x 5 mm
6 Safety contact strips, flex contact
7 Roller assembly with motorised drive unit, 0.25 kW
8 Vertical rib, stainless steel, matt
9 Frame, planar-curved tubular steel profile, Ø 140 mm
10 Roller assembly, wheel Ø 200 mm
11 Elliptical stainless steel channel around the perimeter
12 Lower guide rail for wheels
13 Cable channel for safety contact strips

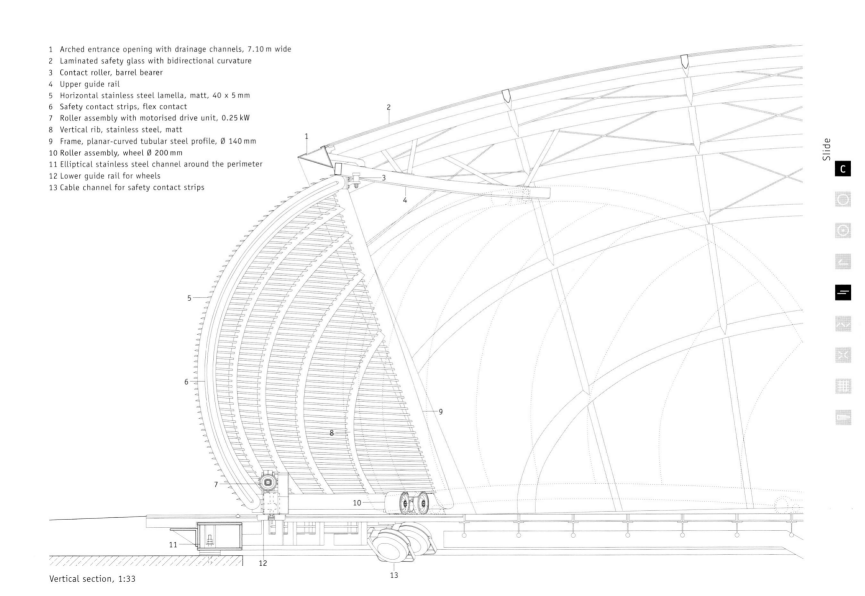

Vertical section, 1:33

Slide

C

Spielbudenplatz

Hamburg, St. Pauli, D, 2006
Consortium Spielbude Fahrbetrieb Hamburg, Lützow 7 Garten- und Landschaftsarchitekten and
Spengler Wiescholek Architekten und Stadtplaner

The Spielbudenplatz is an old historic market square in the heart of Hamburg's St. Pauli quarter. Since the 1960s, several proposals have been made for redeveloping the car park that occupied the site. The aim of the competition initiated in 2004 was to convert it into a multifunctional space for events. The design encloses the square between two mobile stages arranged at each end of the square. The U-shaped volumes of the stages face one another and can be moved towards each other on tracks that run the length of the 300 m long square, allowing a variety of different spatial situations and relation-

ships to be created. Positioned next to each other, they form an enclosed stage space; positioned apart, they enclose a square of a size that depends on how far they are apart.

Each stage has a footprint of 16 x 16 m and is 10 m high. The structural frame is made of closed square-section galvanised steel profiles. The roof of each stage cantilevers forward 12 m, and with a structural depth of only 1 m is particularly slender. The facades of the stage are clad in three layers: behind a metal mesh, which also protects against vandalism, is a layer of translucent glass backlit by LED

modules. The lighting modules can be programmed with animations, and in the evening the stages emit a golden glow from within, revealing the pattern of the underlying structural framework.

Four undercarriages per stage enable the stages to be shifted back and forth along the square along two 210 m long rail tracks. Each set of wheels is powered by an electric motor. Before the stages are moved, they are first hydraulically raised by 15 to 20 cm. This means the wheels do not need to bear the weight of the stage when it is parked and avoids damage to the stage skirting during transit.

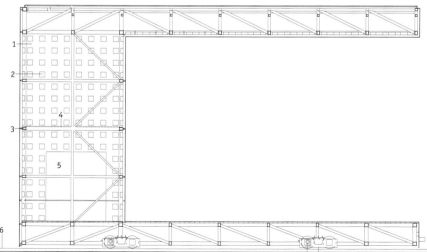

1 Stainless steel mesh
2 LED elements
3 Hollow steel profile, 150 x 150 x 5 mm
4 Platform
5 Control systems
6 Rails
7 Electric motor drive
8 Wheels
9 Transmission

Longitudinal section, 1:150

0:00   0:08   0:16   h:min

Dimensions L x W x H 16 x 16 x 10 m   **Weight** 55 t per stage   **Drive** 4 electric motors per stage   **Travel distance** 210 m

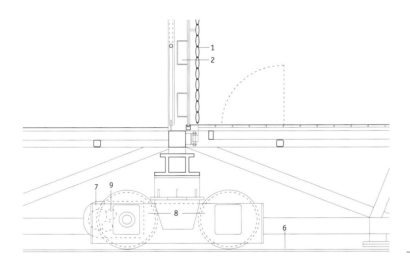

Detail, undercarriage, 1:33

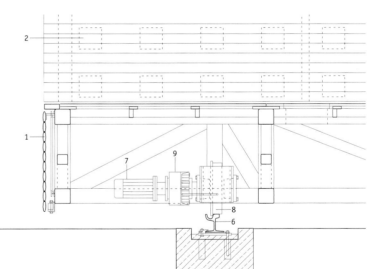

Detail, drive mechanism, 1:33

Slide

C

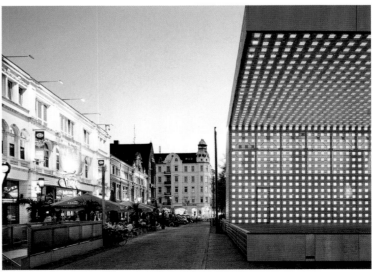

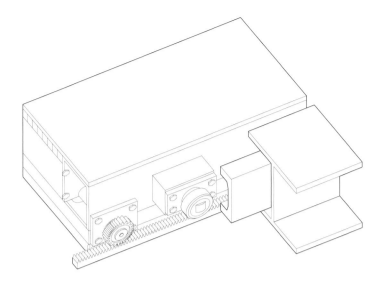

Living Room

Gelnhausen, D, 2005
Seifert.Stoeckmann@formalhaut

The existing building dated back to the 17th century and was an unsightly part of the old town, a conservation area containing the oldest half-timbered house in the state of Hesse. According to the stipulations of the conservation authorities, it was replaced with a building of the same size and external geometry. Artists from different backgrounds were involved in the planning. The architecture is conceived as a system that brings together the different positions of the artists – poets, painters, sculptors, photographers and acoustic artists – and expresses their connection to the building and place.

The ground floor, visible from outside, fulfils the needs of an outdoor space indoors, presenting a stone landscape complete with a large sandstone monolith measuring 4 x 6 x 1.30 m. The interior extends from the ground floor to the roof creating a sense of spaciousness within the small building. The first floor is conceived as a box inserted into this space beneath the gable, with the roof space and fireplace above it. A "thick wall" at the rear contains the tightly-dimensioned service spaces.
When additional space is required, the bedroom can be extended outwards to project like a drawer some 2 m outside the box. A key-operated switch turns on

two 360 V electric motors that set the 24 m² large "drawer" in motion, causing it to travel outwards along its axis on two racks. Automatic switches at the ends of the rails shut off power after the 3-minute journey. The "drawer" rests on six roller bearings, mounted on the rearward edges of the moving element, that travel along C-section guide rails. A lightweight steel frame construction clad with OSB panels minimises the force required to set it in motion.

0:00   1:00   2:00   3:00   min:sec

Dimensions L x W x H 8 x 3 x 2.20 m, max. extension of the drawer 2.64 m   **Weight** 1 t   **Drive** Geared motor 0.12 kW   **Speed** 0.9 m/min

1 Connecting shaft, 20 x 2850 mm
2 Geared motor, 0.12 kW, 7.5 U/min
3 Extended edging piece, 48 mm
4 Spur gear, M 2.50, 25 teeth
5 Winkel combined roller bearing, ø 77 mm
6 C-section guide rail, standard 2-Nb profile
7 Box section, 180 x 100 x 10 mm
8 Toothed rack, M 2.50, 3 m sections
9 Main HE-B 180 wide flange beam

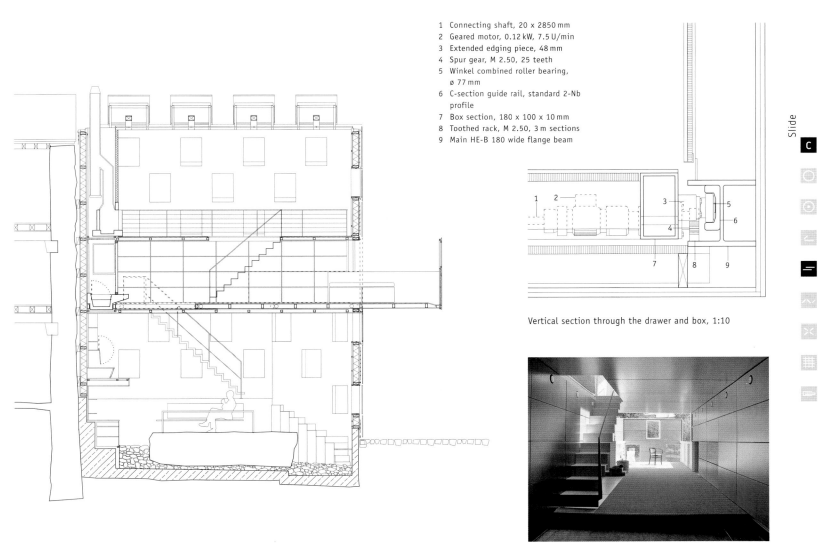

Vertical section through the drawer and box, 1:10

Slide

Vertical section, 1:125

An indoor space becomes an outdoor space

Theresienwiese Service Centre

Munich, D, 2004
Staab Architekten

The Service Centre on the Theresienwiese in Munich houses a police station, a fire station, the Bavarian Red Cross and other services as well as the offices for the Oktoberfest. For several decades until 2003, these had previously been housed in a cluster of containers at the edge of the festival grounds as the historic site had been kept free of buildings for hundreds of years. For this reason, the appearance of the volume of the new building needed to be as discreet as possible, particularly during the months between each Oktoberfest. The facades of the build-

ing play a major part in this. Clad in copper, they will over time acquire a typical green patina, allowing the building to gradually blend more and more into its surroundings.

At the beginning of the Oktoberfest when the building is opened for use, the external appearance of the otherwise closed and monolithic volume changes markedly. Three large gates open vertically upwards, signalling the public entrances far and wide. Each of the rising gates is inscribed with words in large letters that mark the respective entrances:

"Organisers", "First Aid" and "Police". The three rising sections are powered by two synchronously driven electric motors with cable winches that are concealed in an underfloor channel at the base of the gates. Rollers at the sides of each gate section travel along steel channels. The raising mechanism is operated by a key switch with a dead man's control from which the operator has a clear view of his gate. This obviates the need for a photoelectric beam or contact switch.

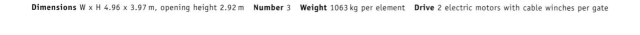

| 0:00 | 0:19 | 0:38 | 0:57 | 1:16 | min:sec |

Dimensions W x H 4.96 x 3.97 m, opening height 2.92 m   **Number** 3   **Weight** 1063 kg per element   **Drive** 2 electric motors with cable winches per gate

1 Overhead pulley, ø 155 mm
2 Hanging bracket in open position
3 Panels with backlit lettering
4 Bottom edge of gate frame in the open position
5 Guide rollers in the open position
6 Steel box profile, 140 x 80 x 6.3 mm
7 Framed door construction, 2 double leaves
8 Hanging bracket for tension cable
9 Perforated copper panel
10 Guide rollers
11 Drain pipe
12 Electric motor with cable winch
13 Steel channel profile, 200 x 100 x 8 mm as lateral guide rails

Slide

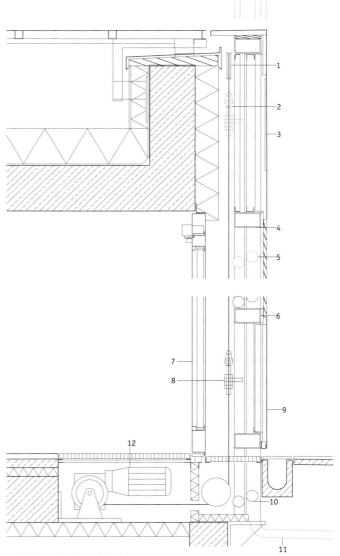

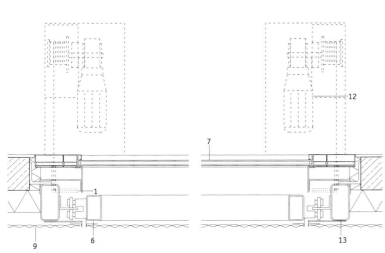

Horizontal section, drive mechanism, 1:20

Vertical section through facade, 1:20

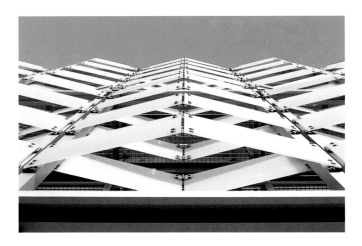

House at the Milsertor

Hall, A, 2008
Arch. Orgler ZT GmbH

The Milsertor Service Centre in the town of Hall in Tyrol occupies a corner site close to the historic city centre and houses a local bank branch as well as several doctors' surgeries. The corners of the building are clad with a system of folding sunscreen elements.

The arrangement of the folding sunscreens picks up the banded pattern of the prefabricated concrete elements of the main facade. Each folding sunscreen is made of 6 mm thick white plexiglass panels that when closed allow diffuse light into the interiors. A total of 1504 elements have been fitted. Each element consists of two panels, connected to one another with a hinge fastened by rubber-mounted point fixings. Altogether, 18 different individually adjustable sections of the facade have been fitted with sunscreens, each with 25 elements.

The construction is operated by a specially developed system of connecting rods. Two guide rails, one at the top of each section and one at the bottom, contain a gliding rod that is controlled by a toothed belt. Half of the vertical posts are mobile and slide back and forth with the gliding rod; the other half remain stationary and are fixed to the guide rail. The motor is located at the end of the lower guide rail adjacent to the solid construction of the central section of the building. A bevel gear system drives a synchroniser shaft that connects the upper and lower guide rails. This is necessary to ensure even parallel movement of both upper and lower gliding rods so that the vertical posts do not snag or twist.

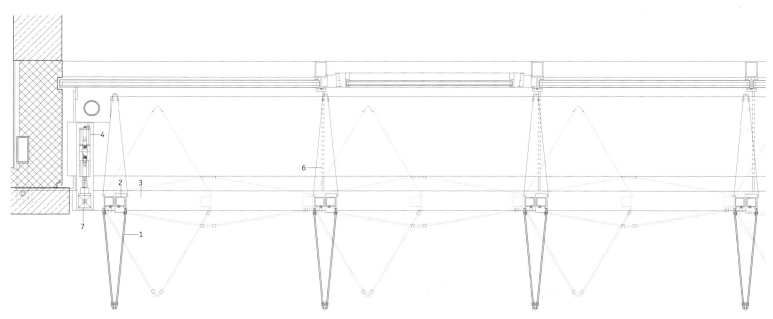

Horizontal section, 1:20

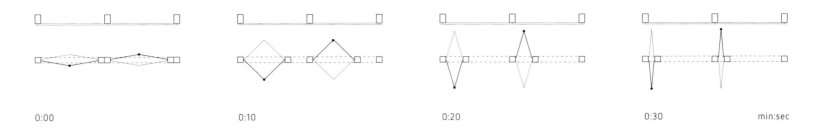

| 0:00 | 0:10 | 0:20 | 0:30 | min:sec |

Dimensions W x H 53.50 x 53.50 cm per acrylic glass panel   **Number** 1504 elements   **Drive** 18 electric motors, 1 per storey section

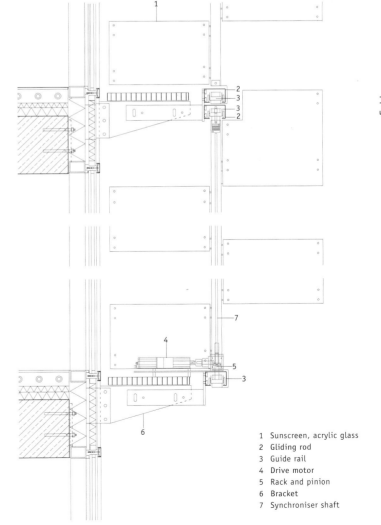

1 Sunscreen, acrylic glass
2 Gliding rod
3 Guide rail
4 Drive motor
5 Rack and pinion
6 Bracket
7 Synchroniser shaft

Section through facade, 1:20

Fold

Horizon House

Atami, J, 2005
Shinichi Ogawa & Associates

This two-storey house with a floor area of 314 m² is located on a plot totalling some 700 m². The design makes the most of the exceptional site and unobstructed view of the sea by glazing the entire 3 m high frontage of the house and the balcony parapet. The glazed balustrade is let into the cantilevered floor slab and held in place with steel angles. The butt joints between the glass balustrade panels are bonded where surfaces are visible. On each facade, two of the six full-height, 3 m wide glass sections can be slid to one side, allowing a direct connection between inside and outside.

To protect against the sun, large 3.40 m high, folding shutters are arranged externally in front of the facade and draw back to reveal the leading edge of suspended ceiling when open. Four of the 730 mm wide and 80 mm thick shutters cover exactly one pane of glass. The careful placement of the hinges means that when closed the shutters fold out to form a single plane and when folded in they occupy as little space as possible. A total of 48 shutters are needed to fully cloak the building on both sides. They fold away in pairs, sliding to the side to reveal an ever larger section of the view. The sunscreens are clad with opaque metal panels. The sliding glass panels travel on rollers along triangular rails let into a channel in the floor and are held in place laterally at the top by a track.

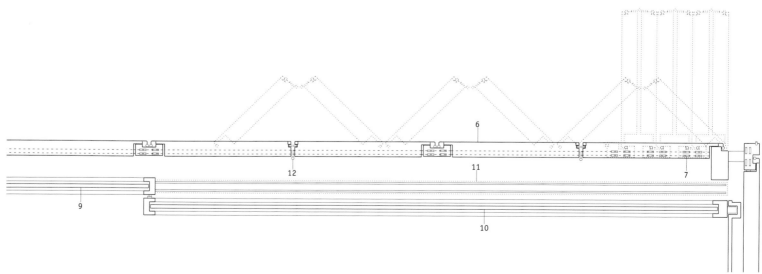

Horizontal section, 1:20

Dimensions W x H x D 0.73 x 3.40 x 0.08 m per shutter   **Number** 48 shutters, 4 per facade section   **Drive** manual

No threshold between the living room and terrace

1 Balustrade, fully-glazed, bonded butt joints
   between panels
2 Balustrade fixed to the reinforced concrete
   roof slab with L-profiles
3 Cantilever beam, H 80 mm
4 Canopy, fully-glazed, bonded butt joints
5 Upper track for the shutters
6 Shutter, 730 x 3400 mm, ø 80 mm
7 Wheels for the shutters
8 Upper tracks for the glass panels
9 Sliding glass panel, insulating glazing (18/16/18)
10 Fixed glazing (18/16/18)
11 Rails for sliding glass panels
12 Hinge between shutters

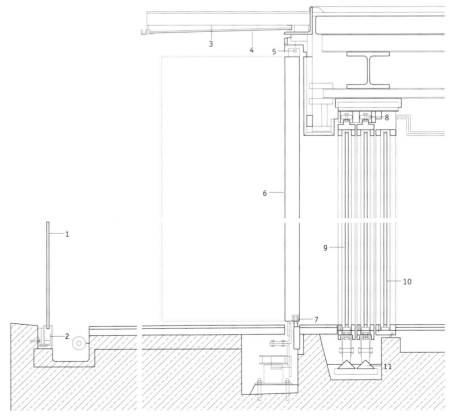

Vertical section, 1:20

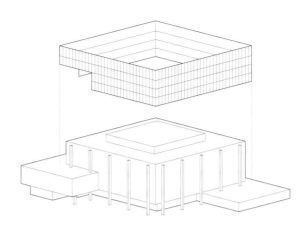

St. Ingbert Town Hall

St. Ingbert, D, 2009
schneider+schumacher architekten

An ideas competition for the remodelling of the town hall facade was won by schneider+schumacher with their proposal for an intelligent facade coupled with a sustainable building concept.

The open interior courtyard was covered over and closed off with full-height glazing to form an enclosed atrium that serves as a buffer zone for night-time cooling and allows the ground floor to be used all year round. The existing, defective external cladding was removed entirely and replaced with new high-performance windows and 120 mm of thermal insulation to provide adequate winter insulation.

Special attention was given to the problem of solar gain in summer which is prevented using a modern interpretation of window shutters. The externally-mounted system of shutters is burglar-proof and air-permeable and also functions as an effective weather barrier, even in stormy weather. The folding shutters are made of electropolished expanded metal sheeting with an embossed pattern, mounted on a tubular frame of extruded aluminium profiles, which together give the entire facade a strong graphic appearance. An oak leaf pattern symbolises the origins of the city and lends the town hall an appropriate sense of decorum.

Due to the building's geographic location in one of the sunniest regions in Germany as well as its orientation, the window shutters are mounted on all four sides of the building. A central control system adapts continuously to the changing conditions to avoid excessive solar gain. Individual users can override the system when desired.

Each set of folding shutters consists of a pair of hinged panels, one fixed and one with a movable roller bearing. A push rod system powers the folding mechanism by a lever fixed to the top of the vertical rotating axis of each shutter. The small lever arm allows the drive mechanism to remain largely concealed. The second shutter is connected to the first and travels along an upper and lower channel on two sets of rollers. Steel fins at 2.64 m centres anchor the framework, holding the shutters and the maintenance catwalks to the concrete structure of the building.

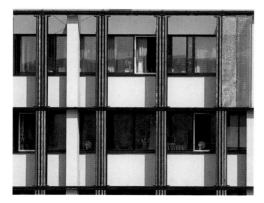
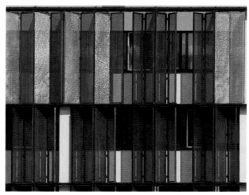
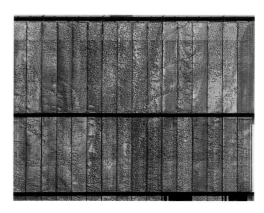

Folding shutters made of electropolished embossed expanded metal sheeting

| 0:00 | 0:07 | 0:14 | 0:20 | min:sec |

Dimensions W x H 132 x 350/422 cm per folding shutter   **Number** 444 elements each with 2 folding shutters   **Drive** electric push rod system

1 Cantilever bracket, steel flat, 120 x 8 mm
2 Stainless steel strip, 4 or 5 per element
3 Tubular frame, extruded aluminium profile
4 Stainless steel expanded metal, electropolished, embossed
5 Suspender, steel flat, 60 x 15 mm
6 End stop for folding shutters
7 Guide rail and pin with sliding block
8 Drive lever, open position
9 Roller assembly, open position
10 U-profile steel, 100 x 58 x 6 mm, with bottom track for elements above
11 Bottom track HELM 300
12 Non-sliding pivot point of drive lever
13 Vertical pivot point, stainless steel angle with bearing pins and bushes
14 Push rod motor, electric
15 Non-sliding pivot point of push rod motor
16 Stopper for roller assembly, top

Fold

C

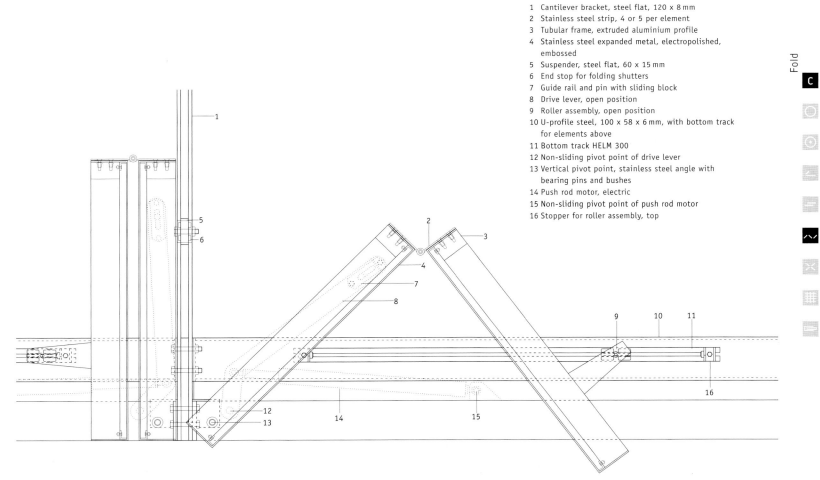

Detail showing layout of folding shutters, 1:7

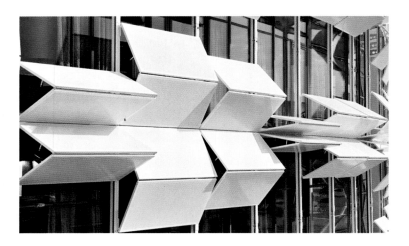

〜〜

Kiefer Technik Showroom

Bad Gleichenberg, A, 2007
Ernst Giselbrecht + Partner

The showroom for the company Kiefer Technik is the public face of its business premises. The building, which one sees on arrival in Bad Gleichenberg, takes its cue from its surroundings, employing the same aluminium panelling as the adjoining offices. These elements have been reconceived to develop a facade that can change its appearance. Along the 28.75 m long southwest facade of the building, 112 aluminium panels in the form of horizontal folding shutters have been mounted on a 7.75 m high supporting aluminium framework arranged in front

of the showroom's glazed facade. The supporting framework carries the guide rails for the 56 folding shutters and is anchored to the building by stainless steel brackets. Rollers and electrically-operated motors are integrated into the guide rails and allow the elements to be raised, lowered and folded together. To open the shutters, the elements at the top of each floor are raised and those at the bottom lowered, folding together to create horizontal cantilevered sun canopies. In the closed position, light passes into the showroom through perforations in

the aluminium panels as if through a veil-like material. To create a carefully orchestrated harmonious effect, the motors accelerate gradually and come to a halt gently. Each of the elements can be individually controlled using a programmable BUS/PLC system and can be extended or retracted to the degree required. As a result, the facade serves not only a shading function but can also assume a continuously changing appearance that can be choreographed at will.

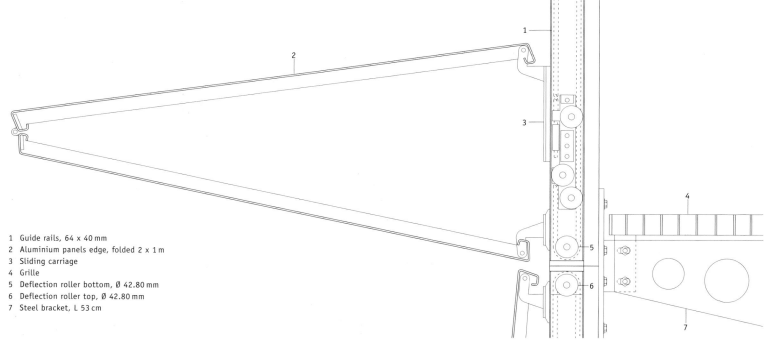

1 Guide rails, 64 x 40 mm
2 Aluminium panels edge, folded 2 x 1 m
3 Sliding carriage
4 Grille
5 Deflection roller bottom, Ø 42.80 mm
6 Deflection roller top, Ø 42.80 mm
7 Steel bracket, L 53 cm

Detail, 1:7

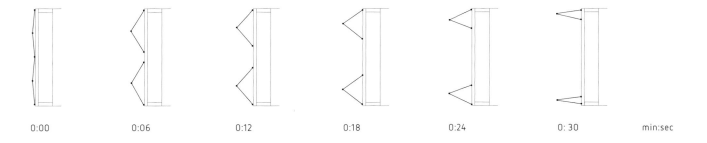

| 0:00 | 0:06 | 0:12 | 0:18 | 0:24 | 0:30 | min:sec |

Dimensions W x H 2 x 2 m folding element   **Number** 56 folding shutters, 2 per facade element   **Weight** 50 kg/m²   **Drive** electric motors

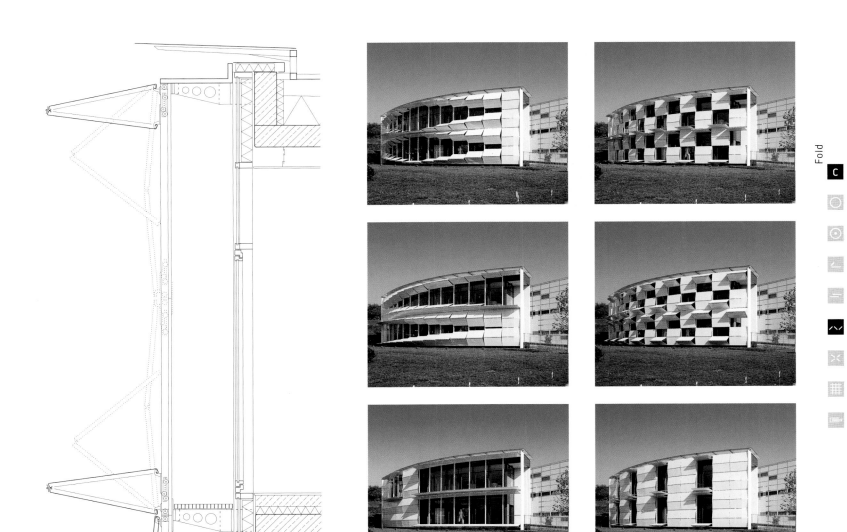

Section through upper part of facade, 1:33

Fold

C

Fabio's Restaurant

Vienna, A, 2002
BEHF Architekten

The ambience of the restaurant, which can cater for 140 guests at a time, is dominated by wood, leather and glass. The continuous surfaces of the floor and ceiling planes define a horizontal space divided into different spatial zones. Its most distinctive architectural feature, however, is a glass extension to the interior fitted snugly into a recess in the building's facade. The frontage of this so-called "glass squirrel's nest" can be raised, allowing passers-by to partake momentarily in the spectacle of fine food and drink.

The entire length of the glazed facade of the restaurant can be folded in sections vertically. Each of the eight elements has its own electric motor concealed within the suspended ceiling, allowing each element to be controlled individually. When opened, the facade elements serve as a canopy, when closed as a glazed and insulated external wall. The glazed sections open from the bottom upwards: the lower edge of each element is raised by cables concealed in the uprights on either side. The self-weight of the facade panels is sufficient to lower the elements with the motor functioning as a braking mechanism.

The open facade panels provide a canopy

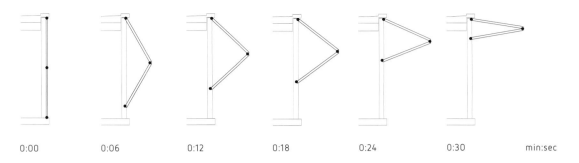

0:00   0:06   0:12   0:18   0:24   0:30   min:sec

Dimensions 2 x 190 x 190 cm edge length   **Number** 8   **Drive** electric motors with cable hoist

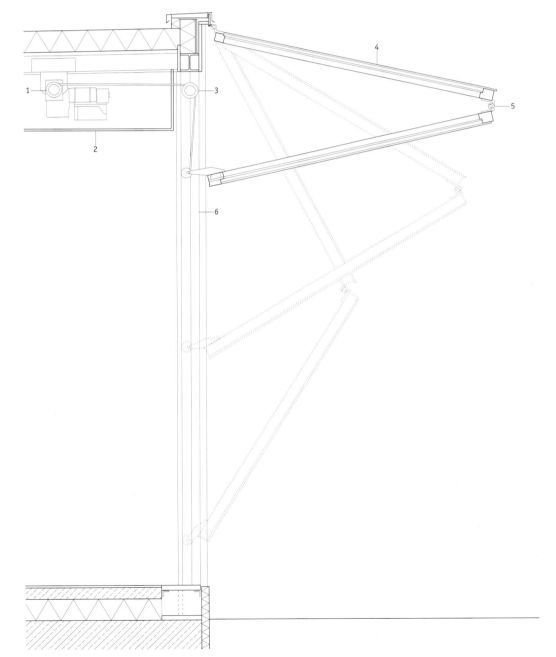

1 Electric motor
2 Suspended ceiling
3 Pulley wheel
4 Facade panel
5 Hinge
6 Channel guide

Each facade panel can be operated individually

Section through the facade, 1:25

Fold

C

Erika Mann Primary School

Berlin, D, 2007
Susanne Hofmann Architekten and the Baupiloten

The renovation of the Erika Mann Primary School was the first project by the Baupiloten, a group of students from the Technical University of Berlin led by the architect Susanne Hofmann. Together with the children and parents, they devised a fantasy world entitled "The Silver Dragon". The individual architectural elements on each storey symbolise the personality of a fictional dragon.

In the corridor on the second floor, this conceptual idea has been realised in the form of folding tables and benches around which groups of four to five children can congregate. When not needed, these elements fold up to the wall. Tailor-made fabric webbing of different lengths and elasticity fixed with rivets between the seats and the box profiles ensure that the individual flaps of the tables and seats open in a concerted, fluid movement while also preventing the children from falling between them. Only the lower two flaps can be used to sit on; the upper flaps function as backrests. Folding cupboard elements, behind which the children can hang their jackets and leave their shoes, are arranged alongside the seats. The cupboard "doors" are simply pushed upwards, folding horizontally so that they can be parked in a raised position. Side-mounted castors on either side of the door panel run in U-profile channels. For smooth operation, sliding stays with integral torsion springs prevent the panels from snapping open and shut. To close the folded panels, the children pull on a fabric tag riveted to the bottom of the panel. Because each folding flap and panel can be halted at any position as needed, they form an ever-changing modular system of movable elements in the corridor that offer the children an engaging area to sit, meet and play.

Working surface and wardrobe cover

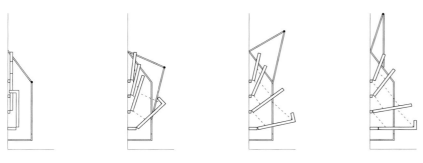

Dimensions D x H 349 x 1470 mm wardrobe, length of folding elements 579 and 923 mm   **Number** 39 wardrobe covers, 27 folding elements   **Drive** manual

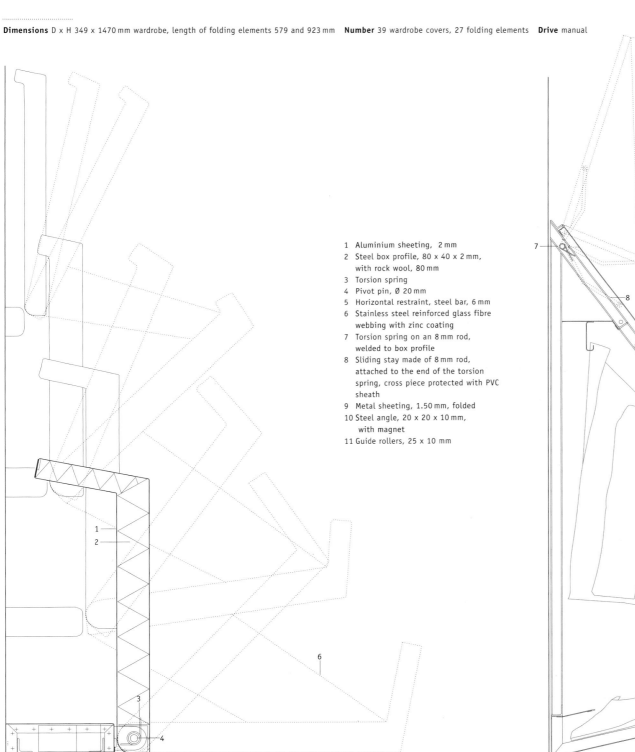

1   Aluminium sheeting, 2 mm
2   Steel box profile, 80 x 40 x 2 mm,
     with rock wool, 80 mm
3   Torsion spring
4   Pivot pin, Ø 20 mm
5   Horizontal restraint, steel bar, 6 mm
6   Stainless steel reinforced glass fibre
     webbing with zinc coating
7   Torsion spring on an 8 mm rod,
     welded to box profile
8   Sliding stay made of 8 mm rod,
     attached to the end of the torsion
     spring, cross piece protected with PVC
     sheath
9   Metal sheeting, 1.50 mm, folded
10 Steel angle, 20 x 20 x 10 mm,
     with magnet
11 Guide rollers, 25 x 10 mm

Section, folding element, 1:10

Section, wardrobe cover panel, 1:10

Fold

C

Hoberman Arch

Salt Lake City, Utah, USA, 2002
Hoberman Associates

Designed for the Winter Olympics in Salt Lake City in 2002, Chuck Hoberman's stage construction demonstrates the impressive representational possibilities of kinetics. The stage curtain, whose form and movement resembles that of the human iris, opens and closes to mark the beginning and end of the games, as well as for special attractions such as the awarding of medals. The curtain-like construction is now situated in the grounds of the University of Utah.

The construction of the Hoberman Arch can be considered in two parts: a matrix of movable sections and a structural arch that supports the movable elements. The construction has a width of 21.5 m and a height of 11 m. The individual elements are made of sandblasted aluminium profiles and 96 translucent fibre-reinforced panels. Four different forms are used and fixed in a polysymmetrical, overlapping arrangement so that they enclose the stage entirely when the construction is lowered. The outermost panels are anchored to the structural arch at 13 points; the nodes at the bottom are connected to runners that travel along a rail in the floor from the centre of the stage to the base of the arch as the curtain opens. This lends the lattice construction the necessary structural stability. The mechanical curtain is driven by two 30 PS electric motors which hoist the elements upwards and fix them in the open position. When opened, the folded-together curtain construction is only 1.80 m deep. More than 4000 individual pieces were machined for the construction, fixed together with around 13 000 steel rivets. The visual impression is heightened by more than 500 computer-controlled lighting elements that follow the scissor-like movement of the elements as the stage opens. When the curtain is closed, the construction can withstand wind speeds of up to 80 km/h.

Opening sequence of the mechanical stage curtain

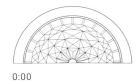 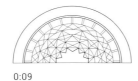  

| 0:00 | 0:09 | 0:21 | 0:30 | min:sec |

Dimensions W x H 21.50 x 11 m   **Weight** 6.8 t   **Drive** rope hoist with 2 electric motors

Isometric of a panel (second row from the centre)

1 Aluminium corner plate
2 Aluminium square hollow section, 100 x 100 mm, sandblasted
3 Hinged bolt connection
4 Fibre-reinforced plastic
5 Prefabricated steel elements, fixed to runner rail in the floor
6 Machine room, each with a 30 PS electric motor
7 Steel frame: hollow square-section tube, welded, unchamfered edges

Expand and contract

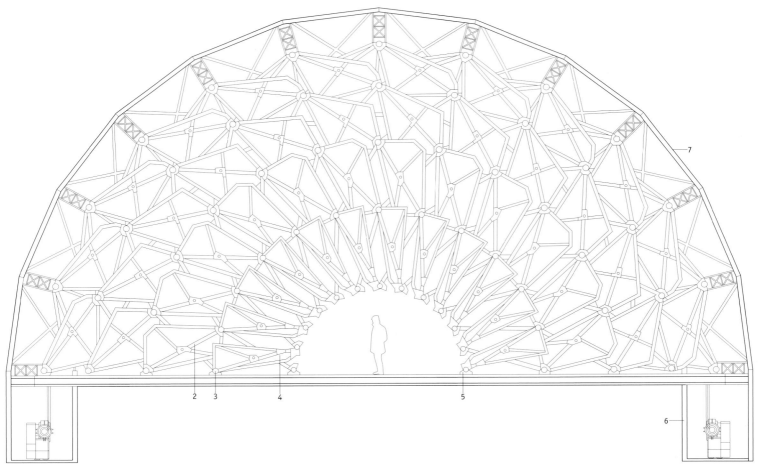

Sectional elevation, stage curtain, 1:120

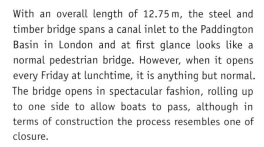

Rolling Bridge

Paddington Basin, London, GB, 2004
Heatherwick Studio

With an overall length of 12.75 m, the steel and timber bridge spans a canal inlet to the Paddington Basin in London and at first glance looks like a normal pedestrian bridge. However, when it opens every Friday at lunchtime, it is anything but normal. The bridge opens in spectacular fashion, rolling up to one side to allow boats to pass, although in terms of construction the process resembles one of closure.

The bridge appears to open effortlessly to allow water-borne traffic to pass: one end of the bridge lifts off the ground and describes a large arc through the air before joining the other end of the bridge. The almost noiseless movement is achieved by locating the plant room, which contains a hydraulic pump and several ancillary hydraulic cylinders, in the cellar of the neighbouring building. Hydraulic rams set vertically into each of the eight sections

of handrail cause the joints in the top of the handrail to lift, the sections to fold and the bridge to curl up.
In 2005, the inventor and architect Thomas Heatherwick was awarded the British Structural Steel Award for his innovative solution.

Footbridge

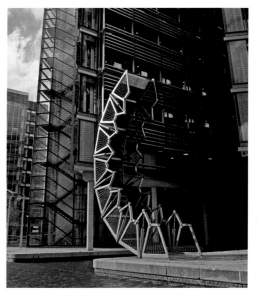

Boat passage

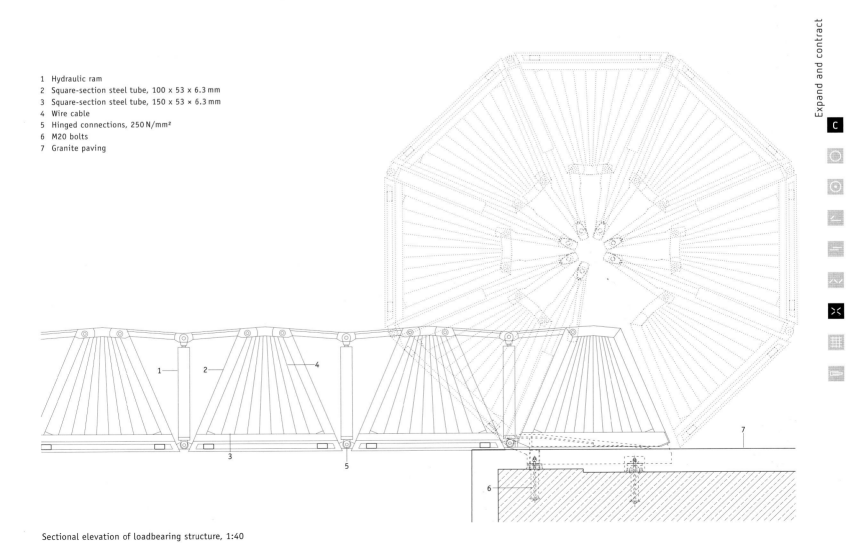

0:00 0:30 1:30 2:00 min:sec

Dimensions L 12.75 m (8 × 1.60 m segments)   **Weight** 4.04 t   **Drive** 14 hydraulic rams

1   Hydraulic ram
2   Square-section steel tube, 100 x 53 x 6.3 mm
3   Square-section steel tube, 150 x 53 × 6.3 mm
4   Wire cable
5   Hinged connections, 250 N/mm²
6   M20 bolts
7   Granite paving

Expand and contract

Sectional elevation of loadbearing structure, 1:40

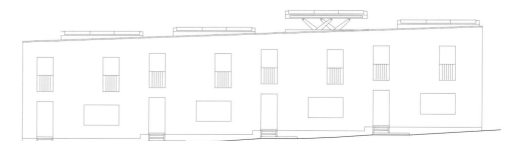

Rebgässli Housing Development

Allschwil, CH, 2004
Amrein Giger Architekten

The Rebgässli Housing Development is located at the edge of the village of Allschwil. The project is the product of an invited architectural competition initiated by Wohnstadt, a housing cooperative in Basel. Two stepped rows of houses are arranged at an angle to one another, responding architecturally to the incline of the topography and the trees on the site. The variously coloured woods in the timber board facades form an intrinsic whole with the park-like environment. For the architects, it was important to establish a direct relationship between in-side and outside and to emphasise this for the residents. The result is a terraced house type with an integral patio in the interior. Each of these is covered by a glass skylight that can be raised hydraulically in a vertical direction by up to 80 cm. This provides natural light and a means of intelligent ventilation.

The roof window consists of a steel frame with aluminium attachments. Its weight of 3500 kg is carried by two chromium-steel scissor levers, which also produce the vertical movement. The scissor levers are positioned differently, depending on the installation situation of each site; offset and parallel to one another on the long sides, or facing and parallel on the short sides. The head and foot points of one side of each scissor lever are fixed in position but have pivoting joints, which means the opposing free bearing points move laterally on a guide rail. The scissor levers are hydraulically driven and have a load capacity of 5 t. Movement is controlled by a manual switch. Sensors and a wind-speed monitor guard against jamming and storm damage.

East elevation, 1:275

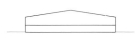

0:00

0:19

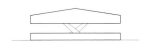

0:38

min:sec

Dimensions W x L x H 388.7 x 529.3 x 66.2 cm **Number** 4 + 5 elevating skylights **Weight** 3500 kg per element **Drive** 2 hydraulic rams, 5 t lifting capacity each

1 Metal casing: anodized aluminium
2 Hydraulic ram, min. 5 t lifting capacity
3 Textile sunscreen
4 Pair of scissor levers, V4A chromium-steel
5 Perimeter frame, steel and aluminium

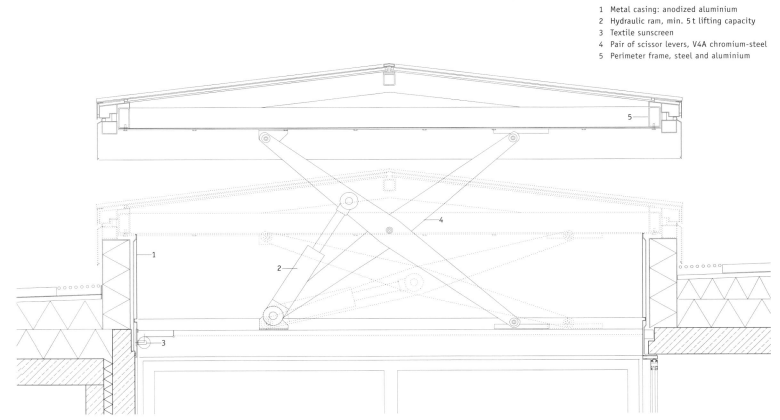

Section, 1:25

Elevating skylights over the interior patios

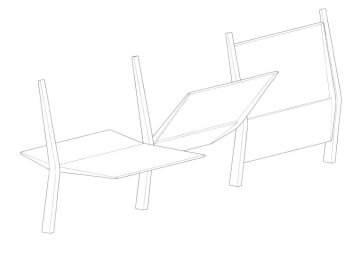

Riva Waterfront Promenade

Split, CR, 2007
3LHD

The waterfront of the city of Split, the Riva, is one of the most interesting and distinctive places in the Mediterranean and embodies the history and character of the Croatian city. It is a public urban space which has recently been restored and remodelled following an architectural competition won by the architectural team 3LHD. The competition site lies between the Mediterranean on one side and the frontage of historic buildings on the other, which are part of the Diocletian's Palace World Heritage Site dating back 1700 years.

The promenade is the focal point of diverse communal activities and one of the most important public spaces in the city; 250 m long and 55 m wide, it is a space for all kinds of social events, ranging from sporting competitions to religious processions and political rallies.

The new design provides a series of sail-like sunscreens that shield the outdoor areas of the numerous waterfront cafés, restaurants and shops by day from the sun and wind. The construction consists of a series of 7.20 m high masts with 6.10 m long pivoting outriggers, which are fixed to the masts with a hinged joint at a height of 2.80 m above ground. The textile sunscreens are slung between each pair of outriggers. Both outriggers on either side of a mast can be raised or lowered using a hydraulic piston with a power unit concealed within the masts.

In the evening, the sails can be raised to a vertical position. The synthetic textile sail material, which provides protection against UV light during the day, can then be used as a projection screen during the evening. The 38.40 m² projection screen is double-reinforced at the corners and has a sewn-in edging profile. An electric motor allows it to be rolled up along the outrigger. To avoid damage resulting from excessive winds, each mast has an integral wind sensor.

Waterfront promenade with sunscreen sails

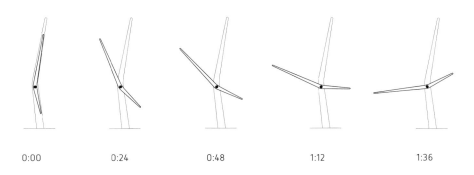

| 0:00 | 0:24 | 0:48 | 1:12 | 1:36 | min:sec |

Dimensions 38.40 m² textile surface area, 7.20 m mast height   **Number** 29 elements   **Weight** 2300 kg per mast with 2 outriggers   **Drive** hydraulic piston with power unit

1 Wind sensor
2 Halogen lamp; size of recess: 440 x 145 mm
3 Mast, rectangular section, 150 – 550 x 320 mm
4 Roller and channel for retracting the sunscreen
5 Pivoting outrigger, rectangular section, 100 – 300 x 150 mm
6 Pivot bearing, Ø 250 mm
7 Electric motor for retracting the sunscreen
8 Synthetic textile sunscreen
9 Hydraulic piston
10 Lighting unit for the sunscreen, 260 x 135 mm
11 Controller for drive mechanism and lighting
12 Electricity connection for lighting
13 Hydraulic power unit
14 Electricity connection for hydraulic power unit

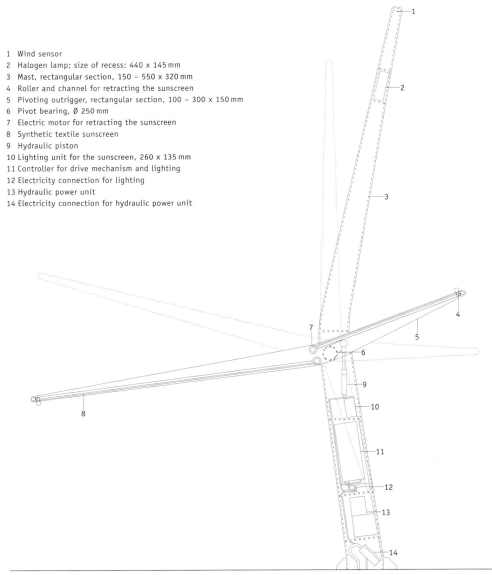

Vertical section, 1:50

The sunscreens shield against the sun and wind

Hinged connection of the outriggers to the mast

Gather and roll up

Houses on Hohenbühlstrasse

Zurich, CH, 2004
agps.architecture

In 2004, two new houses, designed by the Swiss architects agps.architecture, were built on the grounds of the luxurious site "Am Hohenbühl" in Zurich.

The design for private clients consists of two simple volumes positioned slightly offset to one another. Each floor contains a single apartment with views in all four directions.

A multi-layer facade construction, consisting of continuous full-height glazing, sliding internal wall panels and external metal curtains for shading, all of which can be moved independently or in conjunction with one another, allows the residents to vary the desired degree of privacy.

The articulated wire-braid textile made of stainless steel was originally developed as a material for conveyer belts for use in large bakeries. The metal curtains are hung from rails attached to sturdy frames that hold the glazing, which in turn are anchored to the leading edge of the reinforced concrete floor slabs.

Every 400 mm a flat bar is integrated into the textile mesh at the top and bottom to which the guide rollers are attached. A geared electric motor with chain drive and an additional transmission from the lower to the upper rail, is used to move only the first set of rollers in each rail. When the textile is moved back and forth, the sun shade folds or unfolds.

Each curtain has its own dedicated motor. The curtain rollers function in such a way that when closing the curtains, the folded leaves of curtain unfold neatly one segment at a time. The curtain rollers move at a speed of 135 mm/s.

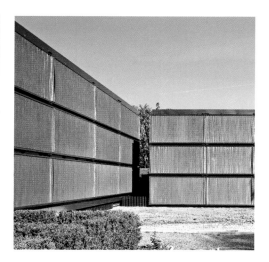

0:00	0:10	0:20	0:30	0:40	min:sec

Dimensions W x H 5.40 x 2.80 m   **Number** 60 curtains   **Weight** 18 kg per m² metal textile

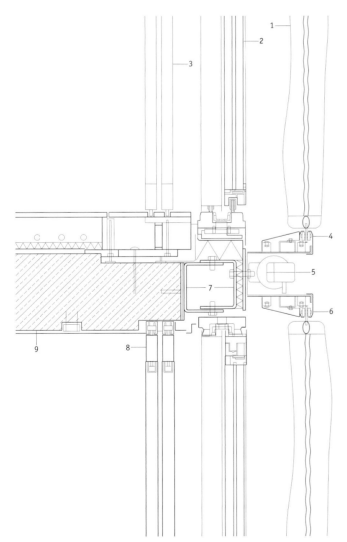

1 Metal textile curtain
2 Sliding window element
3 Internal sliding wall panel
4 Runner rail with rollers beneath
5 Chain drive for curtain
6 Hanging rail for curtain, top
7 Facade U-profiles bolted to RC floor slab
8 Hanging tracks for internal wall panel
9 Reinforced concrete floor slab

Detail, sun shade fixture, 1:10

Gather and roll up

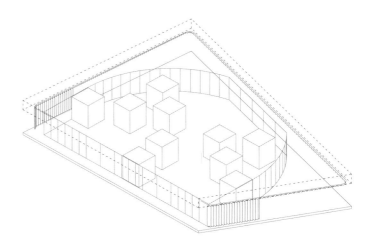

47°40'48"N/13°8'12"E House

Adnet, Salzburg, A, 2007
Maria Flöckner and Hermann Schnöll

The 47°40'48"N/13°8'12"E house is situated in Adneter Riedl in the Tennengau region near Salzburg. The longitude and latitude of the building's name denotes its geographic location. The house lies far from the nearest village and a car is necessary to run daily errands. The remote building looks out over both the landscape to the north and the road to the south, mediating between the two. Inside the building, the only fixed elements are nine geometrically identical hollow boxes measuring 2.40 x 2.40 m. These partially top-lit boxes house private spaces such as the bathroom, dressing room and storage. Steel columns embedded in the walls of these wooden boxes support the structure of the building and bear the weight of the reinforced concrete roof that is in parts up to 1 m thick. The open living area is almost entirely free of columns. The only evident columns are in the glass facade. The exposed concrete roof slab cantilevers outwards up to 8 m, so that the glass facade functions less as a visual boundary and more as a kind of curtain. One's view is directed towards the Alpine panorama and the sky.

The view of the panorama is defined by a movable black curtain on the outside of the building that hangs from a track set into the reinforced concrete ceiling. The curtains can be moved at will around the entire building and define spaces with different degrees of enclosure and illumination. Over the course of a day, or a year, the external curtains can lead one's view in particular directions.

Sliding curtain acts as an outer skin

 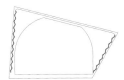 

Dimensions L x H 10 x 2.70 m per curtain, rail 75 m   **Number** 10 curtains   **Weight** 240 g/m²   **Drive** manual

1   Reinforced concrete roof slab
2   Track, 38 x 38 mm
3   Triple glazing
4   Poured asphalt with diabase aggregate
5   Polyethylene textile curtain, hem 5 cm

Dining area with 2.40 x 2.40 m hollow box in the background

The space between the glass facade and the curtain

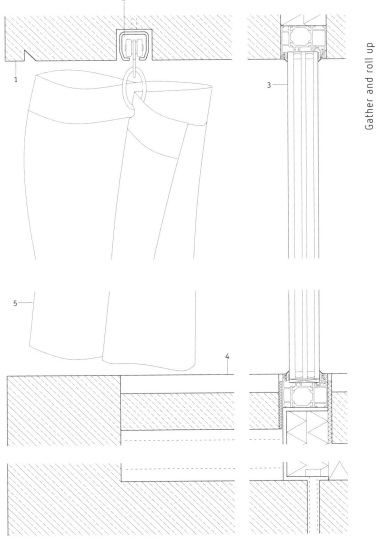

Curtain fixture, 1:5

Gather and roll up

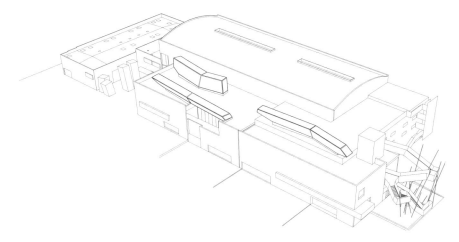

South Campus of the Art Center College of Design

Pasadena, California, USA, 2004
Daly Genik Architects

The South Campus of the Art Center College of De-sign lies around 12 km southeast of Downtown Los Angeles. Prior to conversion, the building was used by the California Institute of Technology (the aca-demic seat of the NASA Jet Propulsion Laboratory) and was upgraded in the 1950s to house one of the world's first supersonic wind tunnels.

The conversion to the Art Center changed the ap-pearance of the building only slightly. The semi-transparent additions to the roof are the most dis-tinctive new feature. Their amorphous form and over-sized scale turn the complex into a landmark. They serve as skylights, allowing filtered light to illuminate the ateliers below. At night the effect is reversed: the skylights become lanterns, illuminated from within.

The system of skylights consists of a steel struc-tural frame filled with ETFE membrane cushions that incorporate three layers of film. The outer and mid-dle layers are printed with a shading pattern. Inflat-ing or deflating the cushion moves the position of the central film, changing the degree of overlap of the two patterned films. This method allows the amount of natural light entering the spaces below to be varied from 16 % up to 60 % light transmit-tance. The use of this technology led to the build-ing being granted the highly coveted LEED certifica-tion (Leadership in Energy and Environmental De-sign).

Skylights in the form of variable light transmittance ETFE membrane cushions

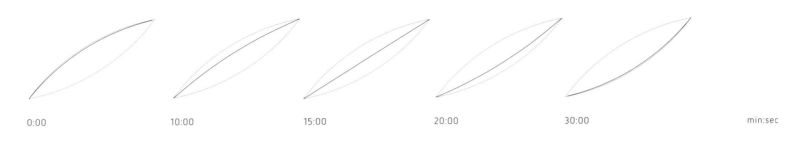

| 0:00 | 10:00 | 15:00 | 20:00 | 30:00 | min:sec |

Dimensions variable **Number** 28 **Drive** pneumatic

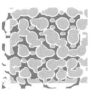

16 %

22 %

60 %

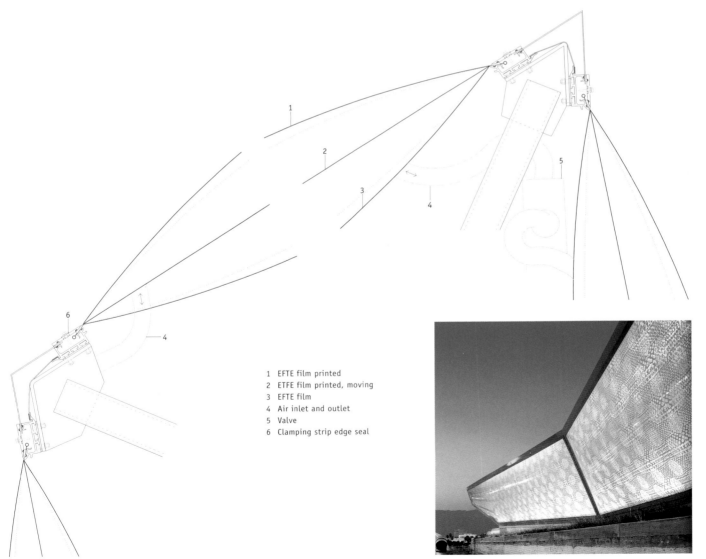

1 EFTE film printed
2 ETFE film printed, moving
3 EFTE film
4 Air inlet and outlet
5 Valve
6 Clamping strip edge seal

Detail, membrane connection, 1:10

Overlapping patterns on the printed films

Pneumatic

About the authors and contributors

Prof. Michael Schumacher, born in 1957, studied from 1978–1985 at the TU Kaiserslautern, followed by postgraduate studies at the Städelschule in Frankfurt am Main under Peter Cook. After working freelance in 1987 for Sir Norman Foster in London and Braun und Schlockermann in Frankfurt am Main he set up schneider+schumacher architekten together with Till Schneider in 1988. From 1999–2000 he was visiting professor at the Städelschule in Frankfurt and in 2002 he took up responsibility for scholarship mentoring at the Designlabor Bremerhaven. In 2004 he became board chairman of the BDA Architects' Association in Hesse and in 2007 was appointed Professor of Design and Building Construction at the Institute of Design and Building Construction, Leibniz University Hanover. In 2008, together with Oliver Schaeffer and Michael-Marcus Vogt, he set up the research group MOVE. He is a member of the Urban Planning Advisory Committee for Frankfurt am Main and a member of the AIV Association of Architects and Engineers.

Oliver Schaeffer, born in 1975 in Munich, studied architecture from 1995–2001 at the TU Munich under Professor Thomas Herzog among others, from 1999 to 2000 at the MIT in the USA. In 1998 he was admitted to the German National Academic Foundation. His diploma project under Richard Horden was awarded, among other commendations, the Contractworld Newcomer Award in 2002. From 2001–2004 he worked with Sir Michael Hopkins and Partners in London, from 2004–2007 with Wöhr Heugenhauser in Munich. In 2007 he became freelance; he also works as a member of Professor Michael Schumacher's team at the Institute of Design and Building Construction at the Leibniz University Hanover. He is a founding member of the research group MOVE and heads the kinetics group at schneider+schumacher architekten in Frankfurt.

Michael-Marcus Vogt, born in 1972, studied from 1991–1997 at the Leibniz University Hanover, under Professor Peter Schweger among others. His diploma project under Professor Peter Kaup was awarded the Laves Prize. After working freelance for Venneberg & Zech Architekten and in the design department of Professor Michael Lange's facade engineering office, in 2000 he became a member of staff under Professor Kaup, later under Professor Michael Schumacher, at the Institute of Design and Building Construction at the Leibniz University Hanover. He is a founding member of the research group MOVE and conducts research into dynamic materials and application technologies for adaptive facade systems. In cooperation with Detter Architekten, he continues to work as an architect on residential, commercial and industrial projects.

This book is the result of collaborative efforts within the Department of Building Construction at the Institute of Design and Building Construction at Leibniz University Hanover. The authors especially thank the students who contributed to this publication:

Lilja Bartuli, Nicolas Bittner, Gesa Brink, Johannes Brixel, Berthold Cloer, Erik Dobewall, Jochen Elies, Anne Hillebrand, Sandra Kock, Frank Lindner, Steffen Neeß, Verena Reinecke, Björn Runow, Raimonda Stasyte

Prof. Dr.-Ing. Martin Becker, born in 1962, studied electrical engineering with specialisation in systems technology at the TU Kaiserslautern. After completing his doctorate in the modelling, simulation and automation of cooling systems, he became managing director of a technology transfer centre for automation technology and information systems. In 1999, he became professor at Biberach University of Applied Sciences for Building Climatics and Energy Systems. He lectures and researches on the topics of room and building automation, facade automation, communication systems and energy and facilities management. He also runs his own freelance engineering office.

Kurt-Patrik Beckmann, born in 1964, studied architecture from 1987–1994 at the Leibniz University Hanover. Since 1994 he has worked as a project manager at Venneberg & Zech Architekten. From 1994 to 2004 he was a member of staff at the Institute of Design and Building Construction, Leibniz University Hanover, under Professor Kaup. From 2003 to 2008 he lectured at the HAWK Holzminden, since 2008 at the Institute of Design and Building Construction, Leibniz University Hanover.

Stefan Bernard, born in 1969 in Merano, Italy, studied architecture in Venice before training to become a landscape architect in Vienna and Berlin. Since 2001, he has worked as a freelance landscape architect in Berlin, with teaching posts at the RWTH Aachen and at the University of Applied Sciences in Wismar. His projects include the gardens of the Offices of the Federal State of Hesse in Berlin and the open spaces of the Eberbach Monastery in Rhinegau. He is author (together with Hans Loidl) and designer of the book *Open(ing) Spaces – Design as Landscape Architecture* (2003), as well as *Nicht Ökologie, nicht Kunst – Gedanken zum Wesen der Landschaftsarchitektur* (2005).

Prof. Brian Cody teaches at the TU Graz and is head of the Institute for Buildings and Energy. The focus of his research, teaching and practice lies in maximising the energy efficiency of buildings and cities. Prior to his appointment at Graz, he was Associate Director of the international engineering office Arup, and Design Leader and Business Development Leader of the German subsidiary Arup GmbH. He continues to work as a consultant for Arup and is a member of numerous committees and competition juries. He has also been a visiting professor at the University of Applied Arts in Vienna.

Roman Jakobiak, born in 1963 in Hamburg, studied architecture in Berlin and Marseille. Climatically responsive architecture is both the basis and aim of his architectural endeavours. After several years work in practice for an architecture office in Berlin, he joined the Laboratory for Daylight Planning at the TU Berlin in 1992. From 1996–2008 he worked on research and development projects at the TU's Institute for Building, the Environment and Solar Research. His activities include work in norms committees, teaching, further education and contributions to publications. Since 2008 he works in the field of daylight planning for Licht Kunst Licht AG in Bonn and Berlin.

Andreas Kretzer, born in 1974 in Bodenmais, studied architecture from 1995–2001 at the TU Munich. After working with Hild und K Architekten from 2001–2004, and freelance since 1996, he studied scenography at the University of Television and Film in Munich from 2004–2006, establishing his own office in Munich in 2004. His activities include participations in numerous competitions (among them for ten bridges) and lecturing and workshops at the TU Munich, the TU Kaiserslautern and the TU Graz. Since 2008, he has been a member of staff and lecturer at the Faculty of Architecture at the TU Darmstadt.

Prof. Michael Lange studied civil engineering at the TU Hanover until 1976 and founded Michael Lange Engineers in 1983. In 1987 he became a publicly appointed and certified assessor for facades and facade cladding, windows and doors listed with the IHK Hanover-Hildesheim. In 1992 he was a founding member of the UBF Independent Association of Facade Planners. In 2000, he was appointed a professor at the Faculty of Architecture and Landscape at the Leibniz University Hanover, and since 2007 has lectured on the "Certified Facade Engineering" course at Augsburg University of Applied Sciences. He is a member of numerous associations, including the UBF, VBI, VDI, IFT, BVS, VBD and IKNS, and is a member of the Advisory Committee and Examination Board for Windows, Doors, Portals and Hung Facades at the IHK Munich. He also chairs the VBI task group on the "Integrated planning of building envelopes".

Frank Möller, born in 1974 in Kiel, studied architecture at the TU Braunschweig and the University of North London, graduating with a Master of Arts from the University of North London in 2001 and a diploma from the TU Braunschweig in 2002. After working with well-known architecture offices in Graz, Vienna and Hamburg, he now works as a freelance architect in Hamburg and Lüneburg and is a member of Professor Schumacher's staff at the Institute of Design and Building Construction at the Leibniz University Hanover. In 2009 he was a visiting tutor at the Architectural Association in London.

Zoran Novacki, born 1973 in Regensburg, became a consulting engineer after studying civil engineering at Stuttgart University. In 1996 he founded the office CES civil engineering solutions which has undertaken projects such as the Memorial Bridge in Rijeka, Croatia, together with 3LHD architects. From 1999 onwards he was project manager at the engineering office Seeberger Friedl und Partner in Munich, responsible among other projects for Terminal 2 at Munich Airport. Since 2004, he has been a member of staff at the Department of Structural Design at the Faculty of Architecture, TU Munich.

York Ostermeyer, born in 1976, studied architecture at the Leibniz University Hanover. After working freelance with Professor Ingo Gabriel on energy-efficient single-family houses from 2003 to 2005 and a doctoral scholarship including a period in Kyoto, Japan, he completed his doctorate on "Climatic Responsiveness based on Energy Balancing" in 2008. That same year he embarked on a post-doctorate at the Chair of Sustainable Construction at the ETH Swiss Federal Institute of Technology in Zurich, which he joined as a project coordinator in 2009. His activities include lectures, seminars and project work on energy efficiency and sustainability focussing on the potential of flexible adaptation to regional environmental conditions.

Prof. Andreas Schulz, born in 1959, studied electrical engineering and worked for many years in practice as a lighting planner before founding the office Licht Kunst Licht in 1991, where he is managing director. In addition to high-profile museum projects such as the Louvre in Paris with Adeline Rispal, the Nationalgalerie in Berlin with HG Merz and the Lenbachhaus in Munich with Foster and Partners, Licht Kunst Licht has designed lighting for major government buildings including the new German Chancellery and the parliamentary office buildings adjoining the Reichstag. More recent projects include the former coal refinery at the Zeche Zollverein together with OMA (Office of Metropolitan Architecture), and the Uniqa Tower in Vienna. He was appointed professor in 2001 and in 2003 founded the Chair for Lighting Design at the HAWK Hildesheim.

Agnes Weilandt, born in 1974 in Stuttgart, studied civil engineering from 1993–1999 at the RWTH Aachen with a period of study at the École des Ponts et Chaussées in Paris. Until 2004 she worked at Werner Sobek Engineers in Stuttgart and was from 2001–2005 a member of staff at the ILEK Institute for Lightweight Structures and Conceptual Design at Stuttgart University where she received her doctorate in 2008. Since 2006 she has worked as a project manager with Bollinger und Grohmann in Frankfurt. In 1996 she was admitted to the German National Academic Foundation and was awarded the Schüßler Award, also in 1996, and in 2000 first prize by the Hünnebeck Foundation.

Dr. phil. Isa Wortelkamp, born in 1973, is Junior Professor for Dance Studies at the Institute for Theatre Studies at the Free University Berlin. After studying applied drama studies in Gießen, she completed her doctorate in 2006 at the University of Basel entitled "Sehen mit dem Stift in der Hand – die Aufführung im Schriftzug der Aufzeichnung". In her research work she examines the relationship between performance and reading, choreography and architecture and image and movement.

Jan Zappe, born in 1969 in Siegen, studied chemistry and mathematics from 1988–1993 at the University of Düsseldorf, receiving his doctorate in Physical Chemistry at the University of Heidelberg. From 1997–2000 he studied philosophy, art history and history at the universities of Karlsruhe and Cologne and from 2000 to 2005 media art at Karlsruhe University of Arts and Design, specialising in architecture, photography and digital media. He now works freelance as an artist. Since 1998 he has been a guest artist at the ZKM Center for Art and Media in Karlsruhe. From 2000 to 2007 he lectured in media philosophy at the University of Karlsruhe, Institute of Philosophy. In 2000 he co-founded the art group robotlab at the ZKM, staging art installation projects using industrial robots. Numerous international exhibitions have followed [www.robotlab.de].

Bibliography

Fundamentals of movement

Blokland, Tessa; Keegan, Brian: *Material World 2: Innovative Materials for Architecture and Design*, Birkhäuser, Basel/Boston/Berlin 2006

Brown, Henry T.: *Five Hundred and Seven Mechanical Movements*, Brown, Coombs & Co, New York 1871

Brownell, Blain Erickson: *Transmaterial: A Catalog of Materials That Redefine Our Physical Environment*, Princeton Architectural Press, New York 2006

-- : *Transmaterial 2: A Catalog of Materials That Redefine Our Physical Environment*, Princeton Architectural Press, New York 2008

Calatrava, Santiago: *Secret Sketchbook*, The Monacelli Press, New York 1995

De Certeau, Michel: *The Practice of Everyday Life*, University of California Press, Berkeley 1984.

Fernandez, John: *Material Architecture: Emergent Materials for Innovative Buildings and Ecological Construction*, Architectural Press/Elsevier, Oxford 2005

Haberhauer, Horst; Bodenstein, Ferdinand: *Maschinenelemente – Gestaltung, Berechnung, Anwendung*, 15th revised edition, Springer, Berlin/Heidelberg 2008

Hahn, Achim: *Architekturtheorie*, UVK-Verlagsgesellschaft, Constance 2008.

Hauer, Erwin; Hill, John T.: *Architectural Screens and Walls*, Princeton Architectural Press, New York 2004/2007

Hight, Christopher; Perry, Chris: *Collective Intelligence in Design*, AD/Wiley, Chichester 2006

Huber, Anna: "Raum nehmen | Raum geben – ein Gespräch zwischen Anna Huber und Isa Wortelkamp über das Projekt *umwege,*" *Transversale*, 2009, Munich

Isermann, Rolf: *Mechatronische Systeme*, 2nd completely revised edition, Springer, Berlin/Heidelberg 2008

Redtenbacher, F.: *Die Bewegungs-Mechanismen*, Heidelberg 1857

Reiser, Jesse; Umemoto, Nakano: *Atlas of Novel Tectonics*, Princeton Architectural Press, New York 2006

Stattmann, Nicola: *Ultra Light – Super Strong, A new generation of design materials*, Prestel, Munich 2003

-- : *Handbook of Material Technologies*, Av Edition, Ludwigsburg 2003

Stephano, Effie: "Moving Structures," *Art and Artists*, 8 (January 1974), London

Vyzoviti, Sophia: *Supersurfaces*, Gingko Press, Berkeley 2006

Future movement strategies

Addington, Michelle; Schodek, Daniel: *Smart Materials and Technologies for the Architecture and Design Professions*, Architectural Press/Elsevier, Amsterdam 2007

Hensel, Michael; Menges, Achim: *Morpho-Ecologies*, AA Publications, London 2006

-- : Weinstock, Michael: *Morphogenetic Design Techniques and Technologies*, AD/Wiley, Chichester 2006

-- : *Emergence – Morphogenetic Design Strategies*, AD/Wiley, Chichester 2006

Menges, Achim: *Responsive Surface Structures, Future Wood: Innovation in Building Design and Construction*, Riverside Architectural Press, Cambridge (Ontario) 2007

Ritter, Axel: *Smart Materials in Architecture, Interior Architecture and Design*, Birkhäuser, Basel/Boston/Berlin 2007

Yao, J.T.P.: "Concept of Structural Control," in *ASCE Journal of Structural Division* 98 (7), 1972, 1567–1574

Changing and extending uses and functions

VDI-Bericht, *Innovative Fassaden II: Wechselwirkung Mensch-Fassade*, Verein Deutscher Ingenieure, Düsseldorf 2004

Gatermann, Dörte; Schossig, Elmar: *Prozeßsystematik, Prototypenfassaden, Anwendungsbeispiele*, Gatermann + Schossig und Partner, 2003

Hindrichs, Dirk U.; Heusler Winfried: *Facades – Building Envelopes for the 21st Century*, Birkhäuser, Basel/Boston/Berlin 2004

Issel, Hans: *Das Entwerfen von Fassaden*, 1923, Reprint-Verlag, Leipzig 1999

Kronenburg, Robert: *Flexible – Architecture that Responds to Change*, Laurence King Publishing, London 2007

-- : *Portable Architecture – Design and Technology*, Birkhäuser, Basel/Boston/Berlin 2008

Randl, Chad: *Revolving Architecture*, Princeton Architectural Press, New York 2008

Skin: das Fachmagazin für die intelligente Gebäudehülle, Osterreichischer Wirtschaftsverlag, Vienna 2003

Westenberger, Daniel: *Untersuchungen zu Vertikalschiebefenstern als Komponenten im Bereich von Fassadenöffnungen*, Dissertation, Munich Technical University 2005

Energy

Bonfig, Peter: *Wirkungsmöglichkeiten von beweglichen Fassadenteilen aus nachwachsenden Rohstoffen*, Dissertation, Munich Technical University 2007

Cody, Brian: "Die Stadt neu denken," in *Zeno, Zeitschrift für nachhaltiges Bauen*, 2/2009, Callwey, Munich

-- : "Form follows Energy", *GAM 02, Graz Architecture Magazine*, "Design Science in Architecture," Faculty of Architecture, Graz University of Technology (Ed.), Springer, Vienna 2005

-- : "Urban Design and Energy," *GAM 05, Graz Architecture magazine*, "Urbanity not Energy," Faculty of Architecture, Graz University of Technology (Ed.), Springer, Vienna 2009

-- : "Building Energy and Environmental Performance tool BEEP, Entwicklung einer Methode zum Vergleich der tatsächlichen Energieeffizienz von Gebäuden," *HLH Fachzeitschrift*, Verein Deutscher Ingenieure (Ed.), VDI-Verlag, Düsseldorf, January 2008

-- : "Energieeffiziente Lüftung von Bürogebäuden," loc. cit., Nov./Dec. 2005

-- : "Exploring the potential for natural ventilation of tall buildings," 29th AIVC Conference, Kyoto, Japan, 14–16 October 2008

Danner, Dietmar (Ed.); Kähler, Gert: *Die klima-aktive Fassade*, Verlags-Anstalt Alexander Koch, Leinfelden-Echterdingen 1999/2002

Fraunhofer-Institut für Solare Energiesysteme: *MIKROFUN. Entwicklung von Verglasungen mit regelbarem Transmissionsgrad für direktes und diffuses Licht auf Basis von MIKRO-strukturierten und optisch FUNktionalen Oberflächen und Materialien*, Freiburg 2007

Hausladen, Gerhard; de Saldanha, Michael; Liedl, Petra: *ClimateDesign*, Birkhäuser, Basel/Boston/Berlin 2005

-- : *ClimateSkin*, Birkhäuser, Basel/Boston/Berlin 2006

Herzog, Thomas; Flagge, Ingeborg; Herzog-Loibl, Verena; Meseure, Anna: *Thomas Herzog – Architecture + Technology*, Prestel, Munich/London/New York 2001

Lang, Werner: *Typologische Klassifikation von Doppelfassaden und experimentelle Untersuchung von dort eingebauten Lamellensystemen aus Holz zur Steuerung des Energiehaushaltes hoher Häuser unter besonderer Berücksichtigung der Nutzung von Solarenergie*, Dissertation, Munich Technical University 2000

Schüco International KG, *Aktive Fassaden zur Reduzierung der Schallemission in Gebäuden*, Joint report by Schüco KG and the TU Darmstadt, 2006

Interaction – recognizing and directing movement

Bullivant, Lucy: *4Dspace, Interactive Architecture*, AD/Wiley, Chichester 2005

Fox, Michael; Kemp, Miles: *Interactive Architecture*, Princeton Architectural Press, New York 2009

Simmen, Jeannot; Drepper, Uwe: *Vertical Lift Escalator Paternoster: A Cultural History of Vertical Transport*, Prestel, Munich 1984

Illustration credits

A

9 John Jay/MPTV; 10 top, Daimler AG; 10 bottom, Helen Schiffer; 11 Jesper Jørgen; 13 iStockphoto; 15 Ute Schendel; 16 left, Caroline Minjolle; 16 right, Ute Schendel; 17 left, © all photos Bettina Stöß/Stage Picture; 17 right, Matthias Zölle Photography; 18 left, Annegret Motzek; 18 middle, iStockphoto; 18 right, Hedwig Storch; 19 Sandra Hauer; 20 left, Norbert Henschel; 20 right, Johannes D.; 21 iStockphoto; 23 THE MATRIX © WV Films LLC. Licensed by: Warner Bros. Entertainment Inc.; 24, 25 Tokihiro Sato/Haines Gallery; 26 top, © Kuka; 26 bottom, © Nasa; 27 © Jan Zappe; 28, 29 © robotlab; 31 iStockphoto; 32 Hoberman Associates Inc.; 33 Oliver Schuh/Barbara Burg – www.palladium.de; 34 Maurer Söhne Group/Maurer Rides GmbH; 35 left, Jocelyn Vollmar as Myrthe Giselle, nla.pic-vn3421403, National Library of Australia; 35 right, Santiago Calatrava; 36 left, Claude Knaus; 36 middle Bugatti Automobiles S.A.S.; 36 right, photo: Bundesheer/MACHER; 37 Seminar MOVE, Tania Lembke, René Schirrmeister; 38 left, Rondal BV; 38 right, iStockphoto; 39 Markus Lütkemeyer; 40 Loek van der Klis; 41 left, Georges Fessy; 41 right, Solimar marine equipment, Italy; 42 Hoberman Associates Inc.; 44 Paul Warchol; 46 molo; 48 top, JuCad; 48 bottom, iStockphoto; 49 top, Photo – Joe Hutt; 49 bottom, iStockphoto; 50 left, middle, ©Roswitha Natter; 50 right, Création Baumann; 51 top, Freitag lab.ag/www.freitag.ch; 51 bottom, BMW; 52 Photo © Stylepark; 53 left, © Bengtsson design Ltd/Alistair robinson; 53 right, Photo – Joe Hutt; 55 top/middle, top/left, Photo © Stylepark; 55 top/right, Forms and Surfaces; 55 bottom/middle, bottom/left, woodnotes; 55 bottom/right, nya nordiska; 56 top, Zoran Novacki; 56 bottom/left, Anke Barke; 56 bottom/right, Günter Trost; 57 left, Atelier Frei Otto + Partner; 57 right, Zoran Novacki; 58 top, iStockphoto; 58 bottom, SL Rasch GmbH; 59 top, Wojtek Gurak; 59 bottom/left, © 2009 Birdair, Inc. N.Y.; 59 bottom/right, Gollings Pidgeon; 60 left, middle, Hettich GmbH; 60 right, dreamstime; 62 Torben Eskerod; 64 left, middle, Winkel GmbH; 64 right, Maurer Söhne Group/Maurer Rides GmbH; 65 Photos: Barbara Burg + Oliver Schuh, www.palladium.de; 66 Photo: Bosch Rexroth AG; 67, 68 Elero GmbH; 70 left, dreamstime; 70 right, iStockphotos; 71 J.A. Becker & Söhne GmbH; 72 Matthew Denton; 73 left, iStockphoto; 73 right, Darren Stevenson, Imaging Group, Beckman Institute, University of Illinois at Urbana-Champaign; 74 top/left, bottom/left, bottom/right, warema; 74 top/right, top/middle, bottom/middle, thiesclima; 75 Gira; 76 Drawing: Patrick Beckmann; 77 left, Sick; 77 right, Photo: ABB; 78 left, MBB Systeme GmbH; 78 middle, right, Hörmann; 80 © Christiane Biergans; 83 iStockphoto; 85 Magnus Sandström; 86 Noebu via Flickr; 87 Outlast; 88 Achim Menges, Steffen Reichert; 89 Continuum Dynamics, Inc.; 90 top, Thom Faulders; 90

bottom, Afshin Mehin, Tomas Rosen, Christopher Glaister; 91 nendo; 92 top, Agnes Weiland; 92 bottom, Institute for Lightweight Structures and Conceptual Design (ILEK) at Stuttgart University; 93 top, Philippe Block, Axel Kilian, Peter Schmitt, John Snavely; 94, 95 Tristan d'Estrée Sterk – The Office for Robotic Architectural Media & Bureau for Responsive Architecture (www.orambra.com); 96 R&S(ie)(n); 97 top, SOA Architectes; 97 bottom/left, bottom/middle, Vorticom Inc.; 97 bottom/right, Helen Schiffer; 98 top, Entwicklungsgesellschaft für Baubotanik, Ferdinand Ludwig; 98 bottom, Anastasios John Hart; 99 top, Entwicklungsgesellschaft für Baubotanik, Oliver Storz; 99 bottom, Center for Regenerative Biology and Medicine (ZRM)

B

101 Biegert & Funk; 103 gruppeomp; 104 © Steven Holl Architects; 105 Shigeru Ban Architects; 106 top, Ignazia Favata/Studio Joe Colombo, Milan; 106 bottom, © paul ott photografiert; 107 top, Ignazia Favata/Studio Joe Colombo, Milan; 107 bottom, all photos: © David Grandorge; 108 top, Laif Agentur für Photos und Reportagen GmbH; 108 bottom, Office for Metropolitan Architecture; 109 top, Stéphane Orsolini; 109 bottom, Sören Grünert; 110 top, © Fabien Thouvenin; 110 bottom, Shigeru Ban Architects; 111 AllesWirdGut Architektur ZT GmbH; 112 © paul ott photografiert; 113 © Geoffrey Cottenceau; 114 Marcio Kogan; 115 Shigeru Ban Architects; 116 Florian Bolk; 117 © Georges Fessy/DPA/Adagp; 118 top, Peter Haimerl; 118 bottom, wilfried dechau; 119 Büro zweieinsdrei; 120 top, © Matthias Rick, Raumlabor Berlin; 120 bottom, Courtesy of Hyperbody, Delft University of Technology; 121 top, Matthew Farag; 121 bottom, Dynamic Architecture; 123 Product by Karlsson, available from Present Time; 124 images supplied by quietrevolution; 125, 127, 129 © Drawings: Brian Cody; 126, 127 Jörg Hempel; 128 left, Andrew Holt; 128 right, BDSP; 130, 131, 132, 133 top, 134 top, 135 top, 136 bottom, 137, 139 top, York Ostermeyer; 133 bottom/ left, René Schirmeister, Tania Lembke; 133 bottom/middle, Shahin Anisi, Erol Slowy, Andreas Walter; 133 bottom/right, schneider+schumacher; 134 bottom/middle, photo © www.e-architect.co.uk; 134 bottom/left, Darrell Godliman; 134 bottom/right, © PAUL RAFTERY; 135 bottom, © ATELIER BRÜCKNER; 136 top, sbp gmbh; 138 SMIT; 139 bottom/right, Thorsten Oechsler; 139 bottom/left, iStockphoto; 140 top, schneider+schumacher; 140 bottom/ right, Peter Bonfig; 141 schneider+schumacher; 142 Paul Warchol; 142 Carpenter Norris Consulting Inc.; 143 Rainer Mader; 145 iStockphoto; 146 Maurer Söhne Group/Maurer Rides GmbH; 147 iStockphoto; 148 Anthony Joh; 149 volkswagen; 150 Lift: Inclino, parking garage St. Moritz, AS Aufzüge AG; 151 Schindler; 152 Daan Roosegaarde; 153

HypoSurface Corp.; 154 Katsuhisa Kida; 155 glas platz gmbh & co. kg, www.glas-platz.de

C

157 iStockphoto; 158 Florian Holzherr; 160 Christian Gahl; 161 Richie Müller; 162, 163 Jens Willebrand; 164 Christian Wachter; 166 Christoph Kraneburg; 168 Roland Halbe; 170 Ned Kahn; 172 Sturm und Wartzeck; 174 Dianna Snape; 175 DesignInc; 176, 177 DOUG SNOWER PHOTOGRAPHY; 178, 179 Robert W. Baron; 180 Katsuhisa Kida; 182, 183 top, Ernst Schär; 183 bottom, Paolo Rosselli/Santiago Calatrava; 184, 185 Jörg Hempel; 186 Miguel de Guzmán; 188, 189 Gerhard Hagen Fotografie; 190, 191 Korteknie Stuhlmacher Architecten; 192, 193 David Franck Photographie; 194, 195 Dietmar Strauss; 196 top, bottom/left, Stefan Müller; 196 bottom/right, 197 Joachim Kleine Allekotte; 198, 199 © Alex de Rijke; 200, 201 Philippe Ruault; 202 Didier Boy de la Tour; 204 Spengler und Wiescholek; 205 Ralf Buscher; 206 seifert.stoeckmann@ formalhaut; 207 Jürgen Holzleuchter; 208 Werner Huthmacher; 210 Colt International; 211 Christof Lackner; „private banking hall in tirol"; 212, 213 Shinichi Ogawa & Associates; 214 Jörg Hempel; 216 Ernst Gieselbrecht + Partner; 217 © paul ott photografiert; 218, 219 BEHF Architekten; 220 Die Baupiloten, Jan Bitter; 222 Hoberman Associates; 224 Steve Speller; 226, 227 Amrein Giger Architekten; 228 Domagoj Blazevic; 229 Damir Fabijanic; 230, 231 Gaston Wicky; 232, 233 Stefan Zenzmaier; 234 Nic Lehoux; 235 Daly Genik Architects

Despite our best efforts, we have not always been able to identify the authorship of images. These images are nevertheless protected by copyright. In such cases, we would be grateful for an appropriate notification.

Except where otherwise noted, all drawings have been created specifically for this book. The rights for the drawings lie with the authors.

Sponsoring companies

Hawa AG
Internationally renowned sliding systems
www.hawa.ch

Maurer Söhne
Forces in motion
www.maurer-soehne.com

Schüco
Windows and solar products
www.schueco.com

Sliding systems from Hawa have been used around the world for more than 40 years. The company from Mettmenstetten near Zurich is internationally renowned as a specialist for sliding systems and a leading manufacturer of innovative sliding hardware. Whether for facades, wall systems or furniture, the Swiss company offers high-quality and aesthetic sliding solutions for virtually any requirement, material or door weight. A variety of top-quality technical solutions are available for folding, sliding or space-saving stacking door and wall systems. Among the hallmarks of Hawa's hardware systems are their ease of planning, convenient installation and excellent functionality. Hawa provides architects, designers and installers with specific and detailed documentation for all their products. A comprehensive technical library covering the entire product range as well as a planning tool to assist in visualising configurations in three dimensions are available online.

Maurer Söhne is the market leader in proprietary solutions and products for managing and controlling the interplay of forces in motion in building constructions.
The company's range of "Structural Protection Systems" are designed to prevent damages to structures caused by forces in motion. Maurer Söhne manufactures load-transferring devices which protect structures against the effects of excessive loads and strain. Monitoring systems for forces and movements offer an additional level of safety. The product range includes expansion joints, structural bearings, seismic devices and vibration absorbers.
Maurer Söhne's "Transport & Rides" solutions turn forces in motion into experiences. Maurer Söhne manufactures a variety of specially designed turnkey constructions for leisure facilities that can sustain complex dynamic forces and movements. The product range includes rollercoasters, amusement rides and passenger transportation systems.
Today, the company employs around 700 members of staff at their facilities in Munich, Lünen near Dortmund, Bernsdorf near Dresden as well as in Turkey and China.

Schüco International KG is the global market leader in aluminium, solar, steel and vinyl systems for innovative building envelopes. With more than 5,000 employees and 12,000 partner companies in over 75 countries, Schüco offers advanced window and facade technology, efficient solar solutions and individual consulting for architects, planners, investors and builders.
Schüco is committed to its corporate mission "Energy² – Saving Energy and Generating Energy": thermal insulation and building automation ensure reduced energy consumption. Through the use of photovoltaics, solar thermal energy and heat recovery, buildings have the potential to become standalone power plants, generating electricity, heating and where necessary also cooling.
Schüco's new Technology Center at its headquarters in Bielefeld represents one of the most modern training and seminar centres in the world, and with its innovative energy concept sets new standards for tomorrow.

Layout and cover design
Miriam Bussmann, Berlin

Editor
Andreas Müller, Berlin

Lithography
Licht & Tiefe, Berlin

Printing
Grafisches Centrum Cuno, Calbe

Cover – lenticular printing
Pinguin Druck, Berlin

Translation
Julian Reisenberger, Weimar

Copyediting
Raymond Peat, Alford

Library of Congress Control Number: 2009942366

This book is also available in German
(ISBN 978-3-7643-9985-6).

Bibliographic information published by Die Deutsche Bibliothek
Die Deutsche Bibliothek lists this publication in the Deutsche
Nationalbibliografie; detailed bibliographic data is available in
the Internet at <http://dnb.ddb.de>.

© 2010 Birkhäuser Verlag AG
Postfach 133, CH-4010 Basel, Schweiz

Printed on acid-free paper
produced from chlorine-free pulp. TFC ∞
Printed in Germany
ISBN 978-3-7643-9986-3

9 8 7 6 5 4 3 2 1

www.birkhauser-architecture.com